PRAISE FOR
HYPERSCALE REVENUE

"The hyperscale revenue method has led my teams to secure nine game-changing deals, averaging $15.4 million each—far exceeding our previous large-deal average of $3.8 million at this time. This book provides a clear framework for driving exponential revenue growth, and every CEO should empower their teams to implement these proven, high-leverage strategies effectively."

—ROB SCHILLING, Chief Commercial Officer of C3.ai

"We've always needed these principles but lacked a precise framework—until now. With the Digital-AI Age transforming the economy, *Hyperscale Revenue* serves as a CEO's essential guide to excel today and lead tomorrow. Jim's strategies are practical, well-defined, and critical for navigating the competitive dynamics of the next decade."

—JIM BERRYHILL, Cofounder and CEO of DecisionLink

"Jim rewrote our global sales methodology, driving our average deal size from $335k to $786k, shortening sales cycles by six months and boosting win rates by 23 percent. This positioned us ahead of competitors and ultimately led to our acquisition by a major industry leader for $5.8 billion just one year later."

—LES RECHAN, CEO of Rechan Consulting Group

HYPERSCALE REVENUE

PIPELINE   ACCELERATION   MINDSET

JIM CHRISTEN

RADIUS BOOK GROUP
NEW YORK

Radius Book Group

A Division of Diversion Media and Communications, LLC

www.RadiusBookGroup.com

For more information, email info@radiusbookgroup.com.

First edition: January 2026

Trade Paperback ISBN: 9798895151273

eBook ISBN: 9798895151242

1 3 5 7 9 10 8 6 4 2

Cover design by Will D. Mack

Interior design by Neuwirth & Associates, Inc.

Radius Book Group and the Radius Book Group colophon are registered trademarks of Radius Book Group, a Division of Diversion Media and Communications, LLC

To my incredible wife, Tiffany Christen. Your unwavering support has been essential in sharpening my focus and determination. Thank you for inspiring me to embrace my purpose and for transforming complexity into clarity with your insightful guidance and thoughtful perspective.

CONTENTS

FOREWORD

In every boardroom, at some point during the quarterly sales overview, one board member always seems to ask, "Why can't we push beyond our current pipeline coverage to reliably hit our revenue targets quarter after quarter?" *Hyperscale Revenue* provides the answer; not just for defining a category or market, but for turning growth into an operational system within it. This book isn't about quick fixes or surface-level advice; it's a fully integrated sales operating system designed for the complexities of today's enterprise environment. It doesn't focus on small, incremental improvements to your sales process; instead, it shows you how to completely rewire it, from strategy to execution, rooted in the realities of how buyers make decisions in high-stakes, high-complexity markets. While many sales books promise faster results, this one delivers a set of institutional frameworks that make acceleration not just possible, but inevitable.

Through rigorously tested engagement frameworks, proven sales plays, and a clear sequence of actions, Jim Christen equips companies with the *tools to weaponize their market strategy in the field.* It teaches them how to guide buyers, especially executives, through decision-making processes that are unfamiliar, high stakes, and not just about solving immediate problems, but about shaping long-term business strategies. The result? *The ability to create significant unbudgeted transactions* that are many times larger than the norm, alongside a framework for executive engagement and measurable value realization. This feedback loop strengthens your GTM engine, making it faster, sharper, and more strategic.

Hyperscale Revenue provides the frameworks and sales plays needed to industrialize strategic selling, transform sales teams into trusted business advisors, and build a repeatable engine for sustainable growth.

I've spent much of my career studying, systematizing, and executing the principles behind building and scaling exceptional companies. The strategies outlined in this book are among the most actionable and impactful I've come across for sales leaders, customer success professionals, and C-suite executives who understand the critical importance of enterprise revenue execution but are searching for a structured approach to drive transformative deal momentum.

A seemingly straightforward question reveals a deeper challenge that many leadership teams grapple with: The gap between designing a high-impact product and building a scalable, GTM system. I've developed the Traction Gap™ Framework to systematically bridge this divide, turning early potential into measurable market traction by defining, shaping, and ultimately owning a category and market. This is accomplished by aligning efforts across critical areas, such as demand generation, and creating clear, compelling messaging. The framework provides GTM leaders with a precise, step-by-step operating model to minimize execution risk, enabling them to identify and validate their core markets with confidence. It outlines how to signal readiness to scale and rigorously establish *market/product* fit, while keeping the market as the central focus. The frameworks in my book, *Traversing the Traction Gap*, integrates seamlessly with the principles in *Hyperscale Revenue*. Yet, even with sharp strategy and strong positioning, one essential question persisted: "How do we execute this at scale with consistency, focus, and discipline?"

In enterprise customer value creation, having a complete business strategy earns you a seat at the table. Product quality gets you into the evaluation process. Category leadership puts you on the shortlist. But it's the precision of sales execution at the executive level—driven by strategy, guided by deep insight, and executed with operational discipline—that closes the deal.

Read this book. Then encourage your entire GTM team to do the same to master the art of engaging key executive decision-makers.

It's that important.

Bruce Cleveland,
CEO, Traction Gap Partners

ACKNOWLEDGMENTS

I want to express my gratitude to these visionary leaders whose perspectives have profoundly shaped how I create meaningful value for customers every single day.

Larry Ellison, chairman of the board at Oracle, exemplifies the relentless pursuit of excellence. His ability to consistently outmaneuver competitors, regardless of their market dominance, has instilled a mindset centered on resilience and high performance.

Tom Siebel, CEO of C3.ai, has set the standard for innovation and precision. His mastery in creating and shaping markets, combined with his focus on building strategic alliances with world-class partners, has redefined what it means to execute at scale.

Bill McDermott, CEO of ServiceNow, demonstrates the transformative power of bold vision, compelling storytelling, and a relentless commitment to innovation. His approach consistently drives strategic outcomes that fuel long-term growth.

Ragy Thomas, chairman of the board at Sprinklr, embodies the impact of unwavering persistence. His ability to deliver groundbreaking innovations and inspire teams to exceed their own expectations has been nothing short of extraordinary.

Satya Nadella, CEO of Microsoft, exemplifies a thoughtful and strategic approach to identifying the unique strengths of startups and amplifying those capabilities to expand their presence in the market.

xii
        ACKNOWLEDGMENTS

This book distills the essential strategies and insights from these exceptional leaders. By integrating their approaches, I've developed CEO engagement strategies that have consistently delivered results over the past two decades.

INTRODUCTION

Crafting and implementing a global GTM strategy requires complex process flows that span multiple disciplines, each with distinct objectives. But every company shares the same goal: generate a high-value pipeline that fuels revenue growth. In the technology sector, many GTM experts refer to *Crossing the Chasm*, a seminal GTM and business strategy book that shows how technology products transition from early adopters to the mainstream market. *Hyperscale Revenue* has a different goal: It details how your sales professionals can create significant unbudgeted transactions that drive accelerated revenue growth to outpace even your most ambitious projected operating plans. It draws on thirty years of real-world customer examples, illustrating how executives have adopted new business strategies from sales professionals they hadn't previously considered, betting the next phase of their business on your compelling point of view.

After training twelve thousand elite sales professionals to cultivate and win significant unbudgeted transactions, the most common response I've heard has been, "I had no idea that you could sell this way!" Every sales professional is focused on building relationships and taking guidance from their customer champions at the director level, often neglecting to invest the time needed to be compelling with the executive leadership team. This team doesn't want to know anything about your solutions; they want to understand how leading companies in their industry leverage your solutions to create a unique competitive advantage. These significant transactions are 4.2 times larger than your highly competitive deals. They fall into a category called "confirm fit," where the customer has just enough resources to work exclusively with your company, bypassing the evaluation of other vendors because you're guiding the evaluation process, always staying a step ahead of the newly assembled evaluation team, following the executive team's guidance. These transactions boast much higher margins, often resulting in the largest deals their partner companies have ever executed, as they bypass the standard procurement process.

Hyperscale Revenue is packed with 408 documented and validated GTM plays. While you may already partially be using some of them, this book will show you how to structure them into a series of frameworks to share your elite best practices with your entire GTM organization. Does your marketing team know how to create a pipeline of unbudgeted opportunities without discussing your products? Does your sales team know how to craft a compelling CEO email for your CEO to establish a new strategic partnership, driving $300 million in incremental revenue over the next twelve months? Can your product marketing team definitely provide guidance on the highest-value-use cases to implement in priority order by persona? Does your value advisory team have at least five customers per industry segment who have documented the quantifiable benefits by use case, showing progression of improvement with quarterly scorecards delivered to your customer's executive leadership team so they understand your value? Let's be honest, these are just four of the most challenging GTM issues your company faces in hyperscaling your revenue.

Fortunately, I have compiled the leading practices from diverse elite sellers' engagement styles, which have produced twenty-eight millionaires in sales roles over the past twenty-two years, ultimately achieving 450 percent of quota attainment. Once a sales professional understands how different the decision criteria are for the executive leadership team in allocating unbudgeted funds compared to an evaluation team tasked with selecting the best product at the lowest cost, everything changes. These two engagement strategies are fundamentally different, and pursuing excellence in both methods will open dozens of new avenues to exceed your quotas and revenue goals.

The initial four chapters lay the foundation for all your GTM resources, focusing on the essential elements needed to establish unbudgeted strategic engagements with executives. In my experience, 97 percent of your team members have not encountered the level of investment required early on, nor have they written the personalized content essential to develop a new business strategy that can significantly alter the trajectory of your prospect's business. From there, the next four chapters explore the often-overlooked art of product marketing, highlighting the necessity of industry expertise to prioritize and position your offerings, helping you create a unique differential value by optimizing use cases. Unfortunately, your safe and satisfied customers won't help you reach this goal. Instead, you need to execute this strategy in the field with your most competitive evaluations—the kind that will challenge your go-to-market (GTM) resources and stretch your skill in competitive positioning. Finally, the last four chapters illustrate how to scale these best practices globally, enhancing your GTM experts' capabilities to achieve the ultimate goal of delivering predictable, hyperscaled revenue.

HYPERSCALE REVENUE RESULTS

S — STRATEGIC ENGAGEMENTS

Chapter 1	+73% Deal Size	Create Momentum
Chapter 2	+63% Cross Sell	Gain Alignment
Chapter 3	+34% Win Rate	Establish Credibility
Chapter 4	-43% Sales Cycle	Business Outcomes

V — VALUE DIFFERENTIATION

Chapter 5	+36% Business Acumen	Diamond Teams
Chapter 6	+42% Top Three Projects	Engineer Markets
Chapter 7	-41% New Hire Ramp Time	Executive Frameworks
Chapter 8	+37% Sales Participation	Written Narratives

C — CUSTOMER BUY-IN

Chapter 9	-21% Discounting	Value Realization
Chapter 10	+48% Seller Productivity	Artificial Intelligence
Chapter 11	+24% Achieve Sales Quota	Launch Plans
Chapter 12	+14% Incremental Revenue	Unify Awareness

Pipeline Acceleration

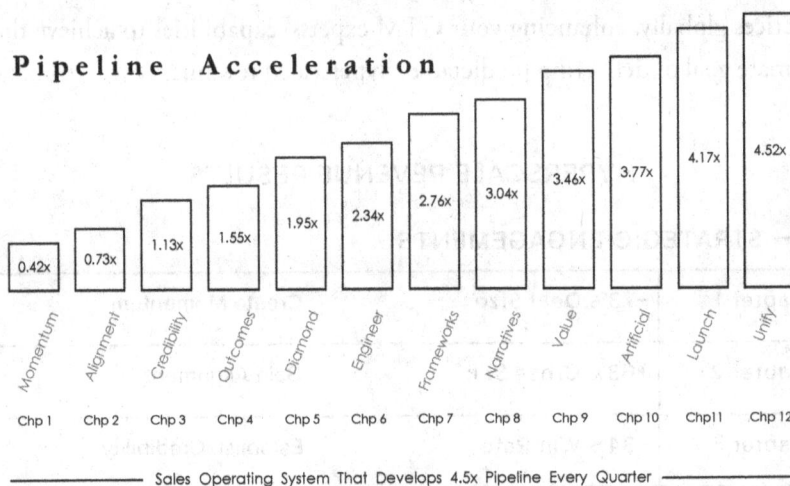

0.42x	0.73x	1.13x	1.55x	1.95x	2.34x	2.76x	3.04x	3.46x	3.77x	4.17x	4.52x
Momentum	Alignment	Credibility	Outcomes	Diamond	Engineer	Frameworks	Narratives	Value	Artificial	Launch	Unify
Chp 1	Chp 2	Chp 3	Chp 4	Chp 5	Chp 6	Chp 7	Chp 8	Chp 9	Chp 10	Chp 11	Chp 12

————— Sales Operating System That Develops 4.5x Pipeline Every Quarter —————

Revenue drives every aspect of your business, from your product roadmap innovation to headcount and future acquisitions. To consistently generate more revenue, you need to develop specialized resources that execute at an elite level—this isn't for everyone. Are you content with just 3 percent of your top sales professionals engaging executives? That approach won't yield the transformative results you're aiming for.

This book brings together the strategies of five renowned CEOs, all of whom have expertly engaged customer executives to forge strategic partnerships that revolutionized their industries. Few sales professionals have had the chance to watch their CEOs in action, structuring pivotal details by crafting materials and proposals custom-made for executive engagement, but all of them can benefit from learning these advanced techniques. Overall, this compilation of 12 engagement theories, 48 concepts, 48 frameworks, 177 sales plays, and 120 tips and tricks offers a proven approach to securing new agreements with C-suite executives. Selling at this level is not about product demos or feature lists—it's about earning the right to become a trusted advisor to your clients' executive teams.

HOW TO OPERATIONALIZE PIPELINE

Sometimes, running a company feels a bit like undergoing open-heart surgery while running a marathon: You have to run your existing processes in parallel with implementing new high-value strategies. I hope you find this book compelling enough to share it with your chief revenue officer, who in turn should review and implement it with their team. Admittedly, this is a significant request, given their current responsibilities and directives. Having led eight global GTM transformations myself, I know firsthand that this endeavor demands a unique approach. Your sales leadership is entirely focused on creating a pipeline and delivering revenue every month. It's challenging to ask them to do more.

To implement these frameworks, I recommend identifying an elite vice president (VP) of sales with at least two years of tenure in your company, one who is respected for consistently overachieving their quarterly and annual revenue targets. This leader should have a robust value-selling background and a team that instinctively engages executives in their accounts to understand the true decision criteria. In other words, this VP must grasp the importance of developing business acumen in sales professionals to create customer value in every interaction.

Once you identify that VP, I recommend taking them out of their current role and having them program manage this approach with two main-focus areas. First, they'll directly manage two specialized value-selling teams that engage six of your highly competitive opportunities every quarter. Second, they will manage the strategic engagement process across your entire North

America sales force, enabling their peers to develop strategic engagements for their own teams. The VP will be the significant transaction investment funnel for each of their peers, who will share a portion of their quota to provide alignment. This provides the focus required to implement this new process in addition to your current sales motion, and more importantly it will triple your number of significant transactions over the next two quarters. The key to success in change management is providing firsthand guidance from one's peers. "Learn one - Do one - Teach one" should become embedded in your team's muscle memory.

Pair this VP of Strategic Accounts with a program management expert who understands industry use cases to track the accountability required to achieve success. *Hyperscale Revenue* growth is a long-term investment that will start producing results within five months, which is not always a timeline your current sales leadership can manage, without dedicated assistance to handle this new strategic sales motion alongside your existing business operations. The goal is to support both approaches, giving you the most optimal way to accelerate revenue—not only in your core solution offering by hyperscaling your edge solutions that otherwise present a challenge.

This book will teach you how to craft hyperscaled deals that once seemed out of reach, using the unmatched power of strategic executive engagement frameworks. Following this model will help you create significant transactions that are four and a half times larger than your average contract value, thanks to meticulous preparation and high-value business strategies. You will be spreading a **Culture of Value Creation** that has existed in pockets of your organization but will become mainstream.

Here's the kind of change you can expect:

The elite sellers in your field organization will increase **from 3 to 12 percent in the next twelve months.**

Equip them with the playbook to generate an additional **forty-six deals** in the next twelve months and **increasing the number of $3.2 million deals and creating new $12.8 million transactions** across five hundred sales professionals.

Create and close forty-one $3.2 million large deals and five $12.8 million significant transactions to deliver **$46.8 million in incremental revenue per quarter and $187.2 million annually,** which is a 31 percent revenue increase.

Guarantee that you exceed your quarterly goals—all while **leveraging only 9 percent of your customer-facing resources.**

By scaling this methodology to 24 percent of your organization in the second year, you will drive **$436 million in incremental revenue** through fine-tuning several critical operational cadences. Furthermore, sharing these frameworks with your global field organization will **shorten their average sales cycles by two and a half months** and accelerate revenue realization by a full quarter, thus **mitigating risk and enhancing overall team revenue performance.** Doesn't that sound better than relying on a select few top performers, hoping that their last-minute heroics will achieve your quarterly revenue targets to balance your books?

HYPERSCALE REVENUE

MOMENTUM

Initiate Strategic Engagements

(Increases Deal Sizes by 73 Percent)

CHAPTER 1

➤ **CHANGE THE STORY:** CEO Engagements

➤ **TRANSACTION SALES:** Empower Your Champions

➤ **STRATEGIC ENGAGEMENTS:** Influence Decision Criteria

➤ **DIFFERENTIATED VALUE IN SALES:** Managing Communication

➤ **TRUTH ABOUT CREATING MOMENTUM:** Net New Meetings

➤ **RAISING BUSINESS ACUMEN:** Executive Conversations

➤ **INDUSTRY BENCHMARKING:** Peer Comparisons

➤ **ARRIVING WITH AN EXECUTIVE POINT OF VIEW:** Shift Mindset

➤ **ENGAGEMENT FRAMEWORKS:** Initiate Executive Meetings

➤ **MOMENTUM THEORY:** Increase Deal Size 73 Percent

➤ **TIPS AND TRICKS:** Engaging Executives

➤ **MOMENTUM WORKBOOK:** Influence Outcomes

➤ **EVERYDAY APPLICATIONS:** Uncover Competing Priorities

➤ **KEY TAKEAWAYS:** Value of Top-Down Engagement

➤ **SUMMARY:** Initiate Strategic Engagements

CHANGE THE STORY

I faced a daunting challenge: Our second largest customer intended to slash their annual expenditures with us in half. If I couldn't swiftly resolve this issue, my tenure overseeing the firm's top fifty global accounts would vanish faster than my first cup of coffee. The customer wanted to renegotiate our agreement within the next week, and the clock was ticking.

My CEO, Reed, was in shock, desperately seeking solutions to avert this devastating revenue reduction, one which would undoubtedly hinder our revenue trajectory in the high-tech sector. A string of positive encounters with the client—a Fortune 50 firm—suggested that we were poised for considerable expansion, so everyone on my team was asking the same question: *What did we do wrong?* Was it in our approach to customer success and their adoption strategy? Were we lacking essential product features? And most importantly, what on earth were we going to do about it?

Just three days earlier, I had started my new role as the company's executive sponsor, specifically tasked with addressing this kind of business challenge. My mission was to establish a comprehensive global account program for our top fifty clients, including this customer, and I got the news of their planned reduction while en route from San Francisco to New York. As soon as I arrived in Midtown Manhattan, I headed straight to the eighth floor, burst through my CEO's office door, and declared, "Here's our plan of action!"

Reed's eyes widened with curiosity, ready to absorb every detail. As I laid out the plan, he was hesitant at first: "This seems incredibly risky. We've never done anything like this before!" "This is precisely why you brought me on board," I assured him. "I've executed this strategy hundreds of times with an 83 percent success rate. The reason it works is simple: It revolves around creating value for the customer's CEO. We're going to give our client's CEO an irresistible opportunity to boost their revenue and secure a new market leadership position, in an area where they have historically struggled." Reed locked eyes with me, scrutinizing my idea while reading my facial expression to determine how confident I really was in my plan.

The first stage of my plan, I explained, involved drafting an email for Reed to send to our client's CEO, Steve, to propose deepening our partnership and creating new market opportunities for both companies. "Not only will this secure a crucial renewal," I reassured Reed, "but it will increase the account's revenue by at least twelvefold. So, here's my question for you: Are you prepared to embrace being uncomfortable in order to radically alter the revenue arc of our partnership with the industry's most prominent brand?"

Such a bold move is never easy, and Reed took a couple minutes to consider the challenge. As soon as he agreed, I headed straight for a conference room, where I secluded myself for the next three hours to draft the email that would make or break our company. Just before 3 p.m., Reed came by to check on my progress. I handed him the draft to read through, but it clearly wasn't the kind of content he'd expected. "Do you think this will work?" he wondered. I confirmed that, "I know it will work."

The succinct email outlined three key value pillars for Steve's GTM approach to customer experience. The first pillar outlined a recent GTM strategy involving an enterprise marketing solution. By enhancing it with social listening and social marketing capabilities, I argued, we could generate an additional $186 million in revenue and foster brand ambassadors—a gap their competitors had already filled. Next, I proposed migrating our solution from cloud competitors to our client's own cloud infrastructure, a move that would boost revenue by $93 million. Finally, I recommended empowering 20,000 of Steve's global sellers with social selling capabilities to cultivate deeper client relationships, projecting an increase in sales by $64 million. Collectively, these three pillars would yield $343 million in additional revenue and give our client a new leadership position in social media marketing, leveraging existing solutions already favored by major global brands.

Like any good CEO, Reed meticulously reviewed my email, seeking places where he could add value for our client. His first suggestion was to move social selling to the top of the list. I knew that Reed was an expert in social selling, but I emphasized that we had to prioritize Steve's needs. That's why I started with his social marketing revenue and his market cloud partnership, before showing how our solutions could support those priorities. Putting our needs first would fail to capture Steve's attention or engagement. This was not a random outreach, but a strategic engagement poised to transform the collaboration between our companies and redefine how we engaged with global accounts.

Reed still wasn't sure, so I shared my own experience solving similar problems. As I recounted a few interactions with other high-level CEOs, both in my own firms and my clients' firms, Reed came to trust my credibility enough to move forward. Still, he asked for a day to have his own sales and marketing advisors review my plan—after all, they had helped him grow his business for eight years while I hadn't even been on the job for seventy-two hours. They were skeptical at best, believing that such an audacious proposal would harm the client relationship. But the more he heard their complaints, the more Reed realized that none of them had ever interacted with a Fortune 50 CEO. Despite presenting numerous examples of how successful CEO-to-CEO communications had accelerated strategic partnerships, he found it challenging to shift their perspective because they had simply never operated at this level.

The following morning, Reed and I met one more time to review the email before he sent it to Steve. He was still anxious and uncertain about the email's success, so I reassured him that I would take full accountability for the outcome. "Go big or go home," I told him. "As long as you're creating strategic value for your customers you have nothing to worry about!"

He grinned, took a deep breath, and reluctantly hit send.

Two hours later, Steve responded favorably, telling us that he'd assigned three members of his executive leadership team to validate our proposed pillars of value. The CMO would handle the GTM social marketing strategy, the EVP of Products would assess what it would take to replace the cloud infrastructure, and the CRO would determine how 20,000 sellers could engage in social interactions with clients. I was pleasantly surprised at the speed of Steve's response, but I knew that Reed and I had made the right call. We had a deep understanding of Steve's business and his company's priorities, and we presented our ideas in a way that resonated with their leadership team and gave them a reason to take strategic action.

Within four months, Steve's company had increased their spending with us from $750,000 to $6.2 million in annual recurring revenue, committing to $18.6 million over three years with a cash payment in thirty days. That immediate cash infusion dramatically shifted the direction of our company. During one of our follow-up meetings, Reed pointed out, "I asked myself why I hadn't considered this approach before and why no one had brought such an innovative idea to me before. I'm so glad we brought you on board!"

This was a great result, but Reed and I weren't content to stop there. We immediately set to work on scaling this approach across the company. The goal was to share customer-centered frameworks with our account teams that they could personalize for their customers, enabling them to create new strategic engagements, without needing Reed's direct involvement from the outset. Overseeing the global account program allowed me to demonstrate the effectiveness of this strategy. Every other week, I conducted reviews of each target account for our next executive engagement. It was a thrilling time in our company, ultimately accelerating engagement with 80 percent of our strategic accounts. Instead of the same old Monday-morning pipeline updates, eight different account executives would spend a Saturday morning combing through our sales professionals' emails. The new strategy soon generated intrigue throughout our sales force, as everyone was eager to find the highest value and capture their clients' engagement.

Here's the point: Most companies are established to target a single ideal customer profile, perfect a single route-to-market, and excel in that one method—even to the point of neglecting world-changing alternatives. These alternatives are often overlooked because they demand pre-work before every communication and meeting to enhance deal size and closing rates. Consequently, the vast majority of GTM teams—around 95 percent—concentrate on the company's flagship solutions and last century's sales methods. This makes it very challenging to grow revenue, especially for edge solutions and acquired product offerings. You have to speak your customer's language before they will take action on the business strategies you're proposing.

As Reed's experience shows, of course, executive engagement is the key piece of this puzzle. Providing tangible benefits to your customer is crucial, yet it doesn't ensure buy-in and support from either your CEO or your customer's CEO. Executive support drives high-value deals, which means your client's C-suite must both see and understand your offering's strategic value. No matter how many everyday improvements you make in your client's workflow, you'll miss the most significant victories if those wins never reach the executive level. Without clearly articulating your strategic impact and communicating it to your customer's leadership, at least once a quarter, you risk down-renewals and even outright cancellations.

Furthermore, failing to explore larger market partnership opportunities can restrict the potential of your client relationships. If you're seen as just another vendor, rather than a strategic partner, you won't be able to show how your solutions contribute to long-term growth or address high-level business goals—and your client's key decision-makers won't fully value your contributions. You must reshape that narrative to stay competitive! By raising discussions to the executive level and focusing on collaborative strategies that go beyond routine service delivery, you can position your company as an essential driver of success. This approach not only strengthens customer loyalty but also ensures that both your CEO and theirs take pride in and advocate for the results you deliver.

TRANSACTION SALES

Our company's early success in the market was underscored by $143,000 in initial contracts that burgeoned into an impressive $1.5 million annual recurring revenue within twenty-four months, showcasing our firm's knack for nurturing and expanding client relationships. Despite this success, we faced challenges in securing significant multimillion-dollar deals that fell outside our primary buyers' budgets, and we seldom involved C-suite executives in the early discussions. I decided to talk to Dan, our foremost sales MVP. Dan had dominated the company's attainment leaderboard for three of the last four years, regularly hitting an extraordinary 187 percent of his annual sales goal. Because he had been so successful with traditional methods, however, Dan had significant doubts about engaging executives in the strategic engagements that I proposed. Why mess with what already works for him?

Typically, B2B salespeople build a relationship with a director-level coach in the client's firm, who helps them navigate the sales process, address potential concerns, and facilitate introductions to some mid-level executives with limited tenure. These directors interact with their executive leadership team two to three times a year, not even once a quarter. In fact, my research shows that a director-level coach will arrange meetings with their executives only 8 percent of the time! They are unlikely to use those rare opportunities to champion your solution.

Sales professionals relying solely on this bottom-up method can expect to achieve 73 percent of their quota if they manage well-established accounts in large, reputable companies. Dan, for example, focused on forging relationships at the director level, leveraging his extensive product knowledge. This strategy enabled him to compete on a level playing field, focusing on feature comparisons and pricing. But many of his colleagues, especially those handling new accounts, reached just 34 percent of their quota, often blaming their shortfall on a lack of meaningful engagement with executives. While a bottom-up sales method like Dan's can deliver some success, it cannot be your only sales motion if you hope to achieve exceptional results every year.

Our goal here is not just to meet your quarterly quotas, but to reach an astounding **450 percent of your goal every other year**. Given typical deal sizes, that would translate to a million dollars in commissions, enough to transform anyone's lifestyle. In the following sections, I will detail how to maximize your potential by filling in the most impactful 30 percent of your week, enabling you to reach the pinnacle of success in direct enterprise business-to-business sales. You'll learn how to create a decisive competitive edge that allows your team to redefine the decision criteria. Using this method, my team and I have boosted our close rates from 34 percent to an impressive 57 percent in significant transactions—the kind that tap unbudgeted funds that directors simply don't have the authority to secure on their own. Therefore, engaging directors should only constitute 70 percent of your client interaction strategy if you aim for consistent success. As the diagram below shows, strategic engagement with potential executive partners can easily outpace hundreds of hours in basic inflight opportunities. Where are you spending your best time and efforts?

ROUTES TO MARKET

BOTTOMS UP	PRIORITY 1	PRIORITY 2	PRIORITY 3
Transactional Seller	Inflight Opportunities 1x ARR	Install Base Expansion 1x ARR	Strategic Engagement 4.2x ARR
160% Attainment	70% Time Qualified Buyer	28% Time Qualified Buyer	2% Time If Blue Bird Appears

Diagram 1.0 Convert 1x Transactions

STRATEGIC ENGAGEMENTS: THE SUMO MODEL

Earlier, we saw how Dan's bottom-up approach provided steady but unimpressive sales. By contrast, Dan's colleague Todd prioritized creating value for his customer executives in every interaction. He invested time and effort into designing engagement strategies, including conversation starters, that zero in on advancing the company's stated priorities and improving their financial performance vs. their peers. The resulting conversation gave Todd's clients fresh, compelling insights that differentiated him as an advisor, not just a vendor. In fact, customer CEOs regularly call Todd to request recommendations on how to move forward on upcoming proposed projects.

Todd includes four essential components in his executive dialogues, which I call **the SUMO model**. First, they feature an *intriguing customer story* from the client's industry segment, ensuring immediate relevance and demonstrating a profound grasp of their business hurdles. Second, they highlight the *top two use cases* that generate the most substantial impact, allowing executives to delegate the appropriate person to assess their viability. Third, they include *metrics with estimates* of anticipated economic value, taking into account the required time and resources compared to other projects. Finally, they illustrate how this initiative dovetails with the client's current strategic priorities, positioning it as one of the leading projects with one of the highest returns on investment. These tactics do more than craft a compelling message: They *create an opportunity for you to make your solution a reality and attract* your client's high-value resources.

To make your conversation impactful, it's crucial to present your insights in this specific order. Leading with the opportunity, for example, is likely to alienate your audience because you haven't shown the context or relevance of your solution. Likewise, leading with financial aspects implies that you can manage their business better than they can. By contrast, presenting both stories and use cases helps everyone understand the context of the problem you're addressing and how other companies have resolved similar issues, building your own credibility to quantify the impact of your solution. Essentially, you're turning a complex topic into a consumable narrative that respects your audience's time and intelligence, proving you belong in the room.

THE EXECUTIVE CONVERSATION

S	U	M	O
STORIES	USE CASES	METRICS	OPPORTUNITY

Diagram 1.1 The SUMO Model: Conveying Value to Executives

I developed and perfected this clear communication framework through 532 net new executive conversations over the span of two years, all while training forty-two global business development representatives to apply this strategy in their own outreach. Adopting it will greatly enhance your chances of leaving a memorable impression, thus nurturing a valuable partnership that accelerates revenue growth for both companies. Executives value actionable insight above all else, ideally from advisors who combine business acumen with subject-matter expertise. That can make for challenging and unpredictable meetings if you do not possess these dual skill sets. But if all you're doing is discussing product features and taking orders, you're in customer service, not executive sales.

This experience solidified my belief that while many top-tier sales professionals shine when customers are ready to buy, few of them know how to create opportunities from the ground up. Unfortunately, books on this crucial art form are few and far between—and the few books out there are heavy on theory and light on practical application. To correct this imbalance, we'll analyze each of our case studies from two key angles, illustrating a systematic and repeatable approach, which is not for the meek of heart. When widely implemented under your leadership, this method can expand your organization's total addressable market by 70 percent, offering a unique opportunity to significantly increase revenue. Additionally, it will enable you to engage with prospects in new segments, creating additional routes to market and safeguard your business model against economic downturns.

TWO TYPES OF SALES ENGAGEMENTS

TRANSACTION SALE	STRATEGIC ENGAGEMENT
Qualified Buyer	Undefined Need
30% of the Market	70% of the Market

Diagram 1.2 Balancing Transaction Sales and Strategic Engagements

What key insights should an executive derive from your expertise? A good starting point is to pinpoint the crucial use cases within their industry that drive other firms' unique competitive edge and propel other leaders' career advancements. These case studies can help you positively influence your client's strategic planning, by showing that you are focused on their business challenges. They are far more important than memorizing product features! Your goal is not to describe your solution but to build trust and credibility, so you can secure a referral with top-down sponsorship.

To show you how this works, let me tell you more about Todd's story. Todd built his work ethic in high school, where he played intensely competitive travel basketball alongside NBA All-Stars Elton Brand, Lamar Odom, and Ron Artest. Competing at such a high level demanded meticulous preparation long before stepping onto the court—especially for a five-foot, eleven-inch point guard! That same readiness informs every one of Todd's professional interactions and helps set him apart, with a 2-percent edge, from his transactional competitors.

For example, in one case Todd discovered that his client's CEO idolized Kareem Abdul-Jabbar, a former high school teammate of Todd's father. Todd could have easily exploited this connection, perhaps having Kareem send the CEO a signed ball, or set up a business dinner next time Kareem was in town. But Todd knew that meeting a sports hero would ultimately create no business value for his client. Instead, he dedicated an entire week to crafting the ideal message for the CEO, collaborating closely with non-traditional influencers from the company's investor relations department, who offered deep insights into the CEO's future strategy.

Ultimately, this work paid off in a customized message that offered significant, differentiated value that captured the CEO's interest. Despite having no firsthand executive experience, Todd demonstrated remarkable dedication to understanding the company's strategic goals and validating his findings with his trusted advisors.

LEAD WITH STRATEGIC ENGAGEMENTS

TOP DOWN	PRIORITY 1	PRIORITY 2	PRIORITY 3
Strategic Seller	Strategic Engagement 4.2x ARR	Inflight Opportunities 1x ARR	Install Base Expansion 1x ARR
275% Attainment	30% Time Customer Value Creation	50% Time Qualified Buyer	20% Time Qualified Buyer

Diagram 1.3 Create Significant 4.2x, Unbudgeted Transactions

This kind of mindset change requires starting everyday thinking about how to solve business challenges for your client executives, based on their strategic priorities. Even if it's mainly in the background, this analysis will help you plan strategic advancements as you handle tactical challenges in your inflight deals. Executives never stop thinking about improving their results, and neither should you! It will take time to craft compelling messages that unlock new avenues for competitive advantage, but you can't create transformative outcomes by doing the same thing as everyone else.

The foundation of this approach, both in captivating storytelling and interesting use cases, lies in leveraging pivotal successes achieved by your most accomplished customers. By centering your prospecting messages around these high-impact achievements, you provide tangible proof of value and drive meaningful engagement from the outset. These insights should illuminate paths for surpassing the competition, demonstrating not only what is possible but how specific strategies and technologies can directly influence your client's market positioning and profitability.

CEOs respond best to narratives that are grounded in measurable results and real-world successes in their industry. Collaborate closely with the executive staff to refine your message, ensuring that it aligns with their strategic goals and speaks directly to pressing business challenges. This partnership helps distill complex achievements into compelling insights that highlight potential competitive advantages. In my own experience, significant transactions secured through this process have featured a 57 percent close rate and overall revenue amounting to $12.8 million. This success enabled 12 percent of our top-tier sellers to exceed their annual quotas by 250 percent, a dramatic rise from the previous 3 percent.

DIFFERENTIATED VALUE IN SALES

This book will help you escape the drudgery of using the same old sales methodology every time. Not every baseball player can (or should) swing for the fences with every pitch, and not every prospective deal is a good fit for executive engagement. In fact, you often need a foundation of positive transactions with a client before you can move on to top-down value creation. The allocation of your efforts should be tailored to the specific demands of your territory, balancing your capacity for planning to meet your unique individual objectives.

I'm not talking about abandoning transactional sales in favor of pursuing 100 percent strategic engagement deals. Transactional deals are the baseline of your business, after all. But you should rethink how much work time you're investing in each category. Enterprise sellers, I believe, should invest around 30 percent of their time in preparing strategic engagements, while devoting the other 70 percent to transactional sales that deliver consistent quarterly revenue. For sellers to surpass 135 percent of their quota, they must invest at least ten hours per week in researching and preparing to connect with executives in new accounts. Meanwhile, every GTM organization needs a clear understanding of how and when to activate both tracks—top-down and bottom-up—so teams can determine the best way to move forward on each transaction. This can be uncomfortable at times, but agility is required to achieve any lasting success in sales.

TWO PIPELINE APPROACHES

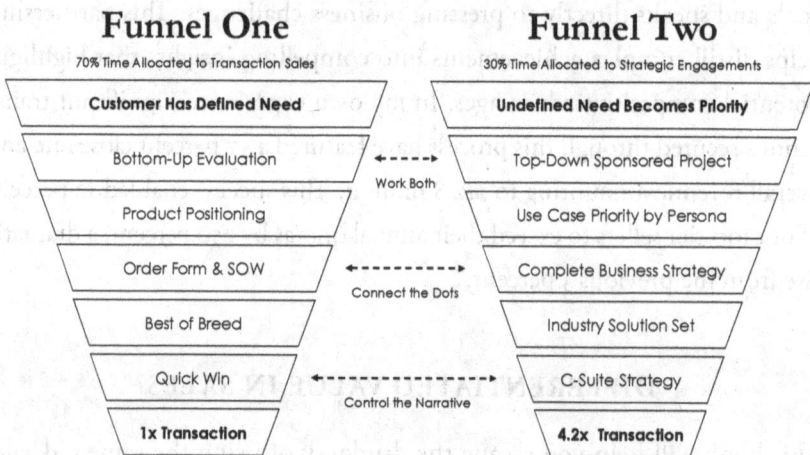

Funnel One
70% Time Allocated to Transaction Sales

Funnel Two
30% Time Allocated to Strategic Engagements

Funnel One	Funnel Two
Customer Has Defined Need	Undefined Need Becomes Priority
Bottom-Up Evaluation	Top-Down Sponsored Project
Product Positioning	Use Case Priority by Persona
Order Form & SOW	Complete Business Strategy
Best of Breed	Industry Solution Set
Quick Win	C-Suite Strategy
1x Transaction	4.2x Transaction

Work Both

Connect the Dots

Control the Narrative

Diagram 1.4 Time Allocation to Optimize Revenue Attainment

Each GTM professional should determine the time they dedicate to target account selling in Funnel Two, based on their territory's accounts. It's essential that everyone on your sales team allocates focused time to fostering strategic engagements, ensuring impactful and meaningful connections.

As the diagram that follows reminds us, effective selling relies on effective communication across levels of engagement. Engagements initiated at the highest levels in an account often lead to several referrals across the organization, garnering accelerated buy-in along the way, and opens the door for progress reports directly to the CEO. But momentum within accounts is also fostered by offering quarterly partnership summary readouts across different levels in the organization. Executives value the ability to scrutinize these details, both to inform their teams and to track the most deal-relevant information. To maintain control over the flow of information from the bottom up, ensure that your champions are always equipped with the latest updates *before* your executives reach out to validate with their teams and engage in executive bridging. Your champions can brief their executives internally without being caught off guard. Remember, executives can easily distinguish mere vendors—those who only want to sell their solutions—from the trustworthy advisors who provide complete business strategies that drive their executive compensation. What kind of partner will you be?

THREE LEVELS OF ENGAGEMENT

CEO	SVP	DIRECTOR
Value Creation Top Down	Business Challenges by Operating Unit	Product Capabilities Bottom Up

Diagram 1.5 Manage the Flow of Information Between These Levels

THE TRUTH ABOUT CREATING MOMENTUM

Though most sales professionals create demand, a significant percentage of them do not optimize either their transaction sales or their executive engagement funnels. In fact, only 3 percent leverage both, largely because executive engagement is far riskier—and far less comfortable—than piecemeal deals with your enamored champion. But that champion will only introduce you to their leadership team 8 percent of the time, a number far too low to rely on for *Hyperscale Revenue* success. Even worse, those accounts often degrade into customer success roles rather than active sales, limiting the salesperson's ability to develop net new executive relationships.

Why is this the case? Over 92 percent of sales professionals identify building relationships as their key skill in sales. As valuable as that skill can be, do you seriously think that executives care more about conference-room rapport than developing a unique and profitable business strategy? Leading with a business strategy is required to establish the necessary credibility to advise an executive, especially for large, unbudgeted projects. Executives' decision criteria are completely different from their evaluation teams' requirements. Without access to the executive team, your deal will always be a lower priority.

Changing that narrative begins by proactively engaging executive stakeholders early in the sales process. To establish strategic momentum, your sales teams must move beyond transactional conversations focused merely on features and functionality, instead guiding evaluations toward strategic outcomes directly tied to executive-level priorities. This shift requires a comprehensive grasp of executives' objectives, sufficient business acumen to identify and address strategic business challenges, and meticulous alignment with your customers' organizational goals.

Both the comfort and simplicity of transactional sales obscure their inherent limitations. Typically, fragmented and short-term in focus, these deals rely heavily on internal advocates or champions who rarely push past straightforward deal renewals. Consequently, revenue opportunities shrink, and long-term strategic relationships become challenging to cultivate.

Conversely, strategic executive engagement allows sales professionals to directly influence high-level organizational decisions, tapping into broader budgets and more strategic initiatives. This approach significantly enhances deal value, partnership longevity, and organizational alignment, fundamentally transforming transactional interactions into strategic collaborations.

Sales professionals must clearly articulate their unique differential value to effectively engage executives, who typically seek solutions that offer tangible strategic outcomes and competitive differentiation. Therefore, sales teams must clearly and persuasively demonstrate how their offerings uniquely support executives' strategic priorities, emphasizing measurable value and alignment with broader business objectives. That requires substantial and careful preparation: Your team should arrive at discussions armed with an informed executive perspective. Likewise, they should demonstrate strategic depth by delivering strategic insights, understanding relevant industry trends, and offering actionable solutions to executive-level business issues. Not only will this build credibility and trust, but it will clearly differentiate your teams from competitors still confined to transactional selling methods.

Elevated business acumen will support this advanced selling approach. By deepening their understanding of industry dynamics, executive-level key performance indicators (KPIs), strategic decision-making processes, and economic drivers, sales professionals position themselves as trusted strategic advisors. This transition enables more impactful executive interactions, deeper client engagement, increased trust, and more substantial revenue growth. Industry benchmarking further supports this transformation by providing clear, objective metrics against which sales teams can assess performance, identify gaps, and target improvement areas. Benchmarking reveals areas where executive engagement may be insufficient, guiding sales teams toward essential skills and practices needed for successful strategic selling.

Finally, structured executive engagement frameworks provide sales teams with a clear, repeatable roadmap for executive interactions. These frameworks help professionals strategically map stakeholders, develop targeted messaging, effectively prepare for executive conversations, and ensure consistent alignment of sales efforts with high-level executive objectives. Adopting these strategic practices significantly elevates demand creation, unlocking substantial growth potential, deepening client relationships, and securing sustainable competitive advantages.

RAISING BUSINESS ACUMEN

Picture this: As CEO, you have just experienced the single most significant revenue increase in your company's history, all stemming from an email that took merely three hours to write. It quantified your client's value realization and outlined a compelling GTM strategy for both companies. Now, just four months later, your revenue from that client has skyrocketed from $750,000 to an astounding $6.2 million, after five years of modest transactions, all thanks to unwavering dedication from both you and your leadership team. It was a major win, despite the pushback you got from your most trusted advisors about sending that email in the first place.

Now you face another critical decision: Should you take another big risk and implement this executive engagement model in your other top fifty accounts? The executive sponsor who convinced you to prioritize your client's CEO's needs has still only been with the company for a few weeks, while you've spent the last nine years building your teams, winning accounts, and communicating your strategic vision. Can he really persuade 125 key stakeholders to do the research and generate the content they need for similar strategic engagements? Ultimately, you decide to move forward, not just because of one income boost but because you saw firsthand how customer value creation transformed your professional relationships.

Spoiler alert: It worked. With the backing of the CEO, I successfully empowered 1,200 GTM professionals in just three months by overhauling our firm's global sales methodology. This revamped approach established executive-level customer deliverables as the key milestones, resulting in a substantial increase in annual contract value from $384,000 to $786,000 within four months. Additionally, it shortened our sales cycle by seven months and boosted win rates by 34 percent. A year later, our company was acquired for $5.6 billion, as the acquiring firm's sales teams found it virtually impossible to compete with our industry-leading GTM strategies.

The point of this story is that any major change—especially one that overhauls a central workflow—requires strategic decision-making and leadership support, ideally including the CEO. As we prepared to roll out the new method, Reed didn't just announce that we were changing gears. He initiated a global account program call to share his story: the proposal that shocked him, the advice that made him nervous, and of course the achievement that made it all worthwhile. Likewise, when you want to change your company's revenue arc, you have to lead through elite execution. The email to Steve would have meant little coming from me, but coming from Reed it confirmed our company's all-in dedication to our mutual success. When a

CEO commits to a strategy, it can unlock extraordinary professional achievements and unparalleled success.

If only 3 percent of your team currently has experience in crafting strategic engagements, and your goal is to elevate that figure to 12 percent within the next four quarters—potentially generating an extra $187.2 million in revenue—wouldn't it be prudent to invest your efforts in championing this executive initiative?

INDUSTRY BENCHMARKING

If a salesperson offered you detailed industry insights, including practical benchmarks comparing your firm to your competitors, would you take the meeting? Of course you would—the data alone would enhance your outcomes, and the free strategy consultation would be icing on the cake! You can use that same approach to create differentiated value for your own customers, as long as you're willing to put in the work.

You likely have hundreds of customers, with at least ten to fifteen in a given industry that have adopted innovative solutions from your company. So how do you gather actionable insights without the benefit of formal case studies with pre-quantified metrics for every industry segment? A good starting point is to identify your target account's main competitors through a simple web search. From there, you can cross-reference these accounts with your company's Customer Relationship Management (CRM) system, to see whether (and to what extent) they've implemented your solutions.

To gain deeper insights into your potential customer case studies, schedule a thirty-minute call with the sales engineers at your company responsible for each of the competitor accounts. Use this conversation to delve into the customer's journey with your proposed solutions: How did they get started? Which use cases did they prioritize to implement first, and in which sequence? Who are the primary stakeholders or personas involved? Which operating units utilize your insights? Which metrics do they track within their industry? Which metrics do we provide their executives? What business benefits and value have they realized from using your solutions? These details may not be formally documented, but they will definitely help you develop future discovery questions and ultimately engage executives at your prospect's firm. The goal is to start the meeting with an industry expert's perspective.

BENCHMARK COMPARISONS

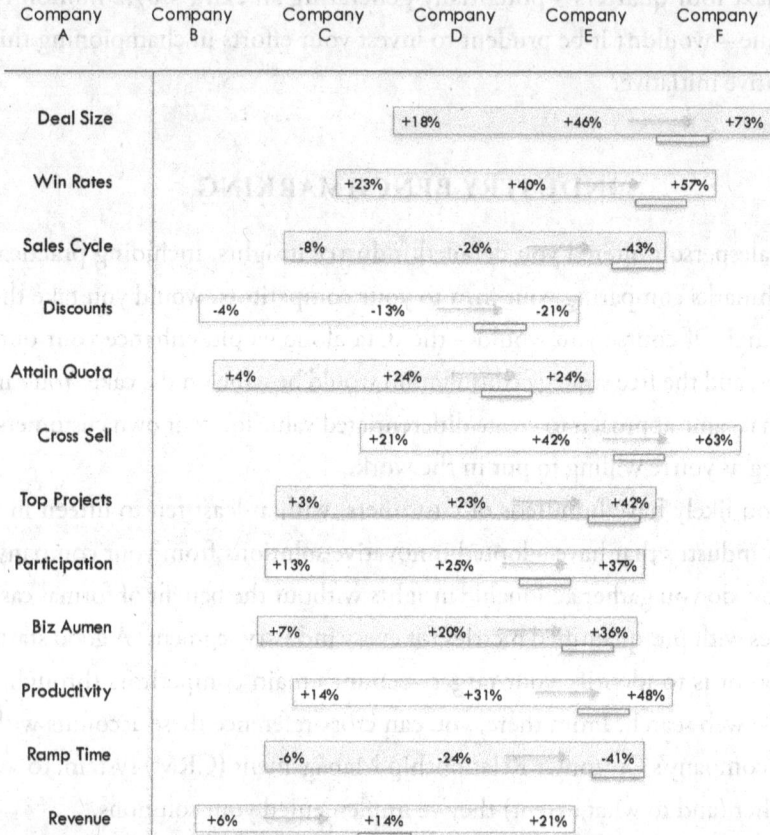

	Company A	Company B	Company C	Company D	Company E	Company F
Deal Size			+18%		+46%	+73%
Win Rates		+23%		+40%		+57%
Sales Cycle	-8%		-26%		-43%	
Discounts	-4%		-13%	-21%		
Attain Quota	+4%		+24%	+24%		
Cross Sell			+21%		+42%	+63%
Top Projects		+3%		+23%		+42%
Participation	+13%		+25%		+37%	
Biz Aumen	+7%		+20%		+36%	
Productivity		+14%		+31%		+48%
Ramp Time	-6%		-24%		-41%	
Revenue	+6%		+14%		+21%	

Data was collected from sales operation teams from 2014 to 2024.

Diagram 1.6 Identify Gaps in Performance

Through these techniques, you can independently craft three distinct account profiles for any industry segment where you already have happy customers. By stepping back and analyzing the roadmaps of each account, then identifying what is lacking, you can effectively amass years of industry expertise from just a handful of thirty-minute conversations with your expert solutions consultants who know their use cases. This method is the most powerful way to gain leverage, positioning you to add significant value for any member of your customer's executive leadership team. Specifically, by providing a scorecard that compares your customer's current results to their peers and offers recommendations for unique competitive roadmaps, you can highlight future competitive advantages. More importantly, documenting use cases enables meaningful business-level discussions with anyone within a target account, broadening your scope of influence with new stakeholders. It's important to note that industry insights are blended to not provide proprietary data to a competitor.

Let me show you how this worked out at one firm. We hired Ben early in his sales career, and at the time of this project, he had only been with our company for six weeks. However, he was an eager and hard worker with business advisory experience. We also had access to an excellent resource: a comprehensive framework of thirty-five use cases, developed over seven months and provided by a renowned global manufacturing brand as a baseline. Ben's goal was to engage executives from an electronics distributor and a separate transportation company. Using the existing use cases as a model, he embarked on a mission to interview customers from each of the two industries.

Through diligent research within our company's CRM system, Ben pinpointed four comparable companies in the electronics distribution sector and another four in the transportation sector. By interviewing five different solution engineers, he developed detailed profiles for each target company that he wanted to engage. This effort enabled Ben to craft a unique perspective, including three-year strategic roadmaps for each of his accounts. The resulting documents identified their business challenges, recommended customer value creation solutions, and articulated the initial economic benefits they could expect.

Ben completed this meticulous preparation before he had ever had his first conversation with either of the executive teams—two very different accounts. As a result, Ben brought a well-informed executive point of view in his very first interaction with each prospect. Could you imagine what would happen if each of your sales professionals took this approach for every new account? You must take time to learn your accounts before engaging the executive teams. Understanding and expertly presenting the top use cases in their industry segment demonstrates significant business acumen, and it will even offer value to executives with decades of experience in their industry.

ARRIVING WITH AN EXECUTIVE POINT OF VIEW

Have you ever paused to contemplate why 82 percent of all the contacts in your CRM system occupy positions at or below the director level? Here's one reason: When onboarding new employees, you meticulously train them in the intricacies and capabilities of your product. Throughout their tenure with your company, these employees find themselves engaging with customer executives and are eager to discuss your product capabilities, only to be referred to the directors who report to them. You are sent to who you sound like, which in this case is someone at the director level. If you can't articulate the value of your business strategy in a few sentences, you will not be granted access to the executive suite to uncover the true decision criteria that form the basis for making an unplanned investment.

Executives, having invested many decades in their respective industries, expect you to convey the value you bring through the specific lens of their industry segment. They seek tangible benefits from your solutions, framed in terms of proven metrics that can provide actionable insights to optimize their business operations. They are not interested in the granular details of how you developed your product to support certain features, or in your company history, or in just how much your CEO "turned the industry upside-down." Unfortunately, this is what nearly every sales professional focuses on, because that is what you have trained them to learn.

Given these trends, wouldn't it be more advantageous to empower thousands of your sellers to collaborate with their peers to create industry benchmarks? Wouldn't you like your GTM team members to evolve into industry experts through focused and relevant research, which they can leverage in every sales conversation? Instead of talking to yet another director, this would enable each seller to engage with a diverse array of fifteen different executives across various departments—including supply chain, finance, product, sales, information technology, and security. They will be experts on far more than your technical features, and more importantly they can retain the knowledge and provide an interesting perspective from your customers' world, utilizing their terminology and specific use cases that drive a unique competitive advantage.

How can you do this? Start by developing a robust executive point of view on the business, tailor it to your audience's persona, and understand the critical use cases that drive substantial business-level conversations. Instead of mentioning your product names, modules, or specific capabilities, discuss the overarching value your clients can derive from them, as outlined in the strategic engagements we've previously covered. Share compelling customer stories within their industry that have meaning to them, prioritize use cases by persona to provide focus, highlight the business metrics that provide clear economic benefit, and document the potential incremental value aligned with their strategic priorities—the same ones you've already clearly articulated within your customer story.

To do any of this work, you may well need to shift your mindset about your strategic partnerships, beginning with a better understanding of how strategic engagements are conducted. I recommend following this proven approach that will allow you to create new strategic engagements by curating personalized content, leveraging virtual teams, and communicating your perspective through your executive sponsor. The best way to master this new process is to see one done for you, do one yourself, and teach one—train someone on your team to prepare and execute the content required to create an effective strategic engagement with a C-suite executive they have never met before.

THE EXECUTIVE CONVERSATION

	S	U	M	O
Customer Value Creation	We have identified three go-to-market strategies that will drive $343 million in the next year	1. Social Marketing 2. Cloud Capabilities 3. Enable Social Selling	Acquisition +12% Interactions +38% Engage +34%	Social selling extends enterprise marketing leadership
Partnership Benefits	Strategic partnership from an average vendor relationship	a. New Route to Market b. 20,000 GTM users	Increase ARR from $750k up to $6.2m in four months	Add enterprise marketing capabilities

Diagram 1.7 Collaborating with an Executive Leadership Team

What proportion of your sales team can come to an initial meeting armed with insights and actionable recommendations to help a prospect begin their journey with you?

As a leader, you must equip your teams to establish industry benchmarks that provide compelling findings that add value to executives. Ask yourselves the following questions.

STORIES: Can you offer industry insights and best practices to executives?

USE CASES: Can you articulate a value proposition tailored to specific personas, aiding executives to refer you to their direct reports?

METRICS: Can you demonstrate the measurable benefit of your solutions? What about the size of the opportunity for the customer?

OPPORTUNITY: How much time will it take from your customer's top resources to make this proposal real? How does it dovetail with their strategic priorities?

Key Practice: Deliver value to executives before every meeting. Communicate ahead of time that you intend to invest your resources in their company to build a partnership.

ENGAGEMENT FRAMEWORKS

Here's how my firm turned a $750,000 down–renewal into $18.6 million dollars within four months, using the unmatched power of CEO sponsorship.

CEO GTM EMAIL

SUBJECT: Go-to-Market Strategy

Hi Stephen,

My team has identified three strategic go-to-market initiatives that will seamlessly integrate into our customer experience offerings, projected to yield an impressive $343 million in additional economic benefits within the next twelve months. The first initiative aims to enhance your enterprise marketing by leveraging sophisticated social listening and engagement tools, potentially generating an additional $186 million in revenue. The second initiative proposes moving our solution from current cloud competitors to your infrastructure, estimated to contribute an extra $93 million in cloud revenue. The third initiative is centered on equipping twenty thousand sales professionals with advanced social selling tools to cultivate stronger client relationships, expected to boost sales by $64 million.

Who on your executive leadership team should we work with to validate these projections?

Warm regards,

Reed

Diagram 1.8 The CEO Email That Changed the Story

The outcome: A Fortune 50 CEO responded in two hours, assigning three EVPs in Product, Sales, and Marketing to review and verify our projections. Four months later, the CEO signed a contract for $18.6 million—at that point, our company's largest prior transaction was $4.1 million.

Every CFO needs to measure the value of their investment before committing to a purchase. Your teams should be able to quantify and project the potential benefits of your solutions before your initial conversion, then commit to providing these readouts once a quarter to the executive leadership team to ensure value expansions. Here's what that might look like:

Partnership Summary
ENTERPRISE RESILIENCE

Accel
Consumer Goods

Industry leading net earnings growth have outpaced your industry competitors. As part of the digital transformation, investing in next-generation supply chain platforms is crucial for enabling real-time visibility, data-driven coordination, and predictive responsiveness across the global value chain. These capabilities are essential in today's volatile environment, where disruptions, fluctuating demand, and evolving consumer expectations require dynamic and proactive management.

Strategies	Consumer Package Goods Best Practices
Market Penetration	Foresee changes, identify emerging opportunities, and respond with agility in product innovation, marketing, supply chain optimization, and customer engagement. Accelerate time-to-market for high-potential offerings. Enhance personalization and relevance in consumer touchpoints. Improve resource allocation and reduce operational inefficiencies. Capitalize on early signals to drive category leadership and growth.
Digital Transformation	Modernized Data Architecture establishes a scalable, cloud-enabled data infrastructure, integrating both structured and unstructured data across the enterprise. This unified data foundation supports real-time analytics across various business functions. Seamless data access empowers cross-functional decision-making, while AI/ML integration fosters adaptive learning and continuous optimization.
Supply Chain Resilience	Swiftly detect and respond to shifts in consumer demand patterns with remarkable speed and precision. This capability enables rapid inventory reallocation, boosts promotional effectiveness, and enhances service levels across both retail and direct-to-consumer channels. Real-time monitoring and analytics throughout sourcing, production, and logistics functions.

Benchmark: Company A   Company B   Company C   Company D

Consumer Package Goods Insights

Industry Solution Set	JUN	JUL	AUG	SEP	OCT	NOV	DEC	JAN
A) Provide CPG AI Innovations	☐							
B) Prioritize CPG Resilient Use Cases		☐						
C) Deliver Quantifiable Metrics				☐				

Diagram 1.9 Collaborate with an Executive Leadership Team

Gaining traction in new accounts is more challenging than you might expect, particularly when your target executive doesn't yet recognize you or isn't aware of the value your company can provide. To encourage them to take the time to read and validate your plan, you will need advanced insights, an innovative approach, and most of all a double portion of tenacity.

MOMENTUM THEORY

When you propose a solution that aligns seamlessly with the executive's priorities, challenges, and goals, and tailor you're messaging to resonate with the executive's strategic vision and business outcomes, it becomes essential.

Why change?

Challenge:	Not able to create enough strategic engagements with executives. Proven way to **engage executives** to secure initial meetings. Create unbudgeted projects that open up new markets.

How do we differentiate?

Concept 1:	**Developing CEO Strategies** begins with a clear vision that aligns with the company's strengths and emerging opportunities. The process starts with in-depth market analysis. Competitor benchmarks, industry reports, and customer feedback shape the landscape.
Concept 2:	**The Executive Conversation** consists of four components that make it compelling to the C-suite. The first is a story to provide context, use cases to identify persona, metrics to determine the size of the impact, and opportunity to make real with expert resource availability.
Concept 3:	**Industry Expertise from Benchmarking** uncovers areas of opportunity to create new areas of competitive advantage to leapfrog the competition by leveraging industry best practices.
Concept 4:	**Influence Outcomes** is having the ability to shape opinions, behaviors, and decisions of individuals or groups. Successful influence outcomes often rely on credibility, emotional connection, and clear communication.

What do we receive?

Result:	Guaranteed sales consistently overachieve their quarterly plans. Providing complete business strategies **increases deal size +73%**. Career development path to evolve into a top-1% sales professional.

TIPS AND TRICKS FOR CREATING MOMENTUM

- Momentum entails transforming demand creation through strategic executive engagement. In my experience, sales professionals frequently gravitate toward transactional methods, appreciating their comfort, predictability, and perceived safety. However, this preference for familiar approaches can significantly limit the potential for growth, scalability, and long-lasting strategic relationships. Recent research underscores this issue, revealing that only 3 percent of sales professionals effectively balance transactional sales with strategic executive engagement. Yet those who successfully combine these approaches experience notably enhanced sales outcomes, deeper executive relationships, and increased strategic opportunities.

- Recognizing and addressing this critical gap is essential. Successful transformation requires sales teams to **embrace structured and strategic engagement practices** designed specifically for executive-level stakeholders. That begins with understanding the intense pressures and demands executives face, particularly in today's environment where virtual interactions dominate. Executives contend with an overwhelming volume of virtual meetings and communications, leading to fatigue and reduced attention spans. Therefore, sales professionals must deliver concise, compelling messages that quickly resonate and directly address executives' most pressing strategic concerns.

- Moving beyond transactional sales is critical. While transactional selling focuses narrowly on short-term gains, it inadvertently restricts access to executive-level stakeholders and limits potential strategic impact. Transitioning away from this transactional mind-set opens opportunities for larger, more impactful engagements. By **strategically positioning solutions** as integral to the executives' broader organizational goals, sales professionals can gain entry into the higher-level discussions necessary for sustained account growth and strategic partnership.

- Strategic executive engagement is indispensable for influencing critical business decisions and achieving meaningful outcomes. Engaging executives early and consistently enables sales teams to align closely with organizational priorities, substantially increasing deal sizes, and enhancing long-term relationship quality and profitability. Clearly **articulating unique differential value** within these engagements becomes paramount, as executives prioritize measurable outcomes and strategic advantages. To build and maintain credibility, sales teams must adeptly communicate precisely how their offerings uniquely address executives' business objectives.

- Preparing for these executive interactions requires enhancing the overall business acumen of your sales professionals. By deeply understanding industry trends, financial metrics, competitive dynamics, and strategic decision-making processes, sales representatives evolve into trusted advisors who consistently provide valuable insights. This elevated status significantly improves their effectiveness in executive-level conversations and strategic engagements.

- Industry benchmarking emerges as a powerful tool in this strategic transformation. By objectively measuring **performance against industry standards**, sales teams can identify gaps in executive engagement capabilities, pinpoint targeted areas for development, and continuously refine their strategies. This rigorous analysis ensures that sales professionals remain aligned with best practices, driving continuous improvement.

- Implementing structured executive engagement frameworks provides a repeatable and consistent roadmap to success. Effective frameworks emphasize targeted messaging aligned with executive personas, strategic communication timing—such as contacting executives at strategic moments before scheduled meetings—and employing advanced outreach methods like FedEx deliveries that require a signature, when conventional communication proves ineffective.

- Sustaining momentum in executive engagements involves coordinated activities with business development representatives (BDRs). By systematically involving BDRs—such as through blind-copying them on critical communications and empowering them to establish rapport with executive assistants—sales teams can create robust internal relationships, significantly enhancing referral opportunities and engagement effectiveness.
- Monitoring and **measuring engagement effectiveness** ensures sustained success. By systematically tracking message impact and internal circulation, sales professionals gain valuable insights into executives' interests and internal dynamics, allowing them to refine their strategies continuously.

In conclusion, by systematically embracing structured executive engagement strategies, your sales professionals can dramatically increase their executive interaction rates—from as low as 1 percent to as high as 41 percent. This strategic approach positions your sales teams as trusted partners, enhances client relationships, and consistently delivers exceptional value through every interaction.

MOMENTUM WORKBOOK
INFLUENCE OUTCOMES

Momentum Frameworks

1 PARTNERSHIP SUMMARY	Strategic document profiles unique value and your expertise • Clearly communicate what sets your organization apart

2 CEO IMPACT EMAIL	Gain initial interest securing a referral to their direct report • Requires precision, credibility, and value-driven narrative
3 BUSINESS STRATEGY	Provide roadmap with goals and actions required to achieve success • Structured plan guides team toward its strategic objectives
4 INVESTMENT STRATEGY	Projected economic benefit in a one-page executive scorecard • Impact allows decision-makers to assess and prioritize value

Momentum Sales Plays

5 OBJECTIVES	Priorities involve actively listening, aligning your solutions • Strategic goals demonstrate your commitment to their success
6 STAKEHOLDERS	• Identify, connect with, and influence key decision-makers, Influencer champions with your industry expertise
7 RESEARCH	Leveraging industry-specific data to create a compelling message • Provocative conversations with executives
8 OUTBOUND	Value-driven messages that capture their attention • Sequenced touches create interest to drive demand
9 SCHEDULE	Efficiently manage time and prioritize high-impact activities • Protect your time allocated to create executive demand
10 INTEREST	Strategically building engagement in a series of well-planned interactions • Optimize revenue, cost, and productivity

11 SPONSORSHIP	Secure high-level support to accelerate deal velocity • Align strategic priorities to drive long-term customer success
12 INSIGHT	Enhance effectiveness leveraging customer insights • Data-driven insights based on segment best practices
13 SUCCESS PLAN	Collaborative framework defines shared goals • Measurable outcomes in quarterly business review readouts
14 LAND	Leverage proven industry success after being live twelve months • Create unique competitive advantage
15 REVIEWS	Assess performance of existing partnership, aligned to objectives • Executive dashboard metrics identify new opportunities
16 URGENCY	Industry-relevant insights to capture executive attention • Motivate immediate action with the art of proactive nudges
17 CHAMPIONS	Identify, engage, and equip key stakeholders to advocate • Actionable deliverables empowered decision-making
18 MEASURABLES	Proven measurable outcomes from your solution impacts • Results provide clear and quantifiable evidence of success
19 PROOF	Case studies showcase the real-world impact of your solutions • Third-party industry success stories with measurable outcomes
20 WORKSHOPS	Consultative sessions leveraging your expertise and insights • Trusted advisors build consensus to redefine decision criteria

21 PROGRESSION	Maintain continuous engagement cadence for consistency • Track executive value engagement each quarter on webinar
22 ABOVE THE LINE	Top-down executive engagement process drives alignment • Secure C-suite referral to direct report critical to secure large deals
23 OPERATIONS	Proven use cases aligned to operational challenges and performance goals • Solution-focused advisor that drives measurable outcomes
24 BELOW THE LINE	Bottom-up director engagement verifies required capabilities • Work with coach for guidance to secure small transactions

Diagram 1.10 How to Create Momentum in Accounts

EVERYDAY APPLICATIONS

In everyday interactions, it is crucial to discern what holds the greatest significance for your audience when they make a decision. What criteria do they take into account when making a purchase? What needs might that purchase meet for them? Have you built sufficient credibility on the topic to earn their trust before you begin to share value with them? If they are willing to disclose their decision criteria, you can then share your own relevant experiences, potentially helping them reassess their priorities. These specific factors underpin their decision-making for a particular purchase.

Moreover, it's essential to step back and recognize potentially competing priorities that might overshadow this individual purchase. What else is on their list of top five priorities, how are they ranked, and why? This broader context of macro factors influences decision-making for any individual purchase, often based on the investment level required.

If you're going to **influence outcomes** you need to share your customers' experiences from their point of view. Use compelling stories to get your prospect to open up to you and share their opinions: What is most important to them and why? Everyone has a unique perspective on their favorite topics. Some people will share readily while others need to be prompted to share the underlying reasons they believe in a certain approach that has worked for them in the past.

You should be thinking about this like a tennis match featuring a consistent back and forth, with insights and value given from both sides. It's not a monologue, and it's certainly not an interrogation where you don't offer anything of substance in response to their information. Most sales approaches recommend a list of discovery questions to ask prospects in rapid succession, leaving your prospect feeling like they have not received any value or guidance they can apply to their current decision. When individuals become uncommunicative, it often indicates that you haven't established enough credibility for them to share their decision criteria or their most pressing competing priorities.

The most impactful way to engage anyone is to do your research ahead of time, so you can come up with a compelling point of view they had not considered before your conversation. Your point of view should come from what your most successful customers have shared with you, based on their experiences receiving value from your solution. This provides third-party validation and guidance for your prospect to share with you what is important to them and why. This is called **reciprocity**, and it's a natural human response: We feel a personal obligation to share our insights after we've received valuable guidance.[*]

MOMENTUM KEY TAKEAWAYS

1. Do your GTM teams have access to 30 percent of your market or 100 percent?

   Profile your industry successes to create newly defined need.

2. Can you quantify customers' measurable results to share with prospects?

   Value realization is required for hyperscale revenue growth.

---

[*] *Influence*, Robert Cialdini

3. Are you waiting for your coach to introduce you to the executive leadership team?

Working with the director level, there's a 23-percent close rate on transaction sales.

4. What gains a CEO's attention more than creating a unique competitive advantage?

Working with the C-suite, there's a 63 percent close rate on significant unbudgeted transactions.

5. Can you build a hyperscale growth company without securing significant transactions?

Increasing sellers that attain 250 percent of plan from 3 percent in the field to 12 percent within twelve months.

6. How many of your GTM team members can orchestrate strategic engagements?

Only 3 percent of your sellers engage executives with new creative business strategies.

7. How many sellers can recommend use cases that create competitive advantage?

Initiate net new meetings with executives that accept 1 percent today up to 41 percent within three months.

8. In initial meetings, do sellers share unique insights with actionable recommendation?

Communicate how your most successful customers have enhanced business results.

SUMMARY

Most companies only tap into 30 percent of their market potential by relying heavily on inbound-qualified leads generated by marketing. This limited approach often results in stagnant pipeline development, as GTM teams passively wait for opportunities to be delivered to them instead of actively generating them. This throttles close rates, often with only one in four engagements yielding revenue. Reactive GTM teams' hesitation to engage without guaranteed revenue creates missed opportunities.

To address these challenges, you must diversify your firm's pipeline development across two primary channels. The first, waiting for inbound leads, works for director-level evaluations driven by marketing efforts. The second, strategic engagements are high-value opportunities driven by executive leadership sponsorship and offer far more potential revenue.

Creating sustainable growth requires structured performance pathways, built around three foundational pillars: strategic leadership that fosters executive sponsorship for pipeline initiatives, GTM strategies aligned with C-suite priorities, and leadership involvement to encourage key engagements.

Overall, you must build and maintain a **culture of value creation** that promotes continuous engagement and customer-focused problem-solving. Develop solutions that extend beyond immediate revenue. Empower your teams to build long-term customer relationships. To reach this goal, you should define daily behaviors that establish clear, measurable activities for GTM teams. Here's a few to get you started.

Prioritize outreach, account mapping, and executive engagement.

Encourage consistent tracking of weekly pipeline development that shows the progression that has been made.

Deliver elite results by setting performance benchmarks tied to strategic objectives.

Conduct regular performance reviews and pipeline assessments.

Implement feedback loops to refine engagement strategies.

Tailoring your engagement strategies to your client CEO's priorities positions your company as a critical strategic partner. Prioritize solutions that drive additional revenue growth, strategies that lower operational costs, and processes that improve team productivity.

Furthermore, CEOs place great value on an executive dashboard that offers unique insights into their current business strategy, especially in areas that have been difficult for them to quantify. In Chapter 2, we will explore how to engage CEOs and their strategic vision to create an ideal executive dashboard, so we can collaboratively manage change in their desired business model.

CHAPTER 2

ALIGNMENT

Curate Executive Insights

(Increases Cross Sell by 63 Percent)

CHAPTER 2

- ➤ **PLAYING FOR THE ENDGAME:** Start with the Answer
- ➤ **EXECUTIVE ENGAGEMENT:** Be Compelling
- ➤ **RELATIONSHIP VS. BUSINESS STRATEGY:** Bet Their Career
- ➤ **CUSTOMER VALUE CREATION:** Add Value in Every Interaction

---

- ➤ **TRUTH ABOUT GAINING ALIGNMENT:** Value in Interactions
- ➤ **REDEFINING DECISION CRITERIA:** Create an Unfair Advantage
- ➤ **THREE-TIER SOLUTIONS:** Personalized by Persona
- ➤ **PROVIDING INDUSTRY INSIGHTS:** Your Successful Customers

---

- ➤ **EXECUTIVE FRAMEWORKS:** Initiate Executive Meetings
- ➤ **ALIGNMENT THEORY:** Increase Cross Sell 63 Percent
- ➤ **TIPS AND TRICKS:** Influence Funding Outcomes
- ➤ **ALIGNMENT WORKBOOK:** Redefine Decision Criteria

- ➤ **EVERYDAY APPLICATIONS:** Understand Buyer Priorities
- ➤ **KEY TAKEAWAYS:** Build Investment Strategies
- ➤ **SUMMARY:** Curate Executive Insights

PLAYING FOR THE ENDGAME

The CEO of a Fortune 100 communications carrier, Dave, was on the brink of awarding my firm a $146 million contract, but his evaluation team had reached an impasse about making such a high-stakes investment. To gain clarity on Dave's strategic vision for the project, I sat down with him one-on-one on a sunny Tuesday morning. During our discussion, Dave shared his long-term goal: deliver an unparalleled level of customer experience to 18 million consumers while also servicing his business customers. To achieve this, he explained, he needed to be able to monitor—in real-time and on a single dashboard—four critical metrics that would allow him to effectively prioritize his time and the company's resources to deliver consistent revenue results. And then came the thunderbolt: "Can you put that together for me in the next three days?"

With only seventy-two hours to execute a huge project, I left the meeting both excited and anxious. Dave articulated four specific requests for his new dashboard. First, he needed visibility into the number of service requests per product line, to determine if a product needed to be pulled from the market due to readiness issues. Second, he needed revenue breakdowns by product line, to gauge how well his teams were driving market demand for each solution offering. Third, he needed a list of the firm's top thirty business accounts that offered the most significant opportunities for executive engagement that quarter. And most importantly, he needed to track the unresolved issues for each of those accounts, so his team could fix those issues before he confidently approached the client CEOs to secure a commitment for new significant transactions.

Before I boarded my plane from Kansas City back to Dulles, I meticulously pulled together a library of seventy-five different analytic dashboard views, to help me craft a dashboard wireframe that would meet Dave's needs. By the time I landed, I wanted a solid foundation that my sales engineer, Lauren, could use to build the software. I gave Lauren a heads-up to clear her schedule, donned my headphones, and got to work. Three and a half hours later, the adrenaline (and the heat from my laptop) had made my dry-fit golf shirt look like I'd just left the gym, but Dave's dashboard was completely designed, anno-tated with the recommended examples, and populated with the correct data ranges for Lauren to begin her work. She did an amazing job configuring the CEO's views to facilitate his business operations! When the dashboards were ready, I printed and laminated them at FedEx Kinkos, sent them overnight to Dave's office, and scheduled a call with him for Friday morning.

Dave was utterly astonished at how well we had brought his vision to life. During our Friday meeting, he exclaimed, "I can't believe you executed this in such a short time when I have been asking my team for this for the past twelve months! I'm ready to sign off on implementing a new order manage-ment and customer experience platform. I appreciate the swift turnaround, which confirms that your team truly understands our business vision." You can check out the dashboard for yourself in the screenshot on the next page.

This experience underscores an important lesson: While engaging with numerous key stakeholders and influencers is valuable, the CEO is ulti-mately the only one capable of making a **$146 million investment decision**. Without engaging the ultimate decision-maker directly and comprehending their unique decision criteria—which often differ from those of their eval-uation teams—you will not be able to close a deal of this magnitude. As we discussed in Chapter 1, it's crucial to engage with all three levels of influence in an organization, and to craft the narrative of your value proposition to each persona's unique interests and priorities. Your goal is to align all three levels, so your company emerges as the clear and unequivocal choice.

In Dave's case, my team had already spent fifteen months crafting a three-year strategic roadmap, tailoring multiple personalized demonstra-tions for different personas, creating a detailed business case, and developing

EXECUTIVE DASHBOARD

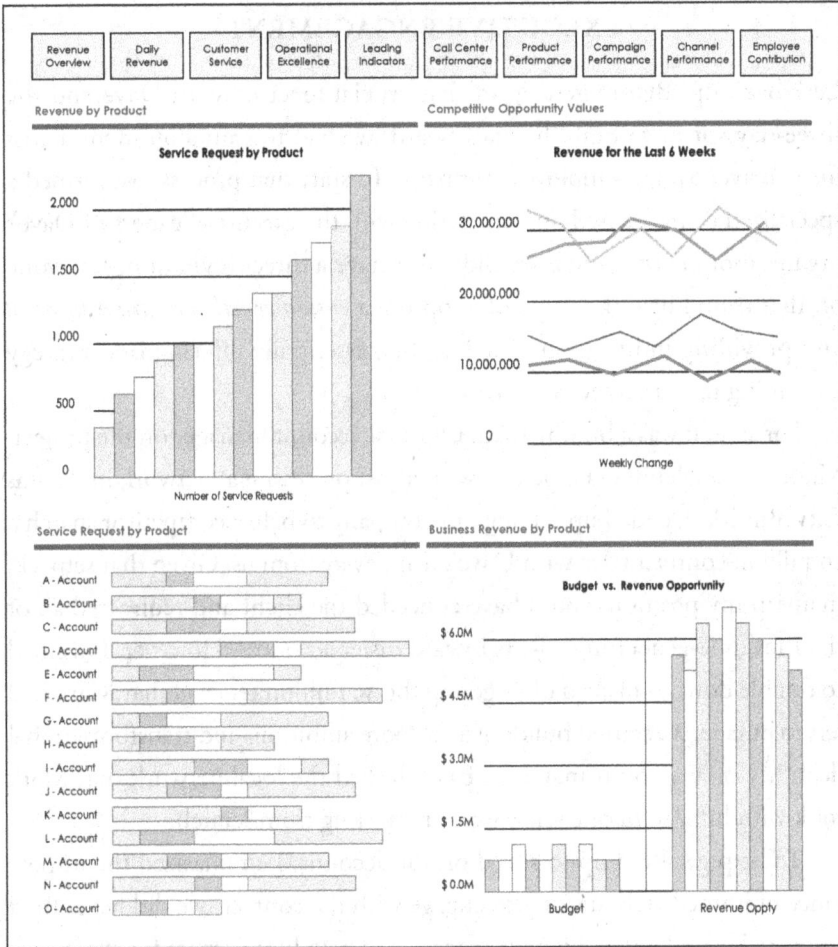

Diagram 2.0 CEO Revenue Dashboard

an implementation plan. But it was the dashboard that persuaded Dave to stand up and make the decision, successfully aligning five separate teams to collaboratively implement a strategic platform for the company. This platform enabled bundled offerings for consumers and provided an executive dashboard to manage organizational change. As a result, customer churn was reduced by 6 percent, and the company generated an additional $487 million in annual revenue.

EXECUTIVE ENGAGEMENT

Let's back up: Before getting to that crucial meeting with Dave and the three-day sprint to build his dashboard, we had to gain alignment across his massive, 63,000-employee company. To start that process, we formed a specialized team focused on connecting with the executive leaders of Dave's organization, even though we didn't yet have a direct invitation. Everyone on that team knew the value of adopting a *customer value creation mindset* and providing industry-specific insights, essentially offering free strategy consulting to our target executives.

For sure, it was a bumpy road. Our first account manager on the project, Mark, was a talented salesperson with a vast professional network in Kansas City. But Mark ended up leaving our company to help a competitor snatch a $9 million contract (also with Dave's firm) away from us. Given that setback, many in my position would have conceded the client and redirected all of their revenue-generating efforts toward easier accounts. However, I decided to double down—instead of targeting the $9 million renewal that Mark had left to pursue, we started building a far more ambitious and transformational deal. My new account manager, Brad, lacked the local network that Mark took with him, so in one sense we were starting from scratch.

To help get Brad up to speed on the account, I emphasized the importance of immediately starting to engage with the contacts we did have. Brad suggested we role-play different scenarios to help him prepare for these conversations, and I was happy to oblige. The next day, we spent several hours simulating interactions with various stakeholders, including the evaluation team, call center management, information technology, and network operations. I managed the engagement with the executive leadership team while Brad became comfortable building relationships with the evaluation stakeholders.

Collectively, we designed personalized content meticulously tailored to each persona we engaged. Enterprise sales is a collaborative effort, where every team member leverages their expertise to contribute unique value. Coordinating all these resources requires significant time and precise planning, and we would often spend a full day preparing for each series of meetings. It took us a month, but through unwavering dedication, compelling messaging, and meticulous organization, we re-established our strategic engagement with the account, eventually facilitating six to eight meetings every day. Those were daunting weeks and months, but we knew we had a unique opportunity to align with each stakeholder's specific business drivers, preparing us to deliver substantial value.

Can you create opportunities with executives that you do not have prior relationships with? Unlike director-level stakeholders, CEOs are looking for complete business strategies to invest in and bet their careers on. Will they bet on you?

RELATIONSHIPS VS. BUSINESS STRATEGY

So far, every candidate I've interviewed for a sales role has emphasized their exceptional talent for forging advanced relationships, a truly commendable trait! But building a professional relationship on personal connections, like cheering for the same sports team, is very different from providing consistently useful strategic insight. Executives don't want ballgame buddies; they want trusted advisors. The best relationships leverage expertise and knowledge of best industry practices to influence unbudgeted funding events. That focus helps you create a documented business strategy that can gain consensus from other executives and secure their backing, no matter who they root for.

In one case, for example, my firm's COO had gone to Harvard Business School with the CRO of our target client's firm. But that prior personal relationship created zero strategic leverage with the CRO because it was based on a completely different set of shared experiences. Instead, the COO should have stressed his professional value: He'd met and worked with dozens of CEOs in the client's industry over the past ten years, advising many of them about effective salesforce implementations. That way, if the CRO happened to remember their time at Harvard, the personal link would be an added bonus instead of the basis for a professional partnership.

Compelling business strategies, confidently delivered through executive deliverables with genuine appeal, will open many more doors than your business school yearbook. Crucially, these deliverables must address and overcome any objections, even those from executives you've never met before. By enabling executive champions to use these documents for indirect selling, you can help them pitch your proposed business strategy as their own. This doesn't mean canceling all your business dinners or forgetting about rapport—but it does mean starting from a strategic foundation and building the relationship from there.

For a company to consider a comprehensive shift in its strategy, a compelling business rationale is indispensable. Let's say they want to streamline the upgrade process for subscribers, allowing them to select bundled packages that include two-year contracts covering up to four service offerings on a single bill. Simplifying the order process for complex services is a monumental task, particularly when you have hundreds of employees who are eager to custom-develop a brand-new solution. A well-documented and compelling business strategy will help your client (and your team) navigate these challenges and drive successful outcomes, based on the measurable case studies you have provided them.

Anytime you can do the work yourself, especially through compelling and unique perspectives, it builds long-term credibility with executives. Executives look for new, creative ideas to stimulate the growth of their business. They also have many inflight projects they need to complete before they can consider yours. But if you work toward long-term outcomes, where every interaction shows your value and builds your engagement brand, you'll be ready when preparation meets opportunity. There is nothing more fulfilling than generating value for customer executives, leading them to expand their strategic partnership with you.

CUSTOMER VALUE CREATION

Code-switching drives executive engagement: You have to speak in their language, not in your company's product vernacular. There is a significant difference between highlighting the benefits of your solution and personalizing a business strategy for your client, based on the best practices that have created a competitive advantage for peers in their industry segment. It's very easy to stay in your mother tongue, especially when everyone in your company is developing white papers and data sheets that are completely focused on your products. It takes real discipline to take a step back, assess your client's landscape, and determine a business strategy that can't be ignored even if the evaluation is still in development. You must understand each client's strategy—and where it comes up short for them—before you can form a reasonable plan to solve the business problem for them.

Specifically, creating customer value involves identifying, enhancing, and delivering use cases (curated by persona) that maximize positive business outcomes for customers. This concept is essential for guiding business strategies that create unique competitive advantages, improve customer satisfaction, and ensure long-term success. Every business has unique differentiation: What unique value propositions distinguish us in the marketplace? It might come through innovation in products, the way services are delivered in phases, different business models, or the way your teams engage customers, but it's never optional. To truly understand your clients' needs and pain points, you must delve deeply into their target customers' preferences and challenges. By identifying these crucial factors, you can collaboratively develop strategies that align seamlessly with customer desires.

Quantifying customer value is vital for defining and assessing value in measurable terms. Metrics such as Net Promoter Score (NPS), Customer Lifetime Value (CLV), and customer satisfaction ratings are commonly used to evaluate how effectively a business is delivering value. Aligning your proposed business strategy with customer value creation ensures that your client's vision, operations, and marketing efforts are all oriented toward delivering value that resonates with the executive leadership team. This alignment ensures that every aspect of the business is focused on meeting and exceeding customer expectations. For instance, a communications carrier client was expecting to convert 12 percent of their consumer customers to bundled service offerings in the first twelve months. With our help, they achieved a 16 percent conversion rate in the first seven months. We provided monthly performance scorecards that highlighted the adoption rate, allowing the client's executives to commit to their stretch goal three months early. Communication is an amazing thing when you provide leading indicators that allow your strategic partners' leadership team to adjust their forecasts.

Customer value creation starts with knowing what is important to executives before you engage them and being able to reference proven, measurable results.

Outcome of Value Creation: Conducting thorough research, referencing best practices, and prioritizing use cases tailored to your audience will enhance your alignment within accounts. Clearly articulate your value proposition and how it aligns with their strategic priorities, emphasizing how you can build on recently completed projects to drive incremental value. Avoid presenting your business strategy in isolation, as this makes it challenging for sponsors to connect it to previous initiatives undertaken by the executive leadership team.

THE TRUTH ABOUT GAINING ALIGNMENT

When you're aiming for meaningful executive engagement, it's essential to begin with a clear vision of the desired outcomes. Starting with well-defined business goals ensures that your conversations remain focused, relevant, and aligned with the strategic priorities and personal aspirations of the executives involved. This initial clarity sets the foundation for a productive partnership and shared long-term success.

Engaging executives requires compelling, personalized communication that deeply resonates with their unique challenges, ambitions, and professional victories. Crafting insightful narratives and evidence-backed stories demonstrates not only your strategic awareness but also your genuine empathy and understanding. Such tailored engagement captures executive attention and fosters an environment conducive to impactful dialogue.

By focusing conversations—especially early ones—around pertinent strategic issues, industry dynamics, and overarching business objectives, you signal your relevance and reliability. Highlighting how your solutions align with their strategic imperatives solidifies that foundation, as it reinforces your dedication to creating tangible customer value. Each interaction should offer strategic insights, comprehensive market analysis, actionable recommendations, or applicable best practices. Such proactive value creation establishes your role as a trusted strategic partner, significantly strengthening executive relationships over time.

Credibility is the cornerstone of influencing executive decision-making processes. Securing the role of a trusted advisor comes only by demonstrating deep expertise, industry understanding, and genuine insight into the challenges and opportunities facing your customers. Your reward is not just a sale, but the opportunity to guide and reshape decision criteria in ways that distinctly favor your differentiated approach.

An effective executive engagement strategy employs a structured, three-layered approach to communication and solutions. At the **strategic** layer, messages must clearly resonate with executive-level visions and objectives. At the **operational** level, discussions should highlight achievable improvements and management-level benefits. Finally, at the **tactical** layer, it is imperative to provide explicit, detailed plans for practical implementation and execution.

Further bolstering your executive engagement strategy involves leveraging success stories and insights from industry-leading customers. Sharing case studies and compelling industry benchmarks underscores the value and relevance of your approach, creating persuasive narratives that directly appeal to executive priorities.

Finally, initiating executive engagement through personalized frameworks demonstrates significant thought, preparation, and respect for each executive's unique context. Customizing your approach through detailed research and tailored strategic frameworks ensures that executives immediately recognize your investment and authenticity, laying the groundwork for a meaningful partnership.

By implementing this thoughtful, narrative-driven approach to executive engagement, you can build robust, strategic relationships and consistently drive meaningful business outcomes.

REDEFINING DECISION CRITERIA

Evaluation teams often begin assessing solutions without consulting the company's executives to understand their priorities. They compile a list of requirements at the project team level, typically assigning them equal weight for scoring. This approach is unrealistic, especially when the evaluators' priorities lack endorsement (or even knowledge) from their decision-making executives. Accordingly, you need to comprehend the unique decision criteria at three levels in the organization—the evaluation team, mid-level management influencers, and the executive leadership team. It is your duty to convey, with deep empathy, how these varying decision criteria intersect and align with one another. Emphasize their commonalities rather than their differences, so you can facilitate communication and consensus within the organization.

Naturally, the executive decision criteria will form the highest value benchmark, one you can leverage to inform and align stakeholders at lower levels. For instance, in preparation for a boardroom meeting, we learned that our customer's sales reps couldn't propose bundled offerings with incentivized pricing during phone conversations with customers. This was an advantage their newer competitors had, allowing them to easily lower customers' monthly rates across four services. This issue needed resolution to significantly reduce our client's high churn rate—the executives' primary decision criterion. Conversely, the directors aimed to optimize four separate best-in-class solutions that didn't integrate together, requiring call-center agents to swivel between four different screens. This illustrates how disparate decision criteria can exist within the same company and evaluation process. The challenge is that evaluation teams are rarely provided access to the executives' priorities throughout the evaluation process, sometimes not until the very end when a decision is made. Whoever gains access to the decision-makers and leverages their decision criteria with the other influencers is in the best position to win the selection.

Navigating the various tiers of decision criteria within an organization demands a sophisticated strategy that runs on multiple tracks. By leveraging executive decision criteria as a foundational guideline, you can effectively redefine and realign organizational priorities. This approach enhances communication management and sets clear expectations across diverse groups, leading to more cohesive and effective decision-making processes. In enterprise sales, controlling the narrative and timing of information, using the language of each level, is crucial for managing communication flow with an account. The most effective strategic sellers understand this program management motion and cover it with their teams, so they can develop the content necessary to influence alignment with customers.

The goal here is to align your solution offerings with the strategic objectives of the customer and position your product or service as the most viable option. Before attempting to redefine the decision criteria, sales professionals must thoroughly understand the existing criteria and the customer's thought process. This entails actively listening to the customer's needs and challenges; identifying key decision drivers such as cost, performance, scalability, or risk mitigation; and uncovering any pain points or gaps in their current approach.

To effectively influence decision criteria, sales professionals need to establish themselves as trusted advisors rather than just another vendor. As we've seen, building credibility with executives requires demonstrating a deep understanding of the industry and expertise in the customer's business. Offering insights that reflect an understanding of the customer's market and long-term goals, as well as sharing relevant success stories that resonate with the customer's situation, are crucial in recommending the next steps in this process.

Customer executives typically focus more on the use cases that drive business outcomes than on specific features or pricing details. Sales professionals must therefore shift the conversation from technical specifications to how the solution can impact revenue growth, cost reduction, market competitiveness, innovation, digital transformation, and risk management or compliance. By directly linking an offering to the executive's strategic objectives, you can redefine what matters most in your client's decision-making process.

Often, of course, there are unstated or hidden criteria influencing decisions, which could be related to internal politics, legacy systems, or risk aversion. Uncovering and addressing these underlying issues is another effective way to reshape the decision criteria. This involves asking probing questions that reveal potential biases, such as a preference for a legacy solution, misconceptions about newer solutions, or organizational resistance to change. By tackling these hidden factors, you can better align your offerings with what truly matters to your customer, thus enhancing your chances of success.

Once you thoroughly understand the current criteria, you often have the opportunity to introduce previously overlooked decision factors that are essential for the customer's success. This involves broadening the scope from conventional criteria such as cost and performance to include modern considerations like innovation, time-to-value, scalability, and customer experience. Additionally, it is important to spotlight opportunities that could redefine the customer's priorities, such as the flexibility cloud storage offers, AI-driven insights, and future-proofing strategies. Presenting Total Cost of Ownership (TCO), Return on Investment (ROI), and long-term benefits in a way that shifts the emphasis from short-term cost to long-term business value can be incredibly compelling.

Utilizing data-driven insights is particularly crucial for convincing executives to reassess their decision criteria. Sales professionals should employ quantifiable benefits from case studies or past implementations, industry benchmarks that illustrate how similar organizations have benefited, and ROI calculators or simulations that show the financial impact of the proposed solution. Keep in mind that enterprise-level decisions typically involve multiple stakeholders, each with distinct priorities. Sales professionals must ensure that the redefined criteria resonate with the entire buying committee, including CFOs and financial leaders focused on cost and ROI; CIOs and technical leaders concerned with industry leadership, innovation, and long-term scalability; and CEOs and other executives who prioritize strategic outcomes that enable growth. By addressing the concerns and objectives of each group, you can craft a unified decision framework that aligns with the company's overall strategy.

Finally, enterprise sales professionals frequently employ competitive differentiation to shift the decision criteria. By emphasizing the risks or limitations of alternative solutions, they can persuade executives to concentrate on criteria that favor their offering. This strategic approach not only positions their solution as the superior choice but also ensures alignment with the customer's long-term objectives, ultimately fostering a stronger, more trust-based partnership.

In essence, by meticulously addressing the evolving landscape of decision factors and leveraging data-driven insights, your sales teams can significantly influence enterprise-level decisions, thereby creating lasting value and securing a competitive edge in the market. Ultimately, the CEO and CFO will make significant investment decisions, taking into consideration the evaluation team's recommendation as a minor portion of their overall decision criteria.

Why are CEO decision criteria the most important area to influence in strategic sales?

There are a number of decision-relevant factors outside of the evaluation team's pay grade:

- GTM revenue contributions from strategic partnerships

- Synergies with common strategic clients who want to invest in product roadmaps

- Time to value, both to deliver capabilities and to provide continuous upgrades from buying versus building internally

Outcome of Redefining Decision Criteria: CEOs are focused on criteria outside the most desirable product fit. They are focused on strategic alignment, risk assessment, execution plan, organizational impact, accountability, industry benchmarks, and differentiation in their market assessments going forward. Do you have a good answer for "How does this help us strategically?"

THREE-TIER SOLUTIONS

To be recognized as a thought leader by your customer's executive leadership team, you must speak their industry language, tailored to the organizational level you're engaging with. Executives focus on key performance indicators in their dashboards. Why would you delve into use case details for end users? VPs prioritize use cases that enhance operational efficiency. Why would you discuss product capabilities? The evaluation team seeks to understand how your solution meets their requirements. Why would you detail unique attributes, customized for each persona, in the data model specific to their industry?

There is a nuanced method to addressing a prospect's question, allowing you to swiftly identify the most appropriate layer for a response. Instead of directly answering from the relevant layer, you should begin at the highest level—an industry executive dashboard. This approach speaks their unique leadership language, focusing on key performance metrics that highlight leading indicators. Next, transition to priority use cases by persona, enabling your team to report on the correct metrics at the executive level. Following this, detail the unique attributes that define the competitive edge within the industry and explain how this specialized data is leveraged within the organization.

Why go into such intricate detail, you might wonder, when the client didn't ask for it? In nearly every instance, this is the first time in several years that the prospect is undertaking such a complex enterprise-level implementation. Your objective is not only to answer their specific question but also to offer guidance on areas they hadn't considered, ensuring their success and maximizing their investment as a strategic partner. You can often discern a customer's priority areas based on how they receive this information and what follow-up questions they ask. Those responses reveal their position within the organization, their tenure, their experience in each area, and their ability to effectively communicate value up the chain to executives. Using this method, I've trained my team to deliver an accelerated level of strategic consulting that prospects may not initially recognize. It's a give-to-get approach: By providing value, the prospect often shares more and provides examples of their current processes and reports.

This is why developing three-tier customer-value-creation conversations is impactful for aligning executives with their dashboards, prioritizing use cases for the VP, and leveraging unique industry attributes for their information technology team. At the end of the day, you need to show how effortlessly your solution integrates across these three tiers, providing a competitive advantage while fulfilling executives' needs for clear visibility, prioritized outcomes, and industry-specific relevance.

The first tier focuses on how your executive dashboards create measurable business impacts. Highlight the most crucial KPIs for executives, such as ROI, total cost of ownership, revenue growth, and customer retention. Employ visual indicators in the dashboards to show KPI trends, illustrating the main drivers behind business outcomes. Explain how your solution aligns with their strategic objectives, industry-specific benchmarks, and trends. These dashboards offer executives real-time visibility into key metrics like revenue growth from digital channels, operational efficiency, and market-share expansion. This visibility is intended to improve strategic decision-making by revealing actionable strategic insights.

The second tier prioritizes use cases by personas within the customer's organization. Each persona has unique needs and goals, and this tier demonstrates how the solution caters to professionals in those roles. Executive personas include the CIO (focused on technology and scalability), CFO (focused on cost and return on investment), COO (focused on operational efficiency), and sales or marketing leaders (focused on customer acquisition and retention).

Highlight the most critical use cases for each persona. CIOs value improved scalability, cloud adoption, and data security. CFOs appreciate enhanced financial forecasting, reduced operational costs, and increased ROI. COOs look for streamlined operations and supply chain optimization. CMOs want personalized customer experiences and increased lead generation. Likewise, demonstrate outcomes for each persona, connecting the use case directly to measurable outcomes that resonate with them, such as increased productivity or cost savings. Tell the CIO, for instance, that this solution enables seamless cloud integration and enhances data security, leading to a 21 percent reduction in system downtime. For the CFO, stress that it offers real-time financial analytics that improve cost forecasting accuracy by 18 percent.

The third tier zeroes in on how your solution captures unique industry attributes to offer your client a competitive edge. Industry-specific challenges, trends, and regulations shape the solution's implementation. Detail how your solution is tailored to meet the specific needs of the customer's industry, whether that's healthcare, manufacturing, retail, or finance. If relevant, discuss how the solution addresses industry-specific regulations or compliance requirements, which can serve as a significant differentiator. Utilize industry benchmarks and trends to underscore how your solution stands out.

For added value, demonstrate that your offering not only meets current needs but also anticipates future trends within the industry. Show how this tailored solution gives the customer a sustainable competitive edge, whether through innovation, operational efficiencies, or customer-centric improvements. In the healthcare industry, for instance, our solution is HIPAA-compliant and optimized for real-time patient data processing, reducing administrative overhead by 32 percent, and accelerating patient care workflows. In a retail context, it enhances omnichannel customer engagement, boosting customer satisfaction scores by 17 percent, and increasing repeat purchases.

THREE-TIER SOLUTIONS

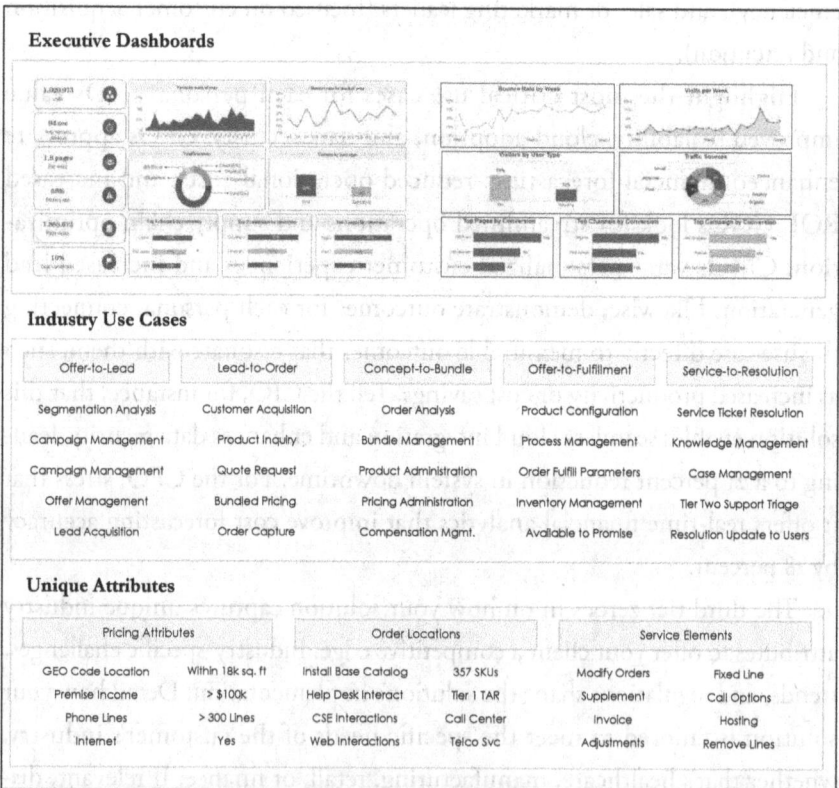

Executive Dashboards

Industry Use Cases

Offer-to-Lead	Lead-to-Order	Concept-to-Bundle	Offer-to-Fulfillment	Service-to-Resolution
Segmentation Analysis	Customer Acquisition	Order Analysis	Product Configuration	Service Ticket Resolution
Campaign Management	Product Inquiry	Bundle Management	Process Management	Knowledge Management
Campaign Management	Quote Request	Product Administration	Order Fulfill Parameters	Case Management
Offer Management	Bundled Pricing	Pricing Administration	Inventory Management	Tier Two Support Triage
Lead Acquisition	Order Capture	Compensation Mgmt.	Available to Promise	Resolution Update to Users

Unique Attributes

Pricing Attributes		Order Locations		Service Elements	
GEO Code Location	Within 18k sq. ft	Install Base Catalog	357 SKUs	Modify Orders	Fixed Line
Premise Income	> $100k	Help Desk Interact	Tier 1 TAR	Supplement	Call Options
Phone Lines	> 300 Lines	CSE Interactions	Call Center	Invoice	Hosting
Internet	Yes	Web Interactions	Telco Svc	Adjustments	Remove Lines

Diagram 2.1 Connect Conversations Between C-Suite, VPs, and Directors

After you address each tier individually, it is crucial to integrate them to demonstrate how the entire solution facilitates a cohesive flow of information benefiting all parts of the organization. The executive dashboard provides a comprehensive view of both strategic business outcomes in Tier 1 and detailed, persona-driven results in Tier 2, while creating unique industry advantages in Tier 3. For example, industry-specific use cases appear on executive dashboards, and persona-level priorities impact broader strategic metrics. A high-level solution diagram illustrates how the different tiers are interconnected, offering a multi-layered advantage that addresses both broad and specific needs within your client's organization.

Would you rather ask basic discovery questions or conduct a three-tier solution conversation?

The best way to uncover each individual's decision criteria:

- Evaluate their level of understanding of dashboards, use cases, and attributes.

- Assess their level of engagement in each topic by studying their eye movement, responses, and follow-up questions.

- Remember that each evaluator's interaction will determine the level of priority for their decision-making process compared to the competition.

Outcome of Three-Tier Solution Conversations: Assess each evaluator's experience level in each area and who is the most qualified to deliver your complete, three-tiered value proposition to the executive team on your behalf. You have to build internal champions who will carry your message and can explain the differential value proposition at all three tiers compared to the competition.

PROVIDING INDUSTRY INSIGHTS

In today's highly competitive business environment, CEOs face immense pressure to drive growth, boost profitability, and ensure long-term sustainability. Customers appreciate understanding critical lessons learned from other industry leaders to improve their competitive position in their market. These insights offer concrete examples of effective strategies and actionable guidance for replicating these successes within their own organizations. By leveraging industry insights rooted in customer success stories, CEOs can accelerate revenue growth by tackling critical strategic, operational, and market challenges more effectively. This approach allows them to navigate complexities with precision and achieve their objectives with greater efficiency.

These industry insights provide more than just anecdotal evidence—they are grounded in data and validated by real-world results. They stem from organizations that have effectively navigated the same competitive, economic, and technological challenges your client currently faces. By thoroughly analyzing their strategies, CEOs can uncover crucial lessons that apply across various functions, including sales, marketing, operations, and customer engagement.

Successful organizations frequently set benchmarks for best practices within their respective industries. When these best practices are implemented effectively, they lead to significant improvements in revenue growth, operational efficiency, and market competitiveness. For example, companies that have mastered digital transformation, customer experience optimization, or supply chain efficiency serve as concrete examples that can be directly applied to your client's business context. When CEOs scrutinize the specific tactics these firms employ to achieve growth, they can implement similar strategies in their own organizations, confident in their potential for success.

On some level, every salesperson knows that executives are more interested in understanding and exploiting the competitive landscape than in how your solutions work. Elite success requires fighting the urge to talk about your solutions anyway, not because they're bad products but because they don't give the executive any need to engage with you. Instead, transform your real-world knowledge into a powerful asset by translating it into strategic initiatives, ultimately accelerating your client's pace of change and fostering a competitive edge.

Successful customers generally share a crucial characteristic: their ability to align business strategies with evolving market needs and trends, thereby differentiating their business. Often, they are early adopters of emerging technologies or business models. By studying these companies, CEOs can stay ahead of industry trends and ensure their organizations are prepared for the next wave of disruption. For instance, many Fortune 100 firms are already heavily investing in artificial intelligence, automation, and sustainability initiatives. By following their lead, CEOs can position their own organizations to thrive in the future.

In summary, leveraging the industry insights gleaned from your most successful customers is not just a strategic advantage—it is a necessity in today's fast-paced business environment. By studying and emulating the strategies of these trailblazing organizations, your potential clients can drive substantial growth, enhance operational efficiency, and ensure their companies remain competitive in an ever-evolving market. Through disciplined application of these insights, CEOs can foster a culture of continuous improvement and innovation, positioning their organizations for sustained success.

Why do your most successful customers hold the keys to success? Can you measure the quantifiable metrics that have improved their business?

Outcome of Providing Industry Insights: Securing approval for quantified metrics in marketing case studies for official press releases can be challenging. Collaborate closely with your advocates to understand the impact of use cases and business metrics on overall business performance. Quantifying these benefits will distinguish your market approach and enhance the value proposition for future customers, creating a competitive edge.

EXECUTIVE FRAMEWORKS

Solution imaging involves crafting a visual representation of a proposed solution, tailored to align with the prospect's specific needs, pain points, and strategic objectives. Within the realm of enterprise sales, this often entails creating executive dashboards that harness data to reveal valuable business insights, guiding decision-makers toward comprehending the potential solution's impact. These dashboards should illustrate how your proposed solution will achieve key business objectives, such as boosting revenue, enhancing efficiency, or improving customer satisfaction. Highlight metrics showcasing the expected return on investment (ROI), providing executives with a transparent view of how the solution contributes to their financial bottom line.

This data should not only be useful but should uncover critical business insights that narrate a compelling story. By highlighting current performance gaps or future growth opportunities, your sales team can clearly articulate the necessity of your solution. KPIs like revenue growth, customer acquisition, operational efficiency, and market share can help you demonstrate the impact of adopting your solution, using predictive analytics to help prospects visualize their future success.

Don't neglect visual indicators—graphs, heatmaps, and trend lines—that can simplify complex information. Not only do these tools help executives easily digest and act on what they see, but they highlight the most important insights that actually drive business decisions, instead of deluging the desktop in data. In certain instances, sales teams might even create interactive dashboards that allow executives to explore various data views and potential outcomes, thereby increasing engagement and buy-in.

Done well, dashboards will create urgency for change, typically by revealing existing risks or inefficiencies that your proposed solution addresses. They can likewise juxtapose the company's performance against industry benchmarks or competitors, underscoring areas where your prospects are lagging and how your solution can bridge that gap. By projecting future growth or improvement metrics with and without the proposed solution, the dashboard makes the value proposition more tangible and time sensitive.

Overall, solution-imaging dashboards function as a potent tool for reinforcing your sales narrative's value proposition with data-backed visuals. Presenting data-driven insights builds credibility with executives, demonstrating that your sales team comprehends their business and can deliver

COMPETITIVE DEAL DASHBOARD

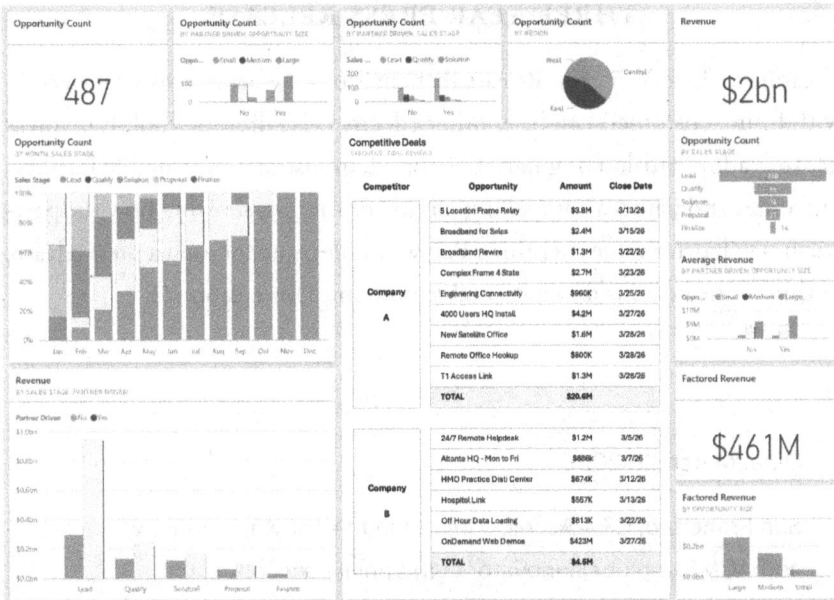

Diagram 2.2 Pattern Matching with Competitors

meaningful, measurable results. These dashboards also create a common language between the sales team and executives, facilitating collaborative discussions on how the solution can address key business challenges.

Dashboards also play a pivotal role in post-implementation success, enabling both the enterprise and the sales team to monitor performance and ensure the promised outcomes are realized. By continually visualizing metrics and performance indicators, the enterprise can pinpoint areas for continuous improvement and ensure the solution evolves alongside the business.

In conclusion, solution imaging through executive dashboards empowers enterprise sales teams to visually convey the business impact of their solutions in a manner that resonates with executives. These dashboards uncover critical business insights, distill complex information, and bolster the sales narrative, thereby aiding decision-making processes and facilitating deal closures.

THREE-YEAR PRESS RELEASE

Creating a Three-Year Press Release that envisions the benefits of a partnership with future customers can be another effective visualization tool. It involves crafting a forward-looking narrative that demonstrates measurable business outcomes and paints a compelling picture of success, showing how the partnership will drive value over time. Below is a template for such a press release, outlining the benefits and measurable outcomes for customers:

Date: March 12, 2026

San Francisco, CA—Accell, a leader in the software industry, and ACME, a global innovator in the anvil semiconductor industry, today celebrated the third anniversary of their strategic partnership. Together, the companies have achieved significant milestones, driven measurable business benefits, and transformed how ACME delivers value to its customers and stakeholders.

Key Partnership Achievements

1. **INCREASED REVENUE BY 12 PERCENT:** Through enhanced market positioning and innovation in the first year of the partnership, Accell collaborated with ACME to optimize its product offerings and expand into new markets. Through this collaboration, ACME increased its market share by 3.6 percent, driving $1.2 billion in additional revenue annually. This success has been attributed to the real-time insights on the manufacturing process, which enabled the company to respond quickly to shifting market demands and customer preferences.

2. **REDUCED OPERATING COSTS BY 4.3 PERCENT:**
   Through operational efficiency and technology integration by implementing Accell's cutting-edge solutions, ACME reduced its operating costs by 1.3 percent, translating into savings of $2.1 billion over the three-year period. This was achieved through streamlined processes, improved supply chain management, and the automation of critical workflows. Additionally, Accell's technology enabled real-time decision-making, reducing operational bottlenecks and improving overall efficiency.

3. **IMPROVED CUSTOMER SATISFACTION BY 5.3 PERCENT:**
   Through the integration of Accell's customer experience management solutions, ACME significantly enhanced its customer satisfaction scores. The companies developed a customer-first strategy, leveraging data analytics and personalized customer engagement tools to improve each customer's journey. As a result, ACME's customer satisfaction increased by 0.8 percent, and its Net Promoter Score (NPS) rose by two points.

Looking Ahead: Continued Innovation and Growth

As the partnership enters its next phase, Accell and ACME are committed to further driving innovation and creating long-term value. With plans to co-develop new products, leverage artificial intelligence, and explore new business models, the companies are poised for continued growth and market leadership.

"This partnership has been a game-changer for us," said ACME CEO Barton Smith. "The measurable benefits we've achieved together—from revenue growth and cost savings to improved customer satisfaction—are a testament to Accell's expertise and our shared commitment to innovation. We look forward to what the future holds as we continue to push boundaries and redefine success in our industry."

"We are incredibly proud of what we've accomplished together over the past three years," added Accell CEO Greg Combs. "The collaboration between our teams has unlocked tremendous value, and the measurable outcomes speak for themselves. We look forward to building on this momentum and delivering even more transformative solutions for ACME in the years to come."

Diagram 2.3 Establish the Vision for Future Partnership

ALIGNMENT THEORY

Generate tailored insights and identify the key themes in the executive's current initiatives. Illustrate the desired outcomes from these insights and demonstrate how they align with the executive's success metrics for optimal impact.

Why change?

Challenge:	Identify areas of opportunity that enhance strategic priorities. Aware of the performance metrics that drive executive compensation. Uncover conflicting decision criteria for executives to resolve.

How do we differentiate?

Concept 5:	**Enable Indirect Selling** of client champions to leverage your executive deliverables branded for them to sell on your behalf when you're not in the room. Partnering with prospects to develop new strategic business strategies sponsored by executives.
Concept 6:	**Three Level Solutions** allow you to determine each stakeholder's level of interest in developing a complete solution. Identifies who has the business acumen to deliver the message to the executive leadership team with impact.

Concept 7:	**Redefine Decision Criteria** alter the factors that a prospect uses to evaluate and select a solution or vendor. It's a strategic move by sales teams to shift the buyer's focus toward aspects where their solutions excel, differentiating them from competitors.
Concept 8:	**Executive Monthly Readouts** provide significant value to key stakeholders by fostering alignment, transparency, and strategic oversight. Provides executives with the ability to inspect toward key objectives, to make course corrections to meet milestones.

What do we receive?

Result:	Become meaningful to executives to influence their business strategies. Master the art of thoughtful research to **increase cross sells +63%.** Influence funding outcomes on future projects and their priority order.

TIPS AND TRICKS FOR GAINING ALIGNMENT

- In enterprise sales, your success depends heavily on strategic preparation and thoughtful execution. One of the most impactful ways to **influence funding outcomes** is creating executive-level deliverables that clearly communicate innovative, compelling business strategies. These deliverables must articulate how your proposal uniquely positions the customer to achieve distinct competitive advantages, aligning seamlessly with their executive priorities.
- The power of established relationships cannot be underestimated. Seasoned, tenured employees with longstanding connections inside the customer's organization play a crucial role. Leveraging their credibility and internal networks can significantly influence key stakeholders, easing the path toward consensus and buy-in.
- Rapid responsiveness is also pivotal. Executives are continually facing new, high-priority challenges. Quickly addressing their inquiries within two to six hours of the request to ensure that your solution remains relevant, **capturing their attention** before they inevitably shift focus to other pressing matters.

- When sales opportunities stall, decisive action is required. Providing tangible, high-value deliverables that executives can easily comprehend and act upon often revitalizes these situations. Clear articulation of immediate benefits facilitates quick decision-making and proactive engagement from the executive team.

- Another essential practice is early empowerment of internal champions. Enterprise evaluations frequently introduce new evaluators mid-process. Preparing thorough, compelling deliverables early allows your internal champions to **perform indirect selling effectively**, maintaining momentum and ensuring influence despite evolving stakeholder dynamics.

- Communication in enterprise sales should be structured and multi-layered. Start by presenting executive dashboards and key metrics to engage senior leadership, follow up with clearly prioritized use cases that address specific business needs, and highlight unique differentiators within your data model. This structured communication helps identify stakeholders who can champion your message to executive leadership effectively.

- Positioning yourself as a trusted advisor is critical in **shaping decision criteria**. Demonstrating expertise in industry best practices early establishes credibility, influencing stakeholders to view your recommendations as valuable and authoritative.

- Consistently demonstrating value is key to maintaining executive engagement. Quarterly structured updates—clearly showcasing business impact, measurable metrics, and demonstrable progress—reinforce your ongoing contributions and solidify your position as a valuable partner in achieving strategic goals.

- Illustrating your long-term commitment through a detailed three-year "press release" provides a visionary perspective on **anticipated joint achievements**. Clearly defined future outcomes and milestones enhance customer confidence and strengthen expectations for shared success.

- Strategically deploying your virtual sales team across key stakeholders at various organizational levels maximizes influence and engagement. Utilizing a structured relationship map ensures team members are effectively assigned based on stakeholder influence, roles, and relationship strength, achieving comprehensive coverage.
- "Solution imaging," or visually compelling executive dashboards, can powerfully showcase potential **future states of the customer's business.** By vividly illustrating transformative outcomes, these dashboards help executives envision and buy into the potential success your solutions offer.
- Finally, disciplined meeting management ensures consistent momentum. Allocating the last five minutes of every meeting to schedule subsequent interactions and promptly following up via email to confirm agreed-upon actions, timelines, and responsibilities maintains accountability and clarity within your mutual action plan, ultimately driving the enterprise sales process forward.

ALIGNMENT WORKBOOK
REDEFINE DECISION CRITERIA

Alignment Frameworks

25 PRESS RELEASE	Announce ambitious three-year strategic vision aimed at driving transformation • Business outcomes with enhanced operational excellence
26 RELATIONSHIP MAP	Visual represents decision-makers and influencers in account • Identify your relationships by levels within operating units
27 SOLUTION IMAGING	Demonstrate CEO's vision in an executive dashboard • Enable quick decision-making from critical data in single view

28 MUTUAL ACTION PLAN	Structured strategy outlines the specific tasks, responsibilities, and timelines • Metrics required to achieve mutually agreed-upon objectives

Alignment Sales Plays

29 CONFIRM	Validate your findings of customer's challenges, objectives, and desired outcomes • Gain agreement or validate use case enhancements
30 OUTCOMES	Solution benefits aligned to quantifiable outcomes • Confirm priority order of industry use case deployment
31 TAILOR	Each executive's role requires a tailored approach for them • Focus on executive core metrics that will impact their role
32 ALIGNMENT	Proactive approach that ensures your business strategy • Customer engagement aligned with impactful industry trends
33 VISION	Position your solutions as industry-standard with executives • Demonstrate leadership that drives measurable outcomes
34 GUIDANCE	Developing multiple coaches who provide unique guidance • Business, Technology, Finance unique points of view
35 CONVEY	Business value you conveyed monthly to the executive staff • Why be in business if you can't quantify your solution value?
36 CONFIRM FIT	Program manage prospect's resource to evaluate your solution • Create significant unbudgeted transaction with no competition

37 INFLUENCE	Provide quarterly recommendations to the C-suite for funding • Define your value with quantifiable business outcomes
38 ACUMEN	Raising business acumen is a journey that deliverables enable • Executive respond to deliverables leverage the top six frameworks
39 SCORECARD	Executive staff manage their business through scorecards • Identify hard to measure metrics that answer tough questions
40 SEQUENTIAL	Orchestrating a minimum of three levels of engagement • Alignment is achieved when levels converse with each other
41 STUDIES	Industry case studies provide relevant use case improvements • Executive case studies require: a story, use cases, metrics, and opportunity to make real
42 PREDICTIVE	Provide predictive analytics from industry benchmarks • Data-driven insights that create competitive advantage
43 ROADMAP	Create roadmap with milestones and metrics to achieve • Path to innovation and competitive advantage
44 REVIEWS	Engage in regular executive joint business planning • Confirm value delivery in executive reviews
45 CONSULTATION	Deliver executive-level consultation that creates value • Industry executive dashboards with best practice metrics
46 MUTUAL	Develop mutual value plans that measure value • Business case details that accelerate operational excellence

47 THOUGHT LEADER	Content is king based on industry best practices • Articulate benefits in dashboards, use cases, unique attributes
48 TRANSPARENT	Building trust requires transparent risk mitigation strategies • Give your content and expertise away for free
49 INCORPORATE	Start early incorporating your future expansion strategy • Path to transformation in horizons captures C-suite attention
50 COMPENSATION	Executive compensation prioritizes initiatives • Are your solutions required to deliver an executive's initiatives?

Diagram 2.4 How to Gain Alignment with Executives

EVERYDAY APPLICATIONS

First and foremost, it's crucial to determine whether there is a genuine and pressing business requirement—without that data, you can't demonstrate any real value. One effective approach is to present a scenario that exemplifies a top-tier solution, then invite your prospect to provide feedback. This method helps clarify their primary concerns and priorities. With this insight, you can then tailor your value propositions to address their most significant needs in priority order.

Take your time here. A common mistake involves hearing one piece of information, immediately assuming it's the top priority, and diving right into your solution pitch. This results in a one-sided exchange before your prospect has fully communicated their insights. But watch out for the opposite problem as well: bombarding them with numerous questions without offering any value in return for their responses.

The most effective way to position your value is to let your prospect speak first, gauging the level of detail they provide. If this area is new to them, share insights from your most successful customers with at least twelve months of implementation. These insights often reveal that what they've learned from using the solution differs from their initial considerations during the evaluation phase. This is also an excellent opportunity to introduce a three-tiered conversation, to uncover what is most important to your client in each area. The prospect will quickly recognize how you are adding incremental value as a thought leader, prompting them to share more information than they initially expected. This approach leverages a give-to-get strategy, enhancing the depth and quality of the dialogue.

ALIGNMENT KEY TAKEAWAYS

1. Are you bothering a CEO if you're bringing them a unique business strategy?

   Encapsulate the CEO's vision in a single executive dashboard personalized for them.

2. Do your GTM teams have the mindset to create value for customers?

   Align to current strategies that drive incremental value executive deliverables.

3. Do your teams rely on relationships to accelerate revenue?

   Enable executives to bet their careers based on your business strategy, not a relationship.

4. Has the evaluation team aligned on the same decision criteria?

   Provide alignment between the evaluation team and the executive leadership team.

5. Will the executives log into your solution, or will they receive insights from dashboards?

   No need to demonstrate your solutions to executive if they will never log in.

6. Executives invest in proven industry best practices that are documented but may not be in the product?

   Have to quantify the value of your solutions within your prospect's industry.

7. Does your team leverage industry best practice selling to create a flywheel of activity?

Executives trust what you say when you put pen to paper to confirm your claims.

8. Can you articulate what your partnership with the client will look like in three years?

Provide the measurable benefits you expect to deliver together through your partnership.

SUMMARY

Can you dive into a CEO's business operations and craft a distinctive perspective that forges a unique competitive edge for their company? Mastering the art of a quick and straightforward industry benchmark can provide you with an invaluable viewpoint for top executives. Industry benchmarking is a crucial tool for assessing a company's performance against peers in the same sector. A swift and efficient approach involves focusing on key metrics, typically leveraging readily available public data or industry-specific reports. Focus on metrics that are crucial to your prospect's business and relevant to their industry, such as revenue growth, profit margins, cost of goods sold, and return on investment.

Once you have gathered the necessary data, calculate the company's metrics and compare them with industry averages. Conduct a straightforward comparison for each metric, placing their company's performance side-by-side with industry standards to quickly gauge their standing. Use percentage ranking data to determine the company's relative position compared to their industry's top performers. Identify areas where your prospect's performance lags behind industry benchmarks and pinpoint where they're excelling. Examine the specifics of their underperformance and identify targeted areas for improvement. Similarly, recognize where they are outperforming competitors and explore strategies to sustain or enhance that advantage.

Leverage the insights from your benchmarking analysis to set practical and achievable improvement goals. Regular benchmarking is crucial for tracking progress and adapting to changes. Implementing this process quarterly or annually helps maintain competitiveness and ensures continuous development over time, as you keep assessing the company's position and identifying growth opportunities. This strategy also fosters meaningful discussions with new executives. Offer them unique insights they wouldn't typically receive from another vendor in your field, thereby distinguishing yourself in the marketplace.

CFOs need access to the improved financial ratios that you have previously provided to other customers as benchmarks in order to establish the credibility of your proposed business case. In Chapter 3, we will explore how CFOs assess the payback of your solution and how you can use that process to bolster your credibility.

CREDIBILITY

Influence Decision Criteria

(Improve Win Rates by 34 Percent)

CHAPTER 3

> **DAVID VS. GOLIATH:** Against Insurmountable Odds

> **DELIVERING PAYBACK TO FINANCE:** Quantify Your Value

> **REFERENCE MATRIX:** Proven Customer Results

> **TRAVERSING THE PROVING GROUND:** Communication

> **THE TRUTH ABOUT ESTABLISHING CREDIBILITY:** Acumen

> **VALUE REALIZATION:** Receive Credit for Your Value

> **ACCOUNT PLANNING:** Written Confirmation with Customers

> **EXECUTIVE DEMONSTRATION GUIDES:** Visual Success Imprints

---

> **RECEIVE UNBUDGETED FUNDS:** Business Justification

> **CREDIBILITY THEORY:** Improve Win Rates 34 Percent

> **TIPS AND TRICKS:** CFO Conversation

> **CREDIBILITY WORKBOOK:** Proven Customer Success

> **EVERYDAY APPLICATIONS:** Measurable Benefits

> **KEY TAKEAWAYS:** Financial Acumen Embedded in Sales

> **SUMMARY:** Influence Decision Criteria

DAVID VS. GOLIATH

My team found out the largest broadband provider for business services was planning to replace their sales applications—and we were not part of their selection process. Kayce, my global account manager, was determined to earn a spot in their evaluation. It took her team three months to secure a thirty-minute meeting with their SVP of Sales, Mark. But that was only the first hurdle: We were competing directly with an industry-leading firm with over 170 customer references in their industry segment, each showcasing success leveraging their sales applications. To earn a spot at the table, we had to prepare something that would change Mark's decision criteria for the entire evaluation process.

Mark's plan was to consolidate fifty-seven contact management solutions down to one by partnering with the industry-leading CRM vendor. This would be a legacy project for Mark—he already had nearly three decades of service with the company, and before that, his father had run the company's global sales division for twenty years. No ordinary blueprint would work here, so we had to add significant differential value. Kayce's opening question to Mark certainly stood out: "Do you want your legacy to be consolidating contact management systems, or do you want to solve your company's most prominent business challenge instead?" You see, Kayce had looked closely at Mark's end-to-end customer journey, and she correctly identified that reducing his company's 92 percent order fallout rate would offer much more value to the broadband sales leader. Mark was taken aback by the question and put his head down to think for a minute. When he looked up, he asked the question that Kayce and I were waiting for: "How do you propose we do that?"

I could see that Mark genuinely wanted to solve that problem, but he wasn't sure where to start. Could he lead a brand-new change-management effort, given that so many of his company's development resources wanted to custom-build a new order management system? After all, they were a broadband company, not a software company, and the clock was ticking. But Kayce knew exactly why this project would appeal to Mark, and she expertly tugged at his heart strings: "Everyone will remember you for this project, Mark, and it's game changing." Mark's face lit up, and our thirty-minute meeting soon transformed into a four-hour strategic whiteboarding session.

Together, we reviewed all of the latent pains, opportunities, and challenges associated with tackling this significantly more complex problem. At that point, Mark's sales team had over 990 versions of their price list on disconnected laptops, making it nearly impossible to coordinate price tables when they created quotes. That led to a tremendous amount of rework and manual intervention, not to mention a lot of second thoughts among their prospects. Mark's internal team had, of course, evaluated the problem in the past, but they estimated a two-year delivery time, a tough sell in a highly competitive market. Instead, we proposed a way to solve the problem in only eight months, leveraging proven solutions and a commitment to deliver on our word. That superior time to market made all the difference, creating a unique competitive advantage for Mark's company and powerfully motivating him to rethink his legacy.

Sometimes executives need a big idea—and a little nudge in the right direction—to take a risk on a highly impactful project. We had to take a risk too: Most consulting firms in our situation would have aligned their recommendations with the company's internal consensus, rather than trying to solve a completely new problem. Those conversations aren't easy, even when you have solid data, so let me walk you through the due diligence that went into preparing for the meeting. Kayce and her team developed a detailed differentiated value blueprint, enabling us to create a significant strategic partnership between Mark's firm and our own. Here's what it included.

Industry Expertise:
- Industry Initiatives - the top trends the company is adapting to in their market
- Case Studies - similar-size companies that have achieved quantifiable results
- Best Practices - ways of running your business processes more efficiently
- Proven Metrics - measuring performance gains by persona on a defined timeline

Company Priorities:
- Corporate Objectives - stated priorities the executives committed to execute
- Investment Strategy - a two-page summary of benefits for the executive staff
- Priority Use Cases by Persona - quick wins delivering immediate results
- Economic Benefit - projections showing revenue, cost, and efficiency gains

Implementation Plan:
- Sponsors from Business, IT, and Finance - recommendations for evaluation leads
- Horizon 1-2-3 - plans for three-time horizons based on investments and resources
- Deployment Strategies - approaches to different implementation strategies
- Agreement on Evaluation Timeline - understand other competing project priorities

Recommended Next Steps:
- Mutual Action Plan - steps and owners assigned to execute the evaluation process
- Monthly Executive Review - how each division will leverage the proposed solution

It's critical to provide executives with a list of best-practice topics a week before your meeting, both so they can determine the meeting's focus and so they can use their own priorities to lead the discussion. In our initial thirty-minute time block, for example, we only had time to discuss three of our fourteen topics. But once Mark saw the value of those insights, and that we had prepared similar material on the other eleven topics, he canceled his next six scheduled meetings so we could continue our conversation. Kayce and I provided expert guidance all afternoon, based on the industry best practices we were proposing and the contingencies required to make them a reality.

This achievement was driven by Kayce's unwavering determination, characterized by the relentless pursuit of goals, consistent follow-ups, and sustained effort despite frequent rejections. A passion for mastery is key, with a deep commitment to continuously improving skills, product knowledge, and closing techniques. View objections as opportunities to enhance your pitch, not as obstacles. Dedicate time to nurturing client relationships, understanding that trust develops gradually. Most importantly, though, you need a long-term perspective, focusing on larger sales objectives and quotas over extended periods, rather than seeking quick wins. In this case, our main competitor had quoted $43 million to advance Mark's initial goal of consolidating his firm's contact management solutions. We turned the tables against that Goliath, ultimately securing a $156 million contract for a much bolder—but much more important—task at hand to accomplish.

DELIVERING PAYBACK TO FINANCE

Before Mark could endorse our strategic approach of replacing his firm's complex order management systems to support bundled services from new web-based applications, he needed Finance to review the business case. This would help ensure that the larger investment would exceed the required hurdle rates, within a time frame that would allow them to expense the investment over the initial eight months before they could start receiving the benefit from the new solution. In other words, was the risk worth the reward? Mark was going to need these financial impact numbers to successfully lead the internal change management effort within his incredibly large, monolithic company, which was used to moving at the pace of an arthritic battleship.

By aligning a project with these core financial metrics, CFOs can create a compelling argument that resonates with stakeholders, justifying strategic investments. This could take several forms: Build projections showing how reduced DSO and error rates lead to improved cash flow and profitability, compare current metrics against post-implementation forecasts to highlight potential gains, emphasize how error reduction prevents revenue leakage and operational risks, or demonstrate how automation supports growth without proportionate increases in staff or overhead. The details vary by project and industry, of course, but they all come down to a rational argument to justify the risk. As you develop your case, here are some finance-related variables your solution should improve.

Cash Flow and Liquidity Ratios:
- Days Sales Outstanding - reducing errors and accelerating billing will lower DSO
- Cash Conversion Cycle - invoicing shortens the cycle, improving liquidity
- Current Ratio - improving collections will increase current assets

Risk and Accuracy Ratios:
- Gross Profit Margin - reduce order errors and manual labor
- Operating Profit Margin - reduce rework, order corrections, and admin costs
- Return on Assets - maximize the utilization of inventory and assets

Efficiency Ratios:
- Order-to-Cash Cycle Time - improve invoicing, shortening this cycle
- Inventory Turnover - increase turnover, reducing holding costs
- Sales per Employee - focus on selling rather than admin tasks
- Error Rate in Order Processing - reduce human error to improve satisfaction

• Order Fulfillment Rate - improve customer retention and reduce operational friction

Growth and Scalability Ratios:
• Revenue Growth Rate - accurate order handling supports higher sales volumes
• Customer Retention Rate - better service drives customer lifetime value

REFERENCE MATRIX

An excellent way to engage finance professionals is to showcase industry case studies where similar-sized companies have achieved significant financial impacts within comparable time frames. A Reference Matrix is a good way to establish your industry expertise in a summary table of contents before you justify (in more detail) each of the finance metrics listed previously.

REFERENCE MATRIX

	Company A	Company B	Company C	Company D	Company E	Company F
Increase Online Revenue	14%	12%	17%	18%	15%	16%
Improve Answer Relevancy	35%	32%	38%	49%	42%	37%
Improve Conversation Rates	27%	---	17%	31%	16%	19%
Sales Leads Generated	---	---	11%	---	8%	---
Customer Insight	24%	16%	21%	27%	23%	28%
Quick Win Deployment	9 weeks	4 weeks	6 weeks	4 weeks	6 weeks	5 weeks
Payback Time Frame	8 months	5 months	7 months	6 months	7 months	6 months
Lowest Cost to Convert	11%	13%	12%	18%	15%	16%
Annual Revenue	80.6B	16.0B	3.3B	30.6B	70.2B	66.3B
Consumer Interactions	10.0m	2.1m	7.3m	8.6m	11.4m	9.1m
Home Page Interactions	595.3m	151.1m	125.5m	128.1m	250.4m	286.9m
Search Effort Before	0.387	0.391	0.318	0.356	0.324	0.367
Search Effort After	0.435	0.453	0.391	0.425	0.382	0.413
eCommerce Index Before	30	40	40	45	40	35
eCommerce Index After	55	70	70	85	75	75

Diagram 3.0 Proven Success to Establish Credibility

This is an ideal way to establish credibility: Identify the highest value use cases, quantify your solution's measurable impact on the business, and leverage that data as a benchmark for your business within an industry. This can be used to confirm decision criteria, expand the existing business case to include new metrics, or even to redefine decision criteria. Based on my experience, it will enable you to increase your win rates by 34 percent as you traverse different operating units and levels within your prospect's organization.

Redefining decision criteria can be a transformative enterprise sales strategy to set your solution apart, influence your buyer's process, and boost your chances of closing a deal. This approach shifts the focus from standard features and pricing to the unique value your solution delivers, changing how the buyer evaluates vendors. Be sure to highlight proprietary features, advanced technology, or exceptional service that competitors lack. By introducing new criteria that emphasize your distinctive capabilities, you position your solution as the optimal choice that meets those needs.

Specifically, by shaping how success is measured, you align the buyer's focus with your strengths. Try introducing new pain points or strategic goals the buyer may not have considered. This creates urgency and drives demand for features that only your solution addresses. By providing clear, differentiated decision-making criteria, you reduce confusion and help buying committees reach consensus more quickly. If you shape these criteria early, there is less room for last-minute objections based on irrelevant comparisons. When decision criteria are value-driven, buyers are more willing to pay a premium for solutions that align with those priorities.

TRAVERSING THE PROVING GROUND

The best enterprise sellers disseminate information across various organizational levels by customizing their communication to align with the priorities and influence of each stakeholder. This approach ensures consistent messaging while addressing specific concerns, effectively steering the narrative and guiding the decision-making process.

At the executive level, emphasize strategic alignment and ROI, showcasing how your solution drives growth, profitability, and competitive advantage.

Utilize presentations, executive briefings, and high-level case studies to capture leaders' attention and align your value with their long-term objectives.

For mid-level managers, shift the focus to operational efficiency and departmental impact. Illustrate how your solution optimizes workflows, enhances team performance, and addresses pain points within your audience's area of responsibility. Workshops, product demos, and benchmarking tools are common methods here to demonstrate relevant value.

Finally, at the end-user level, your communication should highlight ease of use, productivity benefits, and day-to-day improvements. Provide hands-on demonstrations, pilot programs, and user-focused testimonials to secure buy-in and build grassroots support.

If possible, you should also engage internal champions—influential individuals who advocate for the solution internally—to reinforce your messaging at all these levels. By equipping these champions with resources like white papers, ROI calculators, and FAQs, you can extend your influence throughout the organization.

RUN MULTIPLE ENGAGEMENT TRACKS

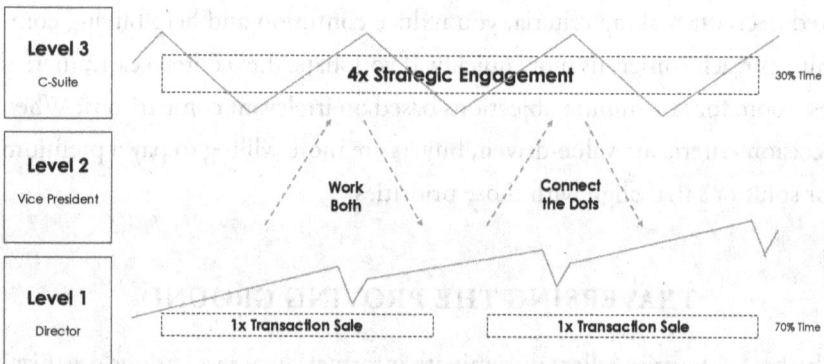

Diagram 3.1 Cascade Communication at All Levels

This top-down and bottom-up approach ensures that your narrative remains consistent, with each level of the organization understanding how your solution benefits them directly. Ultimately, this method reduces friction, accelerates consensus, and enhances the likelihood of closing complex enterprise deals.

THE TRUTH ABOUT ESTABLISHING CREDIBILITY

Strategic selling involves more than simply presenting a product or solution; it requires a thoughtful and proactive approach to shift your customer's perspectives, clearly highlight value, and foster alignment at multiple organizational levels. When you're facing formidable competition or challenging market conditions, you often have to redefine the decision criteria to gain leverage. By introducing innovative and differentiated approaches, you can shift your customers' evaluation frameworks, converting obstacles into significant opportunities favoring your solution.

Quantifying measurable value—ideally through metrics, KPIs, and ROI derived from past customer experiences within the same industry—helps potential customers clearly visualize the impact and benefits of adopting your solution. To further enhance your credibility and showcase tangible outcomes, develop an industry-reference matrix. This matrix should profile five influential industry leaders who previously adopted your solution, detailing their initial evaluation processes and selection criteria, alongside their reflections and insights gained after a year of implementation. Highlighting how these industry leaders' perceptions and expectations evolved demonstrates the transformative power of your solution and offers prospective clients clear, relatable benchmarks.

Equally critical is adopting a balanced approach that engages both top-level executives and operational evaluation teams. Navigating these dual engagements with clarity and consistency ensures alignment and internal consensus, reducing confusion and promoting cohesive support across various organizational layers.

To maintain consistent recognition from senior executives, use periodic performance scorecards to communicate tangible, realized outcomes and benefits. These structured communications help maintain executive visibility of your solution's impact, supplementing the efforts of internal champions who might otherwise be limited by bandwidth constraints. Similarly, establishing reciprocal accountability through formal documentation of agreements, milestones, and action items is essential. Written records clarify mutual roles, expectations, and responsibilities, mitigating risks and fostering a trustworthy partnership.

Given that internal champions retain limited information from detailed presentations, creating concise and visually compelling executive demonstration materials can significantly amplify your impact. These targeted guides empower champions to effectively advocate your solution internally, especially when you're not directly involved in conversations. But be sure you supplement them with comprehensive business justifications, particularly for significant or unplanned investments. Providing detailed financial projections, anticipated business outcomes, and illustrative case studies allows stakeholders to clearly see the benefits and rationale behind their investment decisions, effectively addressing internal objections and reinforcing the value of your solution.

VALUE REALIZATION

Working closely with customer success teams allows you to measure and articulate the economic benefits of your solutions by concentrating on value realization metrics that directly connect to your customer's strategic goals and financial outcomes. Providing these insights to executives, ideally on a quarterly basis, not only underscores your solution's impact but also fortifies relationships and creates avenues for further expansion.

Identify key performance indicators aligned with your customer's goals by collaborating with the customer during the onboarding stage. This will help you determine the KPIs that are most crucial to their business, such as revenue growth, cost savings, and efficiency improvements. Define success metrics that clearly describe what success looks like for them, in consistently measurable terms.

For example, monitor and quantify value realization from operational efficiency gains by measuring time saved, reduced errors, and increased productivity. Assess revenue impact to illustrate how your solution has contributed to increased sales, upselling opportunities, or market growth. Highlight cost reductions by showcasing savings from optimized processes, resource reductions, or lowered risk exposure. Demonstrate risk mitigation by showing how the solution has minimized potential losses or compliance issues.

While detailed analyses have their value, you should also present data in executive-friendly formats, such as concise, one-page executive summaries featuring key metrics, charts, and qualitative feedback. Utilize dashboards and reports that employ data visualization to spotlight trends and results. And once you start a strategic partnership, conduct quarterly business reviews by hosting structured meetings with leadership to discuss value realization and plan subsequent steps.

Align your results with broader business outcomes by illustrating how the solution supports your customer's strategic initiatives, particularly digital transformation and market expansion. Emphasize competitive advantage by highlighting how the solution differentiates your customer in their market. Utilize case studies and testimonials by documenting real-world examples of how your solution delivered measurable benefits. Collect internal feedback from users and department leaders to provide a comprehensive view of the solution's impact.

Your client's executive team will remain unaware of your contributions unless you present them with a quarterly summary of your benefits. After four continuous quarters, they will possess sufficient information to support an expansion of your solution's value. Your high standards will prompt them to request similar performance reports for other solutions they are contemplating for renewal. This will clearly distinguish vendors from strategic partners, reducing your competition and freeing up more funding for your next collaboration—a chance to build on your demonstrated success.

VALUE REALIZATION QUARTERLY SCORECARD

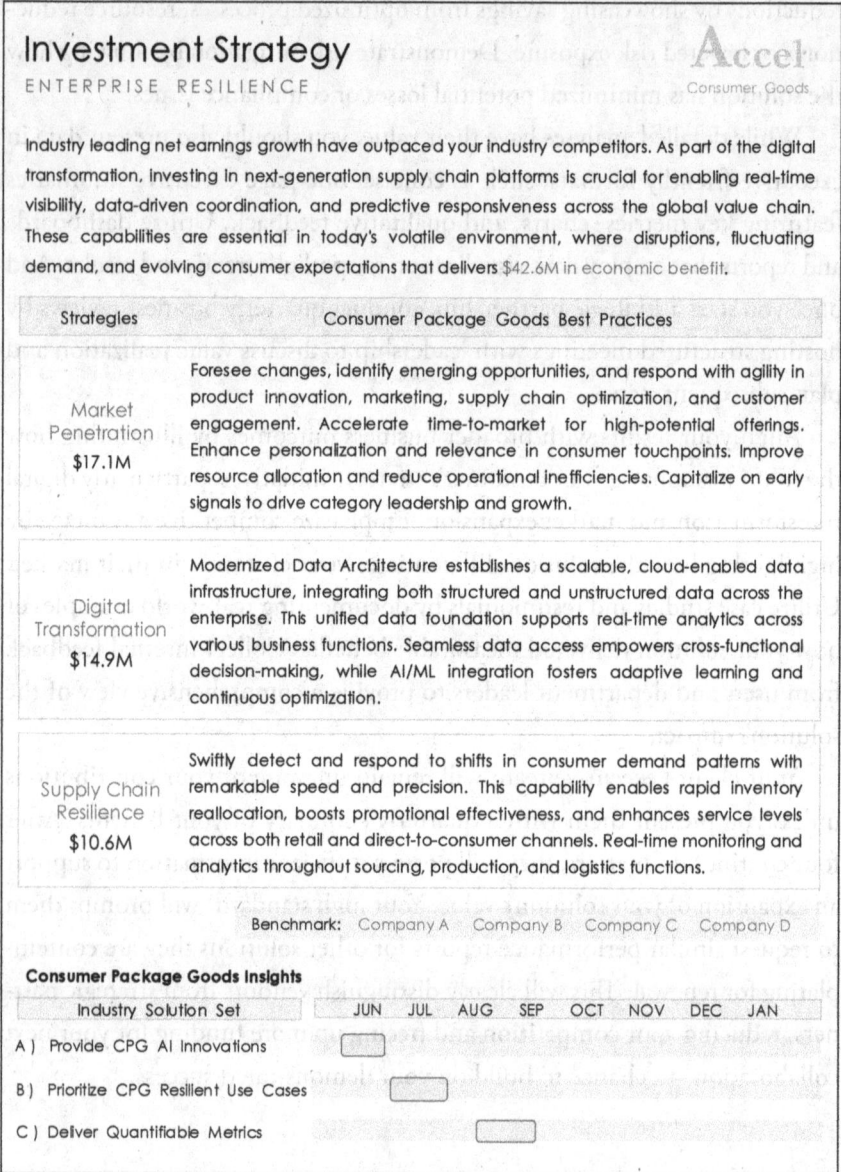

Investment Strategy
ENTERPRISE RESILIENCE $Accel$
                                                    Consumer Goods

Industry leading net earnings growth have outpaced your industry competitors. As part of the digital transformation, investing in next-generation supply chain platforms is crucial for enabling real-time visibility, data-driven coordination, and predictive responsiveness across the global value chain. These capabilities are essential in today's volatile environment, where disruptions, fluctuating demand, and evolving consumer expectations that delivers $42.6M in economic benefit.

Strategies	Consumer Package Goods Best Practices
Market Penetration $17.1M	Foresee changes, identify emerging opportunities, and respond with agility in product innovation, marketing, supply chain optimization, and customer engagement. Accelerate time-to-market for high-potential offerings. Enhance personalization and relevance in consumer touchpoints. Improve resource allocation and reduce operational inefficiencies. Capitalize on early signals to drive category leadership and growth.
Digital Transformation $14.9M	Modernized Data Architecture establishes a scalable, cloud-enabled data infrastructure, integrating both structured and unstructured data across the enterprise. This unified data foundation supports real-time analytics across various business functions. Seamless data access empowers cross-functional decision-making, while AI/ML integration fosters adaptive learning and continuous optimization.
Supply Chain Resilience $10.6M	Swiftly detect and respond to shifts in consumer demand patterns with remarkable speed and precision. This capability enables rapid inventory reallocation, boosts promotional effectiveness, and enhances service levels across both retail and direct-to-consumer channels. Real-time monitoring and analytics throughout sourcing, production, and logistics functions.

Benchmark: Company A   Company B   Company C   Company D

Consumer Package Goods Insights

Industry Solution Set	JUN	JUL	AUG	SEP	OCT	NOV	DEC	JAN
A) Provide CPG AI Innovations	▭							
B) Prioritize CPG Resilient Use Cases		▭						
C) Deliver Quantifiable Metrics				▭				

Diagram 3.2 Receive Credit with Executives for Your Value

ACCOUNT PLANNING

Sales planning is essential for aligning teams, driving revenue, and meeting organizational goals, but several obstacles could impede its success. One major hurdle in sales planning is creating a large amount of content to validate your recommendations that never reaches the customer. The entire hyperscale approach centers on crafting customer-facing executive deliverables as foundational elements to share with the customer for feedback. High-level internal collaborative planning is integral to the account planning process, but attempting to draft a plan in just a few days for an annual review—not to mention using it only once a year—is inefficient.

As you advance through your strategic interactions with each prospect, you must determine which of the sixteen sales frameworks (see Diagram 3.3) to develop based on your personal engagement strategy. Each step simplifies the account-planning process because you gather feedback from various levels within an account about what resonates with them, allowing you to adjust your terminology and industry strategy according to their strategic goals. Meanwhile, each customer deliverable contributes to the account planning document for internal team collaboration. The customer steers the account plan's direction, rather than you creating a plan that is inwardly focused.

Account plans are dynamic documents that need regular updates, usually at least once a month, to stay in tune with market conditions and customers' changing needs. The sixteen frameworks listed previously can be easily updated to elicit customer validation of their changing business needs. Monthly reviews facilitate the incorporation of customer feedback, adjustment of key goals, and refinement of stakeholder maps. This ongoing process makes sure your sales team can adapt to shifts in customer priorities, competitive pressures, and internal changes. It also helps internally, as you can better monitor your progress, spot new opportunities, and manage risks, leading to stronger and more strategic client relationships.

ACHIEVE CUSTOMER INTERLOCK

ACCOUNT PLAN

CUSTOMER-CENTRIC RESEARCH	ALIGN TO BUSINESS OBJECTIVES	COLLABORATIVE PLANNING	VALUE REALIZATION
M	**A**	**C**	**O**
POINT OF VIEW	NEEDS ANALYSIS	ECONOMIC BENEFIT	EXECUTIVE PROPOSAL
Chapter 1	Chapter 2	Chapter 3	Chapter 4
1 CEO Email	5 Relationship Map	9 Value Realization	13 Executive Decision Document
2 Partner Summary	6 Three-Year Press Release	10 Account Plans	14 Procurement Scorecard
3 Business Strategy	7 Solution Imaging	11 Executive Demo Guide	15 Executive Proposal
4 Investment Strategy	8 Mutual Action Plans	12 Reference Matrix	16 Implementation Plan

Customer Value Creation

Diagram 3.3 Elicit Customer Feedback to Validate Your Findings

Viewing account plans as active tools rather than fixed documents improves pipeline accuracy, boosts customer engagement, and keeps your sales strategy relevant and effective over time. This method promotes consistent growth, retention, and long-term value for both the customer and the organization. Accounts should be reviewed during quarterly business reviews to identify future projects with your strategic partners and flesh out their roadmaps of future requirements.

EXECUTIVE DEMONSTRATION GUIDES

Customers generally retain about 10 percent of what they see during technology demonstrations. These sessions often present a vast amount of information in a condensed time frame, leading to cognitive overload. Without consistent reinforcement, much of the detail fades quickly after the demo, especially if the content isn't directly aligned with the customer's specific needs or workflows.

Demonstration guides serve as an invaluable tool by providing a visual reminder of your solution's unique capabilities. These guides reinforce key features, benefits, and use cases, allowing customers to revisit and absorb the information at their own pace. By offering a structured reference, demo guides help bridge the retention gap, ensuring that the most critical aspects of your solution remain top of mind long after the presentation.

Incorporating visual aids and concise summaries into the sales process not only enhances customer understanding but also increases the likelihood of driving engagement and influencing decision-making.

During evaluations, new stakeholders often join the process later. Instead of repeatedly demonstrating your solution, the executive demonstration guide provides a fast-track method to get everyone up to speed. This approach allows evaluators to review the primary use cases as often as they want, at their own convenience, ensuring they grasp your unique differentiation. When the executive team presents the investment request to the board, this guide also offers a clear and concise way for board members to understand the solution they are considering for their business investment.

When implementing this approach within your company, you're likely to get two less-than-helpful suggestions. First, your technical resources department may want to convert everything to a landscape orientation because that's what they have always used in their previous presentations. Landscape orientation is typically favored by technical evaluators who aim to provide detailed insights into product capabilities. On the other hand, portrait orientation is commonly used by executives seeking funding from the board of directors. In either situation, selecting the appropriate format is crucial; the choice should align with the audience's expectations and the presentation's objectives.

Second, some of your advisors may want to brand your dashboard with your company logo and colors. Is this a wise move? In almost every situation, your prospect will need to compare and contrast your solutions against other alternatives, requiring an unbiased perspective. Wouldn't it make more sense to incorporate the prospect's logo and color scheme, to save them additional work during the sales cycle? There is a certain level of healthy confusion that arises when an executive document is branded with the customer's logo and color scheme but produced by your team. This can lead to the executive team questioning whether the document was created by their own team or the vendor, prompting further discussions to clarify the source of the recommendations.

EXECUTIVE DEMONSTRATION GUIDE

Semiconductor Yield Analytics
DIGITAL RESILIENCE

Accel
Semiconductor

Manufacturing analytics capabilities for electrical testing in semiconductor companies focus on providing comprehensive insights into testing processes, improving yield, ensuring quality, and optimizing operations. Collect and aggregate data from various electrical test equipment, including Automated Test Equipment and other diagnostic tools used in semiconductor testing. Continuous monitoring of test parameters and results provides immediate insights into the performance and quality of semiconductor devices.

Defect Rate	First Pass Yield (FPY)	Scrap Rate	Total Defects	Total Downtime	Downtime Minutes
7%	91%	8%	99	63%	426

- Use process traceability to understand where, how long, and how successful production stations are during production runs to reduce scrap, waste, and remanufactured products.
- Increased yield for premium priced components by minimizing station wait times, delays, and error rates.
- Understand the scope of the issues affecting production output and prioritize the changes that need to be made. Simplify the analysis and correlation from different production and test systems to provide a single point of truth eliminating any confusion about what needs to be done to increase production results.

Diagram 3.4 Provide Unique Differential Value

RECEIVE UNBUDGETED FUNDS

Typically, all of a company's funding is spoken for and has already been applied to existing systems and inflight projects, often based on commitments months or even years before your meeting. To justify unbudgeted, out-of-cycle investments to the board, CEOs must present a compelling case that clearly outlines the potential benefits, risks, and resource requirements. This involves addressing key areas with strategic focus and leveraging data-driven insights to ensure alignment with the company's long-term objectives.

CEOs begin by framing the investment within the context of growth, innovation, or risk mitigation, emphasizing how the project seizes an emerging opportunity or addresses an unforeseen challenge. They highlight the return on investment (ROI), showcasing projections of revenue growth, cost savings, or operational efficiencies that outweigh the initial expenditure. To manage board concerns, CEOs likewise conduct a risk assessment, detailing potential obstacles and the mitigation strategies in place. This includes addressing competitive threats, regulatory changes, or market shifts that make the investment timely and necessary. Additionally, they break down the resource requirements, clarifying the financial, technological, and human capital needed to execute the project successfully.

To show your solution's value and strategic relevance, especially when you're seeking unbudgeted funds, you must understand the elements that go into that analysis. Review the below summaries carefully!

STRATEGIC ALIGNMENT outlines the vision and objectives, demonstrating how the investment integrates with the company's long-term strategy. Business opportunities address the specific market need or problem the investment aims to solve. Competitive advantage emphasizes how the investment will differentiate the company or enhance its positioning.

FINANCIAL JUSTIFICATION offers a comprehensive cost breakdown, detailing a precise budget that includes both capital and operational expenditures. Revenue projections clearly outline how the investment will enhance top-line growth, supported by specific timelines and assumptions. Return-on-investment metrics, such as net present value, internal rate of return, and payback period, are meticulously calculated. Financial risks are identified and strategies for mitigation are proposed.

MARKET ANALYSIS reveals the investment's potential given the target market's size, growth rate, and potential. Customer insights offer forecasts on demand or adoption, validating the market opportunity. Competitive landscape analysis outlines strategies for outperforming competitors and sustaining a competitive advantage.

RISK ASSESSMENT identifies operational risks and underscores potential execution challenges, such as supply chain disruptions, resource constraints, or implementation complexities. Market risks encompass external factors like regulatory shifts, economic changes, or competitor actions. Mitigation plans outline strategies to manage and reduce these risks.

AN EXECUTION PLAN provides the project timeline, detailing a clear roadmap with milestones, key deliverables, and expected completion dates. It also outlines required resources such as staffing and technology needed to execute the plan. Partnerships highlight collaborations, vendors, or partnerships essential for the investment's success.

ORGANIZATIONAL IMPACT examines how the investment aligns with the company culture and integrates with existing teams. Employee impacts evaluate whether the investment necessitates hiring, training, or restructuring. Scalability assesses how the investment prepares the company for future growth opportunities.

ACCOUNTABILITY METRICS establish the KPIs that define key performance indicators, crucial for assessing the success of the investment. Monitoring plans outline how progress will be tracked and reported to the board. Governance specifies roles and responsibilities for oversight and accountability.

FUNDING REQUIREMENTS detail the requested amount, explicitly outlining the necessary funds and their breakdown. Use of funds specifies how the money will be allocated and how it will directly support the investment's objectives. Alternative funding options discuss whether external funding sources have been evaluated.

CASE STUDIES AND BENCHMARKS serve as powerful testimonials, showcasing examples of similar investments by competitors or other industries that achieved positive outcomes. Lessons learned integrate insights from past investments, demonstrating a well-prepared and informed approach.

BASIS FOR INVESTMENT DECISION reiterates the strategic importance, financial upside, and readiness for execution. To create a compelling summary, the call to action should conclude with a clear request for funding and a timeline for decision-making.

Transparency is crucial as CEOs provide milestones and KPIs to measure progress and track success, ensuring accountability and demonstrating how the investment aligns with broader company goals. By engaging cross-functional leaders to validate the need and offering scalable or phased approaches, CEOs can present the investment as a calculated, strategic move rather than an impulsive decision.

Ultimately, by addressing each area with clarity and foresight, CEOs can build board confidence, securing approval for investments that drive long-term value and resilience.

CREDIBILITY THEORY

Evaluate establishing financial metrics to assess the value of the business proposal, drawing on industry case studies from your client's success stories as references.

Why change?

Challenge:	Gain access to the CFO to validate desire to invest in your solution. Calculate an outside-in business case based on prior proven success. Identifying the CFO's required hurdle rate to fund a strategic project.

How do we differentiate?

Concept 9:	**Deliver Payback to Finance** is essential to clearly demonstrate the value, return on investment (ROI), and the strategic alignment with the company's goals. Highlight how the project will yield early benefits, ensuring a shorter payback period.
Concept 10:	**Traversing the Proving Ground** involves demonstrating increasing strategic value, aligning with corporate goals, and building influence across the entire organization. Managing the narrative of your value proposition across multiple levels and business units.
Concept 11:	**CFO's Performance Metrics** must align with financial health, operational efficiency, and strategic growth objectives of the business. The CFO will evaluate ROI, TCO, payback period, revenue growth, and cost avoidance to evaluate the viability of a project.
Concept 12:	**Provide Thought Leadership** to executives involves presenting cutting-edge insights, creative concepts, and practical advice that contribute to business expansion. This includes personalized information pertinent to industry changes that align with core goals.

What do we receive?

Result:	Successful quantified value of your solutions from prior customers. Understand the unique industry nuances that **improve win rates +34%.** Identify unexpected costs in TCO to mitigate risk for the CFO.

TIPS AND TRICKS FOR ESTABLISHING CREDIBILITY

- Successfully engaging with CFOs and executive-level stakeholders requires a comprehensive and nuanced approach. At the heart of this strategy is a deep understanding of the **nineteen critical metrics CFOs** rely upon to gauge the overall health and performance of their businesses. By clearly identifying and articulating precisely how your solution positively impacts these metrics, you establish immediate relevance and credibility.
- In practical terms, the effectiveness of your **engagement hinges on aligning priority** use cases directly to tangible, measurable business outcomes that resonate with executives. These outcomes should be framed in terms of revenue growth, operational efficiency, risk mitigation, or productivity enhancement, clarifying how your solution contributes directly to strategic goals.
- To effectively communicate your value proposition, prioritize consistency and structure in your messaging. By carefully orchestrating interactions between executive teams and evaluation groups, you minimize the potential for miscommunication, fostering alignment and internal consensus. This **structured approach builds credibility** and increases your solution's likelihood of gaining internal champions.
- Differentiation through thought leadership further enhances your value. Executives deeply appreciate insights drawn from extensive industry experience, even if the insights provided are not fully complete. Offering unique perspectives, even

with approximately 70 percent accuracy, demonstrates your investment and understanding of their challenges, allowing executives to fill in the gaps themselves. This strategy not only distinguishes you from competitors but empowers executives to redefine their own decision-making criteria, based on your informed perspective.

- Clearly articulating the economic benefits of your solution is equally essential. Precise quantification of expected returns—whether through revenue increases, reduced operational costs, or improved efficiencies—provides CFOs the tangible evidence needed to quickly recognize value. Leading discussions with **concise payback timelines** rather than initial investment requirements shifts the narrative positively, elevating your proposal's priority among top organizational projects.

- It is crucial to align your solution with executive career aspirations and broader organizational strategies. Executives seek projects and investments capable of driving significant business impact, potentially propelling their careers forward. Presenting your solution as comprehensive and strategic positions it as an attractive initiative worthy of executive sponsorship.

- Additionally, implementing structured methods for regularly measuring value realization further strengthens your credibility. By transparently **showcasing the impact through quarterly performance scorecards**, you reinforce ongoing executive trust in the consistent value delivered by your solution.

- Creating high-quality executive deliverables, including detailed strategic documents and visually compelling demonstration guides, provides a lasting and persuasive impression. Executive Demonstration Guides, in particular, succinctly capture your unique differentiators and empower internal advocates to effectively represent your solution during crucial discussions, even in your absence.

- Finally, leveraging a robust Reference Matrix highlights **successful decision-making criteria** adopted by leading industry organizations. This approach further validates your solution's strategic relevance and effectiveness, enhancing its appeal and credibility in executive-level conversations.

- Together, these elements form a comprehensive narrative designed to resonate with CFOs and executives, positioning your solution as both essential and strategically advantageous for their organization's sustained success.

CREDIBILITY WORKBOOK
FINANCIAL ACUMEN

Credibility Frameworks

51 VALUE REALIZED	Customer measurable results by industry and persona • Proven quantifiable benefits from the industry segment
52 ACCOUNT PLANS	Comprehensive plan of an account's future projects • How your roadmap aligns to priority initiatives
53 EXEC DEMO GUIDE	Condensed version of a demonstration on paper • Highlight your unique differentiation by use case
54 REFERENCE MATRIX	Measurable benefits by industry leaders' requirements • Decision criteria in evaluation vs. after being in production

Credibility Sales Plays

55 FINANCE	Speak finance language with measure benefits • Quantify business impacts by capabilities
56 ROI	Customer case studies validate ROI projections • Industry leaders set the benchmarks
57 CONSTRAINTS	Executive allocates unbudgeted funds to priority projects • Overcoming operating unit budget constraints

58 ACCOUNT MANAGEMENT	Scorecard that profiles customer interlock • Confirm project prioritization and participation
59 RACI	Define roles and responsibility of each virtual team member • Ownership to develop customer deliverables
60 COMPELLING EVENT	Thought leadership drives compelling events • Keeping the executives' resources focused on their program
61 TOP TEN	Executives gain consensus on their top ten project • Moving up is based on measurable ROI you can confirm
62 OWNERSHIP	Reduce risk by assigning ownership across multiple stakeholders • Allocate accountability to executive direct reports
63 FINANCIAL IMPACTS	Financial impacts measured by use case studies • Industry-specific process optimization
64 GOALS	Link solution benefits to strategic financial goals • Provide the granular line item detail
65 TCO	Demonstrate an understanding of total cost of ownership levers • Uncover the hidden cost to guarantee project's profitability
66 TRADE-OFFS	Be transparent with risk associated with financial impacts • Allow executive to make choices on risk profiles
67 SCENARIOS	Scenario planning based on detailed financial projections • Business case segmented by horizon and use case grouping
68 MEASURABLE	Balance between delivering customer value creation • Ability to measure value realization

69 ADVICE	Capture executive-level thought leadership to provide advice • Trusted advisor status to recommend solving problems
70 PARTNER	Engage procurement and finance early to understand requirements • Aware of term on condition concessions before discounting
71 REVIEWS	Verify measurable financial impacts during business reviews • Share industry benchmarks comparison with the customer
72 REQUIREMENTS	Demonstrate knowledge of customer's financial requirements • You have been here before as an industry expert
73 CROSS- FUNCTIONAL	Involve each of your cross-functional experts • Program manage their involvement in your overall plan
74 LONG-TERM	Everything should point to your long-term value as a partner • Provide options to benefit from quick wins

Diagram 3.5 How to Create Credibility with C-Suite

EVERYDAY APPLICATIONS

Storytelling significantly enhances credibility by forging genuine connections, clarifying intricate ideas, and showcasing experience in an accessible manner. In daily interactions, sharing personal or professional anecdotes helps build trust and rapport by revealing your character, values, and expertise through tangible examples.

When you share a story, you bring your experiences to life, making it easier for others to connect with and remember your message. This creates a sense of authenticity and openness, both crucial for establishing credibility. People are naturally drawn to narratives, and stories demonstrate not just what you know, but how you've applied that knowledge to overcome challenges or achieve results.

Furthermore, storytelling aids in simplifying complex concepts by providing context and emotional engagement. Instead of merely presenting facts or data points, a well-told story frames information in an understandable and engaging way, capturing the listener's attention. This ability to clearly convey messages reinforces the perception that you are knowledgeable and experienced.

Sharing stories of past achievements or lessons learned provides social proof. When people hear how you've navigated similar situations or delivered value to others, they are more likely to trust your judgment and capabilities. This is particularly impactful in leadership, sales, or negotiations, where trust and influence are paramount.

Ultimately, storytelling acts as a bridge between information and connection, helping you to establish credibility by allowing others to see the depth of your experience and the sincerity of your intentions.

CREDIBILITY KEY TAKEAWAYS

1. Do your sale professionals have the financial acumen to engage CFOs?

   Ability to speak Excel to engage the CFO's office.

2. Can your sellers work accounts bottom up and top down simultaneously?

   Multiple engagement tracks are required to ensure revenue attainment quarterly.

3. Do prospects regard your GTM team members as thought leaders in their industry?

   Establishing credibility allows clients to request recommendations from your team.

4. Can your GTM team members structure a CFO conversation?

CFOs require your findings to be anchored on proven industry quantifiable results.

5. Do your sales teams become the customers' proposal team in evaluations?

If you want to control the narrative and reduce the sales cycles by two months.

6. Can you quantify value realization benefits for your customers?

Capture the improvements of success metrics that guarantee value expansions.

7. Do your teams provide executives demonstration guides for your prospects to review?

Ability to revisit your solution twenty-five times after demo whenever questions arise.

8. Do you engage in bi-directional collaboration on future projects quarterly?

Align customers' future projects to your proposed strategic roadmap for them.

SUMMARY

Establishing credibility with an executive you've just met—especially before a negotiation—involves a blend of preparation, professionalism, and insightful value propositions. The objective is to swiftly build trust by demonstrating expertise, understanding their business needs, and aligning your strategy with their priorities.

Initiate that process by leading with insights: Demonstrate that you've done your research by citing relevant industry trends, company performance metrics, or specific challenges your prospect might be encountering. Tailor your introduction to reflect their strategic objectives, underscoring that you grasp their business environment. This frames you as an informed and prepared partner rather than just another vendor.

Concentrate on building rapport by listening attentively and posing thoughtful, open-ended questions. This allows the executive to express their needs while giving you the chance to show empathy and alignment. Highlight previous successes or pertinent case studies, subtly showcasing your track record without overtly selling your solution.

Transparency and honesty are essential—recognizing potential challenges and proactively addressing risks helps both sides evaluate the fit of your business model and solution. Presenting solutions up front or sharing examples of how similar situations were managed likewise builds trust and positions you as a credible problem solver.

Finally, emphasize the value and business outcomes your solution offers, rather than just focusing on its capabilities and cost. Executives are driven by results, so clearly linking your offering to measurable business impacts helps establish credibility, especially early in the conversation.

CEOs will utilize these conversations to present comprehensive business strategies to their board of directors. In Chapter 4, we will examine how these pillars integrate into an executive proposal designed to address and overcome every potential objection.

CHAPTER 4

OUTCOMES

Uncomfortable Conversations

(Reduce Sales Cycles by 43 Percent)

CHAPTER 4

➤ **DELIVER COMPLETE SOLUTIONS:** Proven Industry Roadmaps

➤ **BUILDING STRATEGIC TRUST:** Recommend Strategies

➤ **IMPLEMENTATION PHASES:** to Achieve Quick Wins

➤ **BALANCING THE HORIZONS:** Measurable Benefits

➤ **TRUTH ABOUT BUSINESS OUTCOMES:** Easy to Work With

➤ **BUILDING AN EXECUTIVE PROPOSAL:** Overcome Objections

➤ **BOARD MEETING QUESTIONS:** Anticipate Needs

➤ **EXECUTIVE DECISION DOCUMENT:** Steps Completed in Process

---

➤ **PROCUREMENT SCORECARDS:** Reduce Requests for Discounts

➤ **OUTCOME THEORY:** Reduce Sales Cycles -43 Percent

➤ **TIPS AND TRICKS:** Brief Executive Leaders

➤ **OUTCOMES WORKBOOK:** Executive Acumen

➤ **EVERYDAY APPLICATIONS:** Metrics That Move the Needle

➤ **KEY TAKEAWAYS:** Deliver Complete Solutions

➤ **SUMMARY:** Uncomfortable Conversations

➤ **MACO FRAMEWORK:** Demand Creation Best Practice

DELIVER COMPLETE SOLUTIONS

I found myself sitting in the CFO's kitchen at 11 p.m. on the last day of the quarter. Both Ryan (the CFO) and his wife, Jane, were in their bathrobes, probably because I'd knocked on their door at 10:30, unannounced. "Uncomfortable" doesn't come close to describing the sheer awkwardness in that room, but I had a good reason to be there. You see, Brad and I had less than an hour to review a contract in detail and secure signatures on the $84 million partnership agreement between our firms. This was a critical transaction for the public company I worked for, one poised to deliver two cents a share, but we had to close it before the quarter ended for the company to make their revenue commitments to the street. "Never underestimate the importance of creating and closing significant transactions within the time frame you've committed to," I reminded myself, "no matter what it takes!"

So how did we get to that point? Well, four months earlier I landed in Dallas, Texas, to work with the account team to create a strategic GTM partnership with Ryan's company, a consulting firm well-known as a systems integrator. Initially, they specialized in bidding for custom outsourced projects—in fact, my firm had competed with theirs on past projects. But between the unpredictability of these projects and their Fortune 100 clients' desire to upgrade every six months, after forty years they wanted to pivot from custom engagements to offering a suite of industry-leading packaged applications.

The executives understood that the key to executing this strategic shift was to leverage compensation as a driving force. They implemented a variable compensation structure, offering 75 percent for custom projects and an attractive 150 percent for projects utilizing industry-standard applications. This approach immediately captured the attention of the entire company, garnering robust support from the majority of the leadership, and catalyzing the transformation of the company's GTM strategy.

To partner with them, we needed to create several industry-specific solution sets utilizing that industry's leading applications. We collaborated on the phased implementation approaches that they would recommend for the first three phases of each project. However, my team prioritized the use cases, business impacts by use case, value realization metrics impacted, executive dashboards for the executive staff, and the unique data attributes that would be shared among the solutions. My team worked closely with Ryan and with his CIO, Charlie, to ensure the industry reference architectures met their standards, and that they had the resources to implement successfully.

Throughout the four-month development process, Charlie assured me that as long as we met all of the requirements, he would be the ultimate decision-maker and the one to sign the agreement. Like many executives, Charlie had the best intentions but not much experience working on a strategic partnership of this magnitude. Soon, it became clear that the CFO would have to sign the contracts instead, even though he hadn't participated in any of our previous discussions.

Fortunately, after some awkward small talk and a final set of contract negotiations, Ryan signed the paperwork—perhaps the largest deal ever finalized in a bathrobe—and we moved forward with the project. Here's the point: Even the best laid plans come across glitches, and both creativity and flexibility are needed to meet both parties' needs within the timelines required. How many sales professionals on your GTM team are willing to prioritize strategic outcomes, even if it means having uncomfortable conversations?

In this case, despite having sponsorship from the CIO and CTO, we needed to engage each of the client's eight different industry teams to present our unique differentiation value. Brad, our account manager, skillfully reached out to the forty different vice presidents overseeing those teams. At first, only two VPs agreed to meet, so we clearly needed a better way to capture their attention. Brad sent out another round of meeting invites, each for an eighteen-minute session featuring a four-bullet point agenda and a personalized industry solution set to review. Remarkably, thirty-eight out of the forty VPs confirmed our meetings within the next four weeks.

You might be reticent to reach out to new stakeholders, fearing they might react negatively. Especially in projects involving multiple industries, each department will have their own specific business challenges they must solve for their customers, and they may be skeptical of you. But I think of it this way: We have unique strategy consulting content that will offer our clients a significant competitive advantage as they go to market. So, I ask those scary new stakeholders whether they'd prefer to meet before or after I brief their division's general manager! Almost invariably, they ask for the earlier meeting so they can see the details before their manager tasks them with follow-up. This proactive approach ensures that everyone is aligned and prepared for the strategic discussions ahead.

BUILDING STRATEGIC TRUST

Becoming a trusted advisor to a CEO requires more than just providing solutions—you have to deliver comprehensive business strategies that align with their long-term vision, address challenges, and seize opportunities. This level of influence often starts with professional respect, but keeping it requires a deep understanding of their business and consistent insights that drive measurable outcomes.

To establish this strategic trust, start by deeply understanding the CEO's strategic priorities and the company's overarching goals. This means not only researching the industry and market trends, but also identifying the internal pain points and growth opportunities the CEO is focused on. By aligning your recommendations with their vision, you demonstrate that you are invested in the company's long-term success.

Using this alignment, offer holistic strategies rather than isolated solutions. CEOs value advisors who can connect the dots across multiple functions—from sales and marketing to operations and finance. Frame your recommendations within a broader context, showing how they will impact revenue, efficiency, and competitive positioning. This positions you as someone who thinks beyond surface-level fixes and is capable of guiding transformative initiatives.

Build credibility by backing your strategies with data, case studies, and financial projections. CEOs are driven by results, so providing clear ROI models, benchmarks, and risk assessments shows that your recommendations are grounded in practicality and foresight. Moreover, be transparent about potential risks and offer mitigation plans, reinforcing that your approach is comprehensive and realistic.

To achieve trusted advisor status, you must add consistent value in every interaction to make the best use of a CEO's time. Maintain regular touch-points, providing updates on market trends and proactively bringing new ideas to the table. This ongoing engagement fosters a relationship where the CEO views you as a proactive partner rather than a reactive consultant. Here are some specific tactics I've found helpful.

- Always send a list of topics twenty-four hours before and ten minutes before each meeting.
- Reduce meetings from one hour to thirty minutes whenever feasible.
- Provide an update on the account's internal status and political landscape.
- Present a new idea the customer has not encountered before.
- Ask a question the executive does not know the answer to, gaining a referral to an expert.
- Offer something valuable to receive something in return.
- Engage distractors to uncover objections and decision criteria to address.
- Conclude each meeting with proposed next steps and confirm future availability. Follow up with an email outlining the milestones, action items, owners, and due dates.

Throughout this process, make sure you demonstrate empathy and adaptability. Understand the pressures and complexities CEOs face, and tailor your communication to their style: concise, actionable, and strategic.

By consistently delivering value, aligning with their goals, and anticipating their needs, you position yourself as a trusted advisor capable of shaping the company's future.

IMPLEMENTATION PHASES

Once you have successfully negotiated the specifics of each implementation phase, you move closer to a comprehensive fit assessment. This step signifies that you are on the verge of being confirmed in the final vendor selection, ensuring alignment with the project's objectives. Navigating the three phases of an implementation necessitates a balance between achieving quick wins that provide immediate value and realizing long-term benefits and ROI as the project evolves. This structured strategy maintains stakeholder confidence while preserving momentum throughout the process.

PHASE 1: Quick Wins—Deliver Immediate Value and Buy-In
The initial phase should prioritize delivering noticeable, low-risk improvements that yield immediate results. Establish clear, short-term milestones that demonstrate measurable progress within the first ninety days. These quick wins are crucial for securing stakeholder confidence, justifying the investment, and building organizational momentum. During negotiations, emphasize small, attainable goals that can be swiftly implemented without extensive resource commitments. Prioritize features or processes that address urgent pain points, along with automation or efficiencies that generate immediate cost savings or productivity gains. And of course, align these quick wins with executive priorities to garner support and enthusiasm.

PHASE 2: Mid-Term Gains—Operational Scaling and Expansion
The second phase centers on scaling the solution across broader areas, enhancing functionality, and boosting user adoption. This phase transitions from tactical improvements to system-wide integration and performance enhancements. In negotiations, highlight that this phase builds on your early success to set the stage for greater efficiencies. Expand the solution to additional departments or workflows. Address secondary pain points that contribute

to larger process inefficiencies. Introduce metrics to monitor adoption and progress, ensuring alignment with organizational KPIs. Secure commitment for training and change management to drive user engagement.

PHASE 3: Full Realization—Long-Term Value and ROI
The final phase involves full deployment, optimization, and the realization of the project's long-term benefits. This is where the most substantial ROI is achieved, often through complex integrations, data insights, and long-term scalability. In negotiations, underscore that investing in this phase ensures sustained competitive advantage and prepares the organization for future growth. Emphasize scalability and the ability to adapt to evolving business needs. Showcase ROI projections, long-term cost savings, and performance improvements. Highlight the risk of not completing the project, such as competitive disadvantages or operational bottlenecks. Frame the final phase as future-proofing the business.

BALANCING THE HORIZONS

To balance quick wins with long-term benefits, manage your client's expectations. Clearly communicate that while Phase 1 offers immediate value, the full benefits materialize over time. Use phased rollouts to reduce risk and adapt based on early feedback, but be sure to show value at every step. Specifically, provide measurable outcomes and performance data at the end of each phase, to keep leadership engaged and supportive, and to allow for adjustments between phases based on evolving business needs and feedback. This phased approach ensures that each stage delivers tangible results, keeping stakeholders invested while positioning the project for long-term success. More importantly, it maintains stakeholder confidence and momentum, ensuring the project remains aligned with the organization's goals and objectives. By following this structure, both you and your client can navigate the complexities of implementation while securing both immediate and long-term value.

IMPLEMENTATION HORIZONS

Quick Win Strategies Rapid Deployments	Application Deployments Channel Optimization	Strategic Roadmap Agent Desktop
6 Weeks – Horizon 1	12 Weeks – Horizon 2	20 Weeks – Horizon 3
P1 Knowledge Management		
P2 Web Self-Service		
P3 Proactive Chat	Social Communities	
P4 Online Digital Care	Online Home Page Experience	
P5 Agent Desktop for Region	Unified Agent Desktop	
	P6 Mobile Field Service, Dispatch, and Advanced Scheduling	

Diagram 4.0 Value Delivered by Phase

THE TRUTH ABOUT BUSINESS OUTCOMES

When preparing executive proposals, it is crucial to effectively justify business outcomes by thoughtfully addressing key expectations and requirements executives typically hold. Executives, entrusted with significant decision-making power and often accountable for obtaining unbudgeted funding, rely heavily on proposals that are not just convincing but demonstrably backed by proven industry success. These features build trust and credibility, demonstrating that your recommendations are grounded in solid experience and profound industry insight. Your proposals must therefore contain robust strategies, supported by relevant benchmarks and compelling case studies that clearly illustrate consistent and achievable results in similar contexts.

A critical element of any realistic proposal is the transparent delineation of trade-offs and clearly structured phased deployment plans. Executives must see precisely how implementation phases can be negotiated, managed effectively, and aligned with quick wins that generate tangible and measurable returns. Highlighting these incremental successes early on assures stakeholders that subsequent phases of the project can potentially be funded through initial gains, significantly reducing financial exposure and risk.

Moreover, your proposals should carefully balance the benefits of new capabilities against the complexity and risks inherent in their implementation. Clearly articulating how incremental capability improvements will strategically manage and reduce complexity, as well as risk, encourages executive confidence in the proposal's feasibility and long-term viability.

Proactively anticipating and comprehensively addressing potential executive objections further strengthens the proposal. Providing executives and their teams with comprehensive documentation and editable source files demonstrates a commitment to collaboration and flexibility. Should executives directly depend upon you for further adjustments, this reflects deep trust and solidifies the collaborative nature of your relationship. Likewise, comprehensive economic transparency is vital. Executives expect detailed responses regarding financial outcomes, specific time frames for achieving returns, clearly articulated risk mitigation plans, and explicit assignment of accountability for each project phase. This depth of economic clarity is critical to securing board and stakeholder approval.

In addition, incorporating an executive decision document into your proposal can significantly enhance executive confidence by clearly outlining critical evaluation steps, highlighting decision rationales, and listing the stakeholders who have explicitly endorsed the proposal. This methodical approach eliminates doubts, mitigates buyer's remorse, and provides a clear validation of the decision-making process.

Finally, a procurement scorecard can substantially streamline negotiations by summarizing negotiated benefits clearly and succinctly. Highlighting previous transaction successes alongside current negotiations equips procurement teams to finalize agreements efficiently, avoiding unnecessary discussions around further discounts. Your goal throughout the process is to provide a clear, compelling rationale for securing necessary funding and approvals.

BUILDING AN EXECUTIVE PROPOSAL

A well-crafted executive proposal, addressing each of the components listed below, presents a compelling case for project approval. By clearly defining your client's needs, demonstrating alignment with their company goals, and showcasing the financial and operational benefits, you can secure buy-in and funding for strategic initiatives.

THE EXECUTIVE SUMMARY serves as an overarching introduction to the project, offering a succinct explanation of the proposal's purpose, aims, and expected outcomes. It is designed to catch the attention of decision-makers by emphasizing the most crucial components. *Project purpose* details how the initiative aligns with organizational objectives. *Key benefits* focus on the anticipated value and impact. *Financial overview* covers the cost, return on investment, and payback period. *Call to action* provides recommendations or subsequent steps for approval.

CUSTOMER REQUIREMENTS delineate the specific needs, challenges, and objectives articulated by internal or external clients. Understanding these requirements ensures the project directly tackles key issues and delivers measurable value. *Problem definition* offers a clear articulation of the issue being addressed. *Desired outcomes* describe what success looks like from the customer's perspective. *Priority needs* are ranked or categorized requirements that must be satisfied. *Stakeholder input* involves feedback collected from key decision-makers and users.

STEPS COMPLETED in the evaluation process illustrate progress, credibility, and thoroughness. This section reassures stakeholders that the project has been meticulously planned and is prepared to advance. *Research and analysis* include market potential, feasibility studies, and competitive assessments. *Stakeholder engagement* tracks meeting notes, feedback sessions, and alignment efforts. *Preliminary work* includes prototypes, pilot programs, or initial deployments.

THE MEETING REQUIREMENTS section explicitly outlines how the proposed solution addresses customer needs and aligns with established requirements. It instills confidence that the project is structured to deliver results. *Requirement to solution mapping* provides a checklist or table showing each requirement and the corresponding solution component. *Compliance and standards* explain how the project adheres to regulatory, operational, or technical standards. *Customization* highlights any tailored features or configurations that meet specific customer demands.

PROJECT BENEFITS underscores the overall value your collaboration brings to the organization. This section should emphasize both tangible and intangible outcomes. *Financial gains* stem from revenue growth, cost reduction, or productivity improvements. *Operational efficiency* focuses on streamlined workflows, faster delivery times, or enhanced automation. *Risk mitigation* discusses how the project reduces exposure to market, operational, or compliance risks. *Competitive advantage* identifies unique differentiators that position the company ahead of competitors.

REFERENCE MATRIX visually organizes data to compare solutions, track requirements, or show dependencies. It ensures decision-makers can quickly assess alignment and completeness. Specifically, the *requirement traceability matrix* links project deliverables to requirements. *Vendor comparisons* examine competing solutions or partners. The *feature breakdown* should include a table outlining solution features, capabilities, and alignment with objectives.

TIME TO IMPLEMENT provides a realistic perspective on the project's timeline, ensuring stakeholders understand the phases, milestones, and expected completion dates. *Project phases* include a breakdown by stages for planning, deployment, and testing. *Key milestones* highlight critical points that must be achieved along the way. Finally, the dependencies section identifies tasks that rely on others to progress, while p*rojected completion date* specifies when the solution will be fully operational.

BENEFITS BY PHASE highlights the incremental value delivered at each stage of the project, reinforcing that the organization will see benefits throughout the process rather than just at completion. As described previously, *Phase 1* includes quick wins or early efficiencies. *Phase 2* focuses on major functional rollouts or measurable productivity gains. *Phase 3* encompasses full ROI realization, scalability, or market expansion.

TOTAL COST OF OWNERSHIP analysis provides a comprehensive view of the full costs associated with the project over its life cycle. This helps to justify the investment by presenting a transparent and long-term financial picture. *Initial costs* cover up-front expenses for software, hardware, or services. *Operational costs* involve ongoing maintenance, licensing, and support fees. *Training and adoption* accounts for resources required to train users and drive adoption. *Scalability costs* relate to future expansion or scaling. *Cost savings* aim to offset expenses through automation, efficiency, or resource optimization.

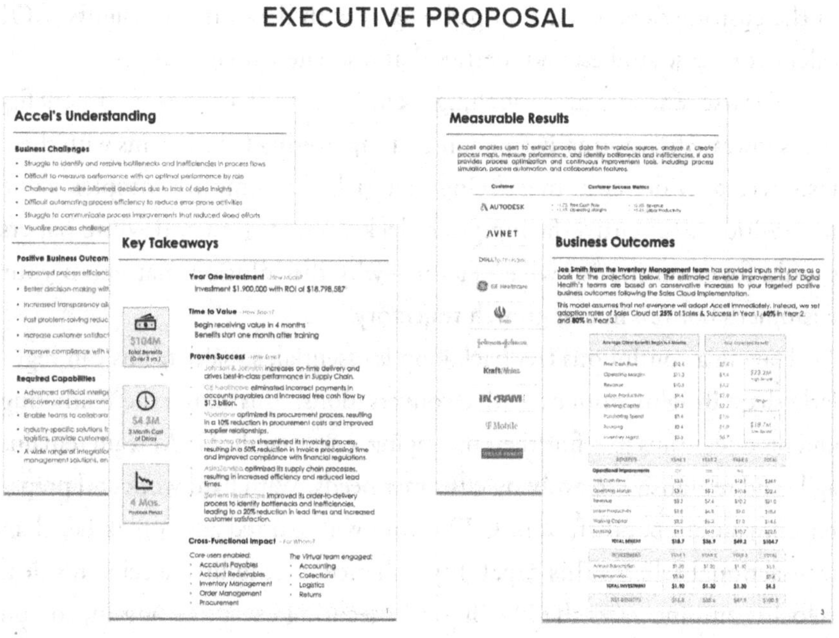

EXECUTIVE PROPOSAL

Diagram 4.1 Anticipate and Overcome Every Possible Objection

To drive successful engagement and win complex deals, your GTM team must be prepared to articulate business outcomes to customer executives. Every team member—from sales to pre-sales and customer success—should confidently and consistently convey how your solution delivers measurable value aligned with the customer's strategic goals.

Aligning your messaging with executive priorities involves focusing on outcomes that drive revenue growth, cost reduction, risk mitigation, and operational efficiency. Rather than focusing on technical details, your GTM team should translate product features into business impact: How does your solution address pain points, accelerate initiatives, or create the competitive advantages that are outlined in the executive proposal?

To prepare for this task, provide regular training and role-playing exercises, including audible-ready conversations, that simulate real-life interactions. Develop talk tracks and value frameworks that align with the top concerns of CEOs, CFOs, and other senior leaders. Focus these efforts on industry-specific use cases to demonstrate how the solution drives outcomes in the customer's vertical. Equip the team with data-driven insights, ROI calculators, case studies, and metrics that resonate with executives.

Likewise, encourage storytelling techniques to share customer benefits that showcase transformative outcomes. Empowering GTM teams with these resources provides customer-facing materials that simplify complex value propositions. Executive-facing pitch decks, one-pagers, and white papers should focus on the "so what" factor—why the solution matters to your customer's bottom line or growth trajectory.

Having a continuous feedback loop is essential, so sales teams can regularly share insights from executive conversations. This allows the marketing and product teams to refine their messaging, ensuring the GTM team remains agile and responsive to evolving customer needs. With hard work and preparation, you can populate your GTM team with trusted advisors rather than transactional sellers. This capability enhances credibility, accelerates deal velocity, and increases the likelihood of securing executive buy-in, so you can ultimately drive stronger customer relationships and long-term growth.

BOARD MEETING QUESTIONS

When evaluating whether to fund a new project, the board of directors focuses on strategic alignment, financial viability, risk, and long-term value. Their questions evaluate whether the project justifies the investment and supports the company's overall goals. Here are the top questions typically asked during board meetings regarding new project funding.

Strategic Alignment and Vision
- How does this project align with the company's long-term strategic objectives?
- Does the project enhance our competitive advantage or open new market opportunities?
- What specific business problem or opportunity does this project address?
- How will this project contribute to our growth, innovation, or digital transformation initiatives?

Financial Justification and ROI
- What is the projected return on investment, and how soon can we expect to see results?
- What are the total costs, including implementation, operational, and maintenance expenses?
- What is the payback period, and how does it compare to similar projects?
- How will this project impact cash flow and overall financial health?
- Are there cost-saving elements or efficiencies that justify this investment?

Risk Assessment and Mitigation
- What are the key risks associated with this project, and how are they being mitigated?
- How sensitive is the project to market, economic, or regulatory changes?
- What are the consequences of not pursuing this project?
- Have we conducted scenario planning or contingency analysis for potential project failure?
- What is the project's risk-adjusted return compared to other investment opportunities?

Market and Competitive Analysis
- How does this project position us against competitors?
- What is the market demand or customer need driving this project?
- Have customer feedback or market studies validated the need for this investment?
- What barriers to entry or competitive threats could affect project success?

Operational and Resource Planning
- Do we have the internal capabilities, resources, and technology to execute this project?
- What external partners or vendors will be involved, and how were they selected?
- How will this project affect current operations, and are there dependencies or bottlenecks?
- What impact will the project have on staffing, and do we need to hire or reallocate talent?

Project Timeline and Milestones
- What is the project timeline, and what key milestones will be tracked?
- How do we measure success, and what key performance indicators will we monitor?
- Is the project scalable or adaptable to future needs and growth opportunities?

By addressing these questions, board members ensure the proposed project is strategically sound, financially viable, and capable of delivering long-term value. This structured evaluation process helps mitigate risks, align leadership, and ensure responsible allocation of company resources.

EXECUTIVE DECISION DOCUMENT

Creating an executive decision document is the fastest way to eliminate buyer's remorse. Executive decision-makers need to know who you have worked with to validate your solution. This one-page framework provides a significant amount of information, making it easy for executives to confirm that the evaluation team has completed their due diligence. It also spreads the risk from a single buyer across multiple evaluators.

Your document should answer several questions:

- How much time have you invested?
- How many meetings have you conducted?
- Who are the key stakeholders in the organization that can verify your findings?
- What deliverables will the customer receive?
- How many managers and end users will benefit from your solution?
- How much incremental pipeline will be generated in the fiscal year?

When I was working with one CRO, for example, he introduced me to a single-value advisory leader to assess our solution. He was pleasantly surprised to find that my team had already engaged seventeen key stakeholders and completed seventeen meetings in four months! Exceeding his expectations allowed my team to secure an initial transaction five times larger than that originally budgeted for the project.

EXECUTIVE DECISION DOCUMENT

Date	Action Item	Attendees	Outcome
Aug 26	Intro call Jim <> Chris	Chris	Chris intro to David + Linda
Sep 11	Accel Introductory Presentation	Linda David	David requested follow up demo and PoV review with broader team
Oct 1	Accel Technical Deep Dive + Review Accel Demand Creation Best Practices	Linda David Ted Marva	• Positive feedback on recommended use cases, one-click PoV's, C-Suite Engagement Best Practices • Work with David C. on business mapping • Work with Marva and Ted to evaluate GTM Pilot
Oct 8	Accel for Strategic Accounts Review	Maureen Ted	Ted shared Walmart PoV with Account Team for feedback on value.
Oct 9	BVC Use Cases | Solution Value Mapping	David	Accel Solution Value Map aligns with Accel Business/Cloud Outcomes initiative. David requested initial draft of Value Map to help connect the dots for BVC Team.
Oct 19	Review Accel Solution Value Map	David	David requested Accel Pilot proposal supporting two industry GTM teams over 4 months
Oct 20	Accel .Conf20	Accel Team	Accel prepared feedback for Marva on Accel LoB Executive positioning
Oct 23	Review Proposal and Business Case	David	Request to consolidate into 4 slide proposal with additional context around services and enablement
Oct 27	Accel Intro for The Magis Group (Per Marva)	Curtis	Curtis thinks Accel aligns well with his C-Suite engagement initiatives. Requested f/u meeting with Ed Nzambi

Evaluation	Engagement	Deliverables	Business Case
4 Months	**17 People**	**Solution Value Map 5 Tailored Exec PoV's**	**$188m Incremental Pipeline**

Diagram 4.2 Remove Buyer's Remorse

I recommend providing a decision document to the economic buyer during the final two months of evaluation for significant transactions over $250,000. Executives often delegate this responsibility to their teams, which can result in excessive detail from all meetings and make it challenging to pinpoint accountability for each evaluation area. This streamlined document is exactly what an executive decision-maker needs to confidently proceed with a selection.

PROCUREMENT SCORECARDS

When the Procurement Department engages in a potential project, they have no idea of the value of the solution and are not interested in understanding the benefits that will be received from the business case. Everything becomes about the terms of the transaction that starts when you initially engage with them. To streamline that process, and (as a bonus) persuade them to stop asking for discounts, you should create a procurement scorecard documenting what they have negotiated with you.

Creating a procurement scorecard for the buyer is a highly strategic approach that reframes the negotiation dynamic, shifting the conversation from price concessions to the total value delivered. This method allows you to proactively outline the cumulative benefits and negotiated wins procurement has already secured, subtly reinforcing the fairness and competitiveness of your deal while minimizing the risk of additional discount requests. Showcase past wins by documenting and profiling all the value-added benefits from previous agreements, which also highlights Procurement's success in prior negotiations. Remind them of discounts, price locks, additional services, extended warranties, and free upgrades. Don't forget favorable payment terms or delivery schedules, or extras like free training, support, or implementation packages.

Quantify the value by attaching financial or operational metrics to the concessions you've already made. This turns intangible benefits into measurable savings, reinforcing the idea that procurement has already driven significant value. Overall, you want to highlight continuity and consistency that will position the current deal as a continuation of their success in previous negotiations. Procurement values consistency and predictability, so presenting the new contract as an extension of favorable terms makes the negotiation seem less contentious.

PROCUREMENT SCORECARD

Hi Mark, the Accel agreement provides the most flexible pricing, terms and conditions. Your agreement is based on a long-standing partnership. Here is a list of industry leading terms that have been provided in our agreement.

> > Pricing certainty with expansion options for the next three years
>
> > $285 per named user price
>
> > $390 per concurrent user price
>
> > Annual pooled capacity over standard monthly use limits
>
> > Annual rebalancing for unused software by moving other services, guaranteeing no shelfware
>
> > Annual rebalance between seats and sessions
>
> > Service level credits
>
> > Dedicated Client Success Manager
>
> > Mixing between named and concurrent users
>
> > No additional usage fees for exceeding 15%
>
> > Capped support costs for premium support

We look forward to continuing our valued partnership with Accel as you look to differentiate your brand.

Diagram 4.3 Reduce Discounting

Frame the scorecard as a value-driven partnership document, not a sales tactic. This shifts the negotiation tone from adversarial to collaborative, reinforcing that both sides are working toward mutual success. Once Procurement sees the total negotiated value, they are less likely to ask for further discounts. And if they continue to push, the scorecard serves as a negotiation anchor, clearly demonstrating the balance between what has already been negotiated and what's being requested. Every time I've used this approach, it has dramatically reduced concession requests and accelerated transaction close times.

Remember, Procurement thrives on measurable wins, and by providing a clear list of negotiated benefits, you fulfill their need for documented success. More importantly, you shift the focus from price to value, transforming the conversation from bottom-line tension to a broader perspective of cost avoidance and added value. This strategy again positions you as a partner rather than just a vendor, enhancing your relationship with Procurement by demonstrating your understanding and respect for their role in securing organizational value.

OUTCOME THEORY

Evaluate establishing financial metrics to assess the value of the business proposal, drawing on industry case studies from your client's success stories as references.

Why change?

Challenge:	Executive sponsors need to be audible ready to articulate the projects value. Answers every objection a board member has to receive funding. Executive proposal with required sections to receive approval.

How do we differentiate?

Concept 13:	**Articulate Business Outcomes** by matching your solutions to the client's strategic objectives and showcasing tangible benefits. Highlight examples of how other companies have successfully implemented the solution. Engage the client in the solution design to ensure it aligns with their internal measurements and procedures.
Concept 14:	**Board Meeting Objections** that are raised to ensure strategic alignment, budget projections, accountability, operational efficiency, stakeholder impact, industry innovation, market competitiveness, risk mitigation, and safeguarding the organization's long-term interests.
Concept 15:	**Required Capabilities** are the minimum core competencies to achieve the essential tasks that are needed to solve the business problem at hand and deliver the positive business outcomes. Identify the basic requirements to overachieve the desired expectations.

Concept 16:	**Executive Sponsor Responses** that are well-articulated can influence stakeholders who are resistant. Addressing objections demonstrates alignment with the organization's goals, fosters confidence across teams, and builds trust to secure critical stakeholder buy-in.

What do we receive?

Result:	Strategy to elevate to a top three project to ensure funding approval. Overcome every objection will **reduce sales cycles by -43%**. Complete solution that ensure TCO and implementation success.

TIPS AND TRICKS FOR BUSINESS OUTCOMES

- Effective executive engagement and strategic partnerships require clear, concise communication and structured planning. When briefing your executives, strive for clarity and brevity by limiting your briefing to one page whenever possible. Begin by explicitly stating the specific request or "ask" of the customer executive they will meet. Structure your briefing to include a succinct overview of relevant background information and a detailed investment strategy that clearly demonstrates the mutual value derived from the partnership. Additionally, including a simplified visual representation of key relationships can significantly enhance understanding and help executives identify the critical contacts necessary for advancing the partnership.

- Identifying joint GTM strategies is equally critical. Clearly articulate specific market opportunities that arise from your partnership, demonstrating how collaborative efforts will enhance your client's market presence and potential. By consolidating your **unique strategic advantages**, you can effectively highlight the distinctive benefits of the partnership, differentiating your collaborative approach from competitors and clearly illustrating its competitive advantage.

- Effective strategic communication plays a central role in aligning executive teams. **Simplifying complex details** to facilitate high-level, strategic discussions ensures that executives fully grasp the critical business outcomes. Clearly distinguishing your proposals from those of competitors is key to securing executive alignment and support.

- Recognizing diverse stakeholder needs within an organization is crucial for the success of strategic partnerships. Different organizational tiers, such as executives and evaluation teams, have unique requirements. Clearly articulating and addressing these separate needs ensures comprehensive internal communication, aligning evaluation insights with executive-level expectations, and preventing potential internal misalignment.

- Engaging executive sponsors early is paramount. When direct interaction with executive sponsors is challenging, proactively uncovering their decision-making criteria through interactions with evaluation teams becomes essential. Documenting these criteria allows for strategic alignment and facilitates **informed internal decisions**.

- Accountability and governance are essential elements of successful executive engagements. Board members frequently emphasize the importance of defining accountability clearly, especially regarding significant investments. To address this effectively, create an Executive Decision Document outlining the top eight to twelve critical steps completed during the evaluation process, along with endorsements from key employees. This document not only clarifies accountability but also alleviates potential buyer's remorse by providing concrete benchmarks of approval and responsibility.

- Effective negotiation strategies are also essential. Provide procurement teams with a **Procurement Scorecard** summarizing previously negotiated benefits, which can effectively reduce additional concession requests and streamline negotiations.

- Preparing for board-level scrutiny demands robust business proposals that anticipate and address potential objections up front. Clearly articulating justifications for the allocation of unbudgeted funds instills confidence and reinforces the value proposition of the partnership.
- Finally, presenting **Investment Strategies** using a structured three-phased horizon approach—short-term, mid-term, and long-term—allows executives clear choices. Because executives typically prefer a balanced mid-term option, providing three clearly defined investment strategies ensures informed, strategic decision-making.
- Adopting this comprehensive and structured methodology ensures clarity, alignment, and confidence at the executive level, significantly enhancing the potential success and impact of your strategic partnerships.

OUTCOMES WORKBOOK
EXECUTIVE ACUMEN

Outcome Frameworks

75 EXECUTIVE DECISION DOCUMENT	Remove buyers' remorse by spreading ownership • Across fifteen key stakeholders to reduce risk
76 PROCUREMENT SCORECARD	Document the negotiation benefits that procurement secured • Current agreement as well as prior agreement benefits
77 EXECUTIVE PROPOSALS	Overcome every possible objection asked in board meeting • Summarize the value of your business proposal
78 IMPLEMENTATION PLANS	Three horizons of implementation success • Each horizon is made up of benefits for each use case

Outcome Sales Plays

79 EXECUTIVE SUMMARY	Summarize your business value on one page • Be compelling when telling your story
80 CHALLENGE	Clearly articulate the current business challenge • Opportunity to improve compared to industry leaders
81 QUANTIFIABLE	Present proven quantifiable business outcomes • Industry leaders set the pace
82 VERIFIABLE	Provide finance-verified ROI and financial impact analysis • Customer industry benchmark examples
83 SCENARIOS	Model scenario planning and sensitivity analysis • Let executives set the parameters on your business case
84 OBJECTIVES	Show your alignment to strategic objectives • Attach yourself to largest problem
85 MILESTONES	Offer a Business Roadmap with key milestones • Executives appreciate when you keep their teams focused
86 MITIGATION	Drive continuous planning to address risk mitigation • Share parameters to reduce risk
87 BENCHMARKS	Measure quantifiable business measure by segment • Make generic to share with customers to set targets
88 DASHBOARDS	Enable executives to drive ongoing outcome tracking • Visibility to change management
89 MUTUAL	Align on mutual value with co-creation approach • Lead with recommendation for executives to edit
90 SCALABLE	Demonstrate scalable long-term value • Quick win foundation to strategic roadmap

91 ADVANTAGE	Articulate the competitive advantage you provide • How this will enhance their market position
92 PHASING	TCO by implementation phase • Uncover hidden costs to build trust
93 CHANGE	Offer executive support for change management • Technology is just one component to enable customer
94 REQUIREMENT	Meet executive requirements to deliver successful project • Deliver all of the required capabilities
95 STEPS COMPLETED	Summarize major steps completed to remove buyers' remorse • Allow economic buyer to spread risk across multiple stakeholders

Diagram 4.4 How to Deliver Business Outcomes to Fund Project

EVERYDAY APPLICATIONS

Effectively engaging executive decision-makers involves deeply understanding their core priorities and expectations. Executives consistently assess solutions by considering whether they directly address key business challenges, support strategic objectives, and deliver measurable ROI. Therefore, successfully positioning your solution requires a narrative clearly aligned with these executive considerations, complemented by highlighting unique differentiators and long-term strategic value.

Executives place substantial importance on a solution's capacity to address specific business needs. Clearly articulating how your solution tackles operational pain points, mitigates risks, or provides competitive market advantages is essential. Beyond immediate challenges, executives also expect alignment with broader strategic goals, such as growth, innovation, efficiency enhancement, risk management, or improved customer experiences. It is beneficial to illustrate this alignment through realistic scenarios or initiatives directly relevant to executive concerns.

Furthermore, a compelling narrative must include clear quantification of expected returns. Providing credible and detailed financial impact analyses (or KPI) underscores your solution's tangible value. Realistic and convincing estimates solidify your argument for executives who need robust justification for their investment decisions.

While tangible benefits form the foundation of decision-making, perceived intangible values also significantly influence executives. Demonstrating innovative features or unique technological methodologies enhances your competitive positioning and demonstrates operational excellence. Ease of use, rapid implementation, and minimal disruption underscore the practicality and immediate usability of your solution, thus reducing hesitation regarding adoption.

Scalability and flexibility resonate strongly with executives who anticipate future organizational growth and evolving business demands. Clearly presenting how your solution accommodates future changes emphasizes adaptability. Additionally, highlighting collaborative advantages—such as increased operational efficiency and improved cross-functional decision-making—further differentiates your solution, appealing to executives' desires for integrated and streamlined operations. Meanwhile, emphasizing your commitment to a sustainable, long-term partnership helps executives envision ongoing strategic collaboration beyond initial implementation. Highlighting continuous support and improvement reinforces confidence and trust.

Preparing for executive-level discussions requires careful anticipation of rigorous questioning. Proactively identifying likely board-level inquiries—such as those regarding financial justification, risk management, or integration complexities—enables you to equip your executive sponsor effectively. Give them comprehensive, persuasive, and concise answers so they can confidently navigate challenging conversations with senior stakeholders.

Identifying and directly addressing the criteria economic buyers use to evaluate solutions—such as total cost of ownership (TCO), financial predictability, risk reduction, and strategic enablement—further strengthens your proposal's alignment with executive priorities. While price remains a crucial factor, successful positioning involves shifting the conversation toward broader concepts of total value. Clearly articulating the long-term cost reductions and strategic advantages associated with your solution, even if it's premium priced, demonstrates a commitment to sustained excellence. Highlighting capabilities that exceed essential requirements further justifies premium pricing by demonstrating added strategic benefits.

Ultimately, effectively engaging executive decision-makers demands a narrative deeply aligned with their essential capabilities and strategic values, reinforced by tangible and intangible differentiators. This approach significantly enhances your solution's perceived value, increasing the likelihood of securing executive buy-in and fostering enduring strategic partnerships.

OUTCOME KEY TAKEAWAYS

1. Can your GTM team members articulate business outcomes to prospects?

   Executives measure success by overachieving expected business results.

2. What's required to truly invest in customer success to earn a value expansion?

   Customers need industry best practices over advanced product capabilities.

3. Are transactional relationships a surefire way to guarantee increasing churn rates?

   Working with multiple levels in an account across business units is required to expand.

4. What do complete solutions consist of to build executives' confidence to provide funding?

   Projected business outcomes with prioritized use cases by implementation phase.

5. What are the top ten questions that need answers in a board meeting to receive funding?

   Your teams need to be prepared to overcome every objective before the board meeting.

6. Are your teams able to gain direct access to economic buyers and funding approvers?

Industry best practices quantified benefits from use cases that deliver proven results.

7. Do your teams have the required sections for an executive proposal to receive funding?

Become the proposal team for your prospects to ensure they can receive funding.

8. Can you remove buyer's remorse by assigning ownership across multiple stakeholders?

Steps completed is an excellent way to verify the evaluation has been completed.

SUMMARY

The ability to drive and communicate business outcomes is a defining characteristic of market leaders. Organizations that excel in this domain do so by weaving a compelling narrative—one that transcends the transactional nature of a sale and instead positions their solutions as transformative. The most successful businesses are those that can vividly illustrate how their offerings address pressing challenges, enhance efficiencies, and drive revenue growth.

For executive teams, the ability to anticipate critical questions is just as important as telling a compelling story. Every major business decision, especially one that involves significant investment, is subject to scrutiny at the board level. Decision-makers demand more than theoretical benefits; they expect data-driven justifications, risk assessments, and an alignment with the company's long-term strategy. Organizations that proactively prepare for these conversations, armed with substantiated metrics and well-structured arguments, are better positioned to secure buy-in at the highest levels.

Yet, beyond the boardroom, businesses must also understand and appeal to the specific decision-making criteria of economic buyers. These individuals, often responsible for budget allocations, are not easily swayed by broad claims of value. Instead, they seek clear, financially sound arguments that demonstrate long-term benefits. Understanding what drives these decisions—whether it is cost reduction, operational efficiencies, or scalability—is essential in crafting a value proposition that resonates.

While vision and strategy are crucial, professional credibility hinges on measurable outcomes. Organizations that can showcase increased productivity, reduced costs, faster time-to-market, and improved customer satisfaction solidify their role as essential partners. Over time, this consistent demonstration of impact strengthens relationships, builds trust, and lays the groundwork for sustainable, scalable growth.

However, value measurement is a dynamic process. It must be woven into every customer interaction, ensuring that differentiation is constantly reinforced. The ability to track, measure, and communicate outcomes in real-time allows businesses to maintain a competitive edge, deepen customer loyalty, and unlock new growth opportunities.

As organizations refine their approach to value articulation, they must also invest in building high-performance teams capable of executing this vision at scale. These elite Diamond Teams—cross-functional groups with deep expertise—will be crucial in ensuring that strategic initiatives translate into real business impact. In Chapter 5, we will explore how to develop these teams, foster their growth, and position them as key drivers of organizational success in an evolving marketplace.

MACO FRAMEWORK (JOIN CHAPTERS 1 TO 4)

Despite the mountain of books and articles on demand creation, so far, we've been missing a framework that empowers sales professionals to have repeatable success engaging net new executives. Faithfully executing the proven MACO framework will enable your GTM team to create significant, unbudgeted transactions—typically converting into at least a 4.2-time opportunity 63 percent of the time when they follow the process for three consecutive quarters.

First, to build **momentum**, you need an industry perspective that is compelling and uniquely differentiated, addressing an urgent business challenge and creating a distinct competitive edge. To engage new executives, you must develop executive deliverables that present your solution up front, securing the meeting. Communicating effectively with the C-suite requires a clear, concise, problem-solving message, so set aside three to seven days (including weekends) to crystallize its form and content. Developing such a message transcends mere concentration; it requires an elevated state of flow awareness where strategic clarity, creativity, and foresight merge. Strategists must look beyond the current moment, identifying patterns others overlook, and crafting visions that shape the future.

Next, gaining **alignment** with executives involves understanding the intricacies of their strategic priorities, including how your solutions and insights can integrate with their commitments to the market and the metrics tied to their executive compensation. Don't just sell products; craft a compelling business strategy that an executive can support, based on the trust you've built through your subject-matter expertise and proven customer success stories from their industry. Your ultimate goal is to uncover each executive's decision criteria and gradually influence them toward standards that favor your partnership. As additional stakeholders are inevitably added to enterprise evaluations, you likewise have to quickly bring them up to speed to secure their buy-in. Indirect selling is crucial to reach both awareness and consensus, especially for large accounts. The only way to achieve this is through executive deliverables that share industry-leading best practices, scalable across multiple business units and personas. Essentially, you need to empower champions to carry your message when you're not in the room with the executive staff, which is, realistically, about 85 percent of the time.

Establishing **credibility** throughout the sale demands a thorough understanding of the financial metrics necessary to meet your client's internal standard hurdle rate for funding an unbudgeted project. Identifying high-impact, low-risk quick wins is crucial to deliver positive payback. You must clearly define and articulate your solution's economic benefits, first with the evaluation team, and then repeatedly as you navigate the proving ground up to the executive suite, ensuring client executives are aware of the work completed.

If you don't take credit for the investment your team has made, someone else will!

In particular, finance departments are eager to make investments that promise exceptional returns, and they require detailed, proven case studies to validate your projections. To develop these resources, make sure your sales professionals are collaborating with their business value consultants regularly, to enhance their business acumen. This can be challenging, as professionals accustomed to structured evaluations must now apply advanced leadership to unstructured evaluations, guiding the customer through a strategic evaluation process.

Finally, delivering business **outcomes** is the culmination of all the work your team has completed, which you should summarize in an executive proposal. The goal is to overcome every potential objection in a board meeting by leveraging your prior industry case study successes. Your team's extensive experience executing multiple implementations will reassure client executives of your skills and knowledge, removing their insecurity about being an "early adopter" of your solution. This experience translates into a unique level of subject matter expertise that enhances their internal teams' understanding of their own process flows.

By establishing a higher echelon of required capabilities, you clearly demonstrate the unique value your solutions provide, making it evident to decision-makers why partnering with your company is the clear choice to improve critical business factors. Concisely articulating key business outcomes in an executive proposal, branded for your customer, is precisely what they need to justify a significant investment. In essence, you have become your customer's proposal team, confirming your trusted advisor status and enabling you to influence the investment narrative and the executive staff's decisions. You have achieved success in creating strategic value for your customer!

CHAPTER 5

DIAMOND TEAMS

Program Management

(Increase Business Acumen by 36 Percent)

CHAPTER 5

➤ **A FORCE MULTIPLIER:** Special Operations

➤ **PROGRAM MANAGEMENT:** Influence Change in Accounts

➤ **CREATING UNBUDGETED PROJECTS:** Endorsements

➤ **DEVELOP LEADING PRACTICES:** Competitive Advantage

➤ **THE TRUTH ABOUT DIAMOND TEAMS:** Deal Follow-Up

➤ **AN INSIGHT-DRIVEN MINDSET:** Be Curious About Challenges

➤ **TIME KILLS DEALS:** Quarterly Revenue Determines Spend

➤ **SPREAD INFLUENCE THROUGH DELIVERABLES:** Proposal Team

➤ **ENABLE INDIRECT SELLING:** Build Champions to Sell for You

➤ **DIAMOND TEAM THEORY:** Increase Business Acumen 36 Percent

➤ **TIPS AND TRICKS:** Proactively Nudge Stakeholders

➤ **DIAMOND TEAMS WORKBOOK:** Scale Client Success Frameworks

---

➤ **EVERYDAY APPLICATIONS:** Overcome Every Objection

➤ **KEY TAKEAWAYS:** Create Flywheel of Engagement

➤ **SUMMARY:** Strategic Oversight Cadence

A FORCE MULTIPLIER

At my firm, our top four sales professionals generate $18 million in revenue per year, each one achieving 450 percent of their annual target. By contrast, 300 of their typical colleagues deliver $1.3 million annually, with an average attainment of 82 percent. Two things enable the first group of sellers to generate fourteen times more revenue. First, as we've seen in the last four chapters, they engage executives leveraging best practices from prior clients who have optimized customer value creation in their industry. But more importantly, they have specialized resources organized in a **Diamond Team**, the subject of this chapter.

As you'll learn, these teams create a force multiplier that accelerates sales cycles due to the immense amount of strategy consulting and specialized content they develop for specific clients, which can be leveraged as frameworks in other accounts to create future demand to hyperscale even more revenue. To personalize these frameworks requires light product marketing skills to modify content on the fly, especially after meetings with executives. Each Diamond Team member thus needs to be able to quickly edit executive documents in Excel, PowerPoint, and Word, skillfully presenting insights they've uncovered from outside-in research merged with client discovery. How many of your sales professionals possess the skills to send an executive a compelling follow-up report within three hours of a meeting?

We've already reviewed four case studies where the clients significantly multiplied their investment by 4.2 times—and switched their partner—based on our Diamond Teams' recommendations. Each team delivered comprehensive business strategies that provided the client with a distinct competitive edge in their industry segment. In turn, the client executives evaluated all aspects of the business case, recognizing the significant impact of advanced use cases that would drive their business forward at an accelerated pace. Diagram 5.0 summarizes how the hyperscaled revenue approach outpaced the competition in each case.

SIGNIFICANT TRANSACTIONS

CASE STUDIES	INDUSTRY	COMPETITORS BID	CLOSED FOR	DIFFERENCE
Chapter 1	Hi-Tech	$29 million	$124 million	4.3x
Chapter 2	Wireless	$34 million	$143 million	4.2x
Chapter 3	Broadband	$38 million	$156 million	4.1x
Chapter 4	Integrator	$19 million	$84 million	4.4x
	TOTAL	$120 million	$507 million	4.2x

Diagram 5.0 Unbudgeted Funding That Was Allocated

What's stopping your company from achieving results like these? Let me highlight a few likely obstacles, based on many conversations with frustrated sales professionals.

1. Your sales teams spend their days waiting for qualified leads when they could be developing business strategies for the executives in their accounts today.

2. Your marketing content focuses on product capabilities, but executives need industry-specific stories to understand why they need your solutions to create a competitive edge.

3. Your virtual teams are waiting to respond to customer requests based on evaluation criteria, when they could be recommending new use cases that generate new funding events for projects that were previously unbudgeted.

4. Only a small percentage of your GTM team members have the light product marketing skill set required to create executive deliverables that will capture the C-suite's attention—and personalize sales frameworks to create momentum in accounts.

Diamond Teams are your secret weapon for creating industry-specific executive content in the field, based on significant transactions requiring competitive evaluations. These teams, featuring collaborative experts in six distinct roles, are willing to push themselves to excellence, far past their normal comfort levels, because 450 percent quote attainment transforms their variable commissions from a nice boost to life-changing commission checks.

Diamond Teams first need an executive sponsor who possesses deep industry knowledge, enabling them to envision big bets and boldly engage the customer executive teams. They're joined by a strategic seller who is committed to investing in customer value creation pursuits, guiding the customer through unstructured evaluations based on their prior proven experience from similar engagements. It takes unique skills to guide clients, including proposing multiple next steps in a complex evaluation process that the customer has never experienced before. This requires continuous planning with your Diamond Team to create an evaluation process for the client that overcomes every objection at all levels in the account.

Next, your teams need a solutions consultant, dedicated to crafting outside-in demonstrations using their industry expertise and documenting use cases in executive demonstration guides, to help the client differentiate your indispensable items. They'll work with a business value advisor who is adept at developing outside-in business case models that can flexibly adjust economic benefits from a consumer to a business perspective, depending on the business unit you're engaged with.

To round out the group, add a professional services expert who is focused on creating proposed implementation phasing strategies that balance quick wins with business case impacts, ensuring the project is strategically sound to achieve milestones. Last but not least, a client success expert can share value realization results from industry use cases from industry-leading clients, having captured the quantifiable metrics over the previous eight quarters.

These last four resources can support two strategic sellers on four strategic pursuits at the same time. Like a special forces military unit who knows the exact roles and responsibilities of each team member, these teams can enhance client deliverables with minimal instruction. They can be pulled out of the field to work closely with their team on an account, developing and delivering industry strategies and executive content that accelerates demand generation in account and can be leveraged by all sales professionals within an industry segment. Diagram 5.1 summarizes how these six roles work together to collaborate.

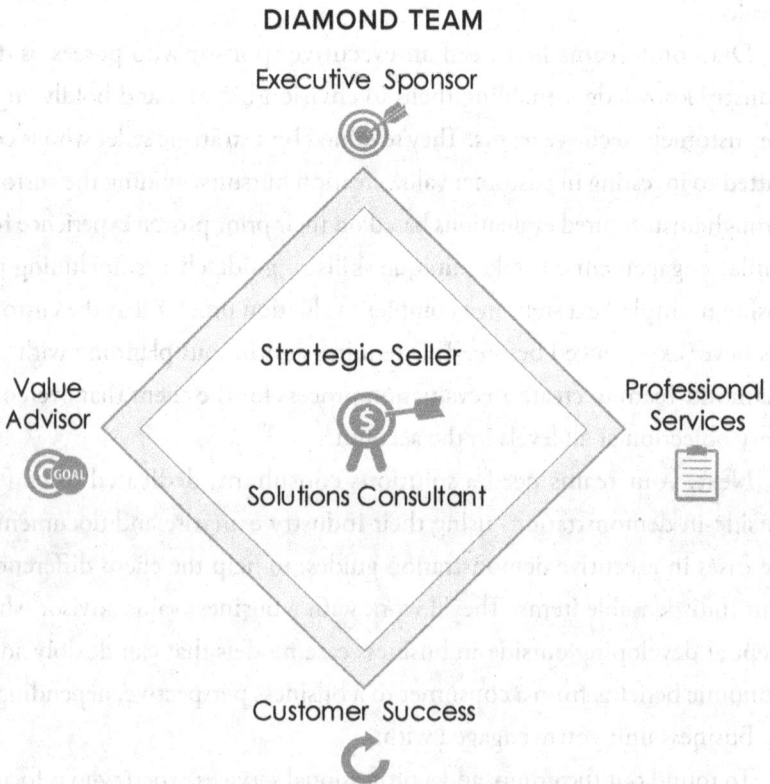

DIAMOND TEAM

Executive Sponsor

Value Advisor

Strategic Seller

Solutions Consultant

Professional Services

Customer Success

Diagram 5.1 Elite Resources Working as a Team in the Field

Beyond their individual expertise, these teams utilize specialized tactics by anticipating executives' needs through prior pattern recognition. They are proficient with the entire array of sales frameworks and know precisely which sections they need to develop to generate momentum within an account. Collaboration is their superpower, as each contributes unique value to enhance and enrich every framework, making the distilled information extremely valuable to client executives. No single person can master every skill required to create elite executive deliverables without advice and support from their teammates.

To start assembling these teams, of course, you need expert resources who can anticipate executives' needs and develop content even before they ask for it. Investing effort into unfunded sales pursuits requires a different kind of dedication: Diamond Teams collaborate not for individual gain but for the greater good of the team and the entire company. It also requires a long-range focus on how these deliverables can be leveraged in future engagements. They'll be creating new materials they (and their colleagues) can personalize to highlight differentiation and earn the attention of executives across industries, providing contexts from adjacent industry successes. While pulling these experts out of the field may incur some extra costs—after all, you have to maintain your regular sales pipeline—it's ultimately a matter of using them where they are most needed, especially if they can help create $187 million in additional incremental revenue annually.

The Diamond Team approach also enables deeper customer engagement through multiple touchpoints across various functions, strengthening relationships and broadening your influence within your customer's organization. Holistic value delivery lets you collaboratively address technical, financial, and operational concerns, resulting in tailored solutions that can scale across business units. The reduced complexity will instill confidence in customers, knowing that a comprehensive team is aligned with their success, thereby minimizing the risks typically associated with complex purchases. This dynamic unlocks upsells and value expansion, with continuous engagement from customer success and executive sponsors creating natural entry points for increased deal sizes over time.

But Diamond Teams really shine after the sale. Having successfully deployed effective product marketing motions with industry-leading charter customers, you can now enable new teams to craft similar executive content to create future deals. Your Diamond Teams gain leverage by working with the most challenging customers in your orbit, producing advanced insights that can be leveraged by the entire global sales force. After all, sales enablement is much more effective when it comes from peers with successful case studies. In turn, this enables more effective change management across your entire organization and, based on your initial pilot programs, you will experience success quickly.

Once you've put a Diamond Team together, I recommend keeping them in this role for twelve to twenty-four months, as they'll need to spend a lot of time traveling and working at your customers' locations. Once they master the advanced program management cadences you've been learning about, they'll be ready to become elite managers based on their specific domain expertise. They will have acquired a master's degree in creating new strategic engagements with executive leadership teams, program managing Diamond Teams and client evaluation processes, and personalizing advanced industry content, all in an effort to provide expert strategy consulting for your most promising and lucrative accounts.

PROGRAM MANAGEMENT

Mimi stood at the helm of a challenging initiative, poised to revolutionize the relationship between our company and a leading vehicle manufacturer. Known for her inspirational leadership and diverse skill set, Mimi understood that while she could address many issues independently, enduring success at this level demanded effective collaboration and scalable solutions. She began her journey by crafting a structured engagement plan designed to empower her elite team—a Diamond Team, of course—to cultivate stronger, more productive interactions with the client's executive leadership.

The mission was clear: Rebuild trust, drive measurable business value, and position the company as a long-term strategic partner. Mimi prioritized enhancing operational efficiencies, reducing incident resolution times, and improving visibility for informed decision-making. The engagement would unfold in three distinct phases, each culminating in a critical executive presentation.

PROGRAM MANAGEMENT

1	Diamond Team	>	2	Sales Frameworks
4	Milestones	<	3	Responsibilities

Diagram 5.2 Managing Diamond Team Engagement

The initial phase, the Business Strategy Framework, laid the groundwork. Mimi aimed to craft a compelling business case that underscored the measurable advantages of collaboration, from cost reductions and ROI to enhanced efficiency. To actualize this vision, she enlisted each member of her Diamond Team, assigning roles that maximized their unique strengths.

Mimi herself took charge as the lead strategist and communicator, responsible for architecting the overall strategy and consolidating the team's diverse insights into a seamless narrative. Ryan, an expert in problem detection and anomaly identification, dove deep into the client's operational inefficiencies to identify vulnerabilities that could derail success. Jay, their data correlation and root cause analysis specialist, worked tirelessly to connect disparate data points and uncover systemic issues. Ray, an automation and monitoring guru, developed frameworks for incident remediation and continuous performance improvement. Meanwhile, Ingrid, an economic analyst, focused on quantifying the potential savings and modeling the economic benefits of the proposed strategies.

DEVELOP A BUSINESS STRATEGY

Business Strategy

The top three quantified benefits:

1. **ROI and Cost Savings:**
   - Deploying visibility resulted on average, a 324% return on investment (ROI) over three years, with a net present value (NPV) of $16.46 million. Implementations lead to considerable cost savings by reducing system outages, consolidating legacy systems, and improving overall efficiency.

2. **Increased Operational Efficiency:**
   - Executive insights reduced system outages by 70% and decreased mean time to resolution (MTTR) by 75%. This improvement in system reliability resulted in 423 additional hours of uptime, translating to $9.8 million in retained profits. Additionally, developer productivity increased significantly, with 34% of one FTE saved and reallocated to innovation driving application code.

3. **Improved Visibility and Decision-Making:**
   - Provide comprehensive, real-time visibility across the entire IT infrastructure. The platform enabled proactive identification and resolution of issues, reducing the number of alerts by 62% and improving decision-making processes. This holistic view facilitated better resource allocation, increased operational efficiency, and supported strategic business objectives.

Data Visualization

Step 1: Data Visualization

Provide real-time, comprehensive views of their infrastructure and application performance across a hybrid environment with Unified Dashboards, KPIs and Business Metrics and Multi-layer Views.

Business Service Health

Overall health of critical services for fleet management systems, product monitoring systems (e.g., autonomous haul trucks), and customer-facing applications.

- **Service Health KPI:**
  - Health score for each business service: Fleet Monitoring, Equipment Maintenance System, Customer Portal, etc.
  - **Color-coded statuses:** Green (healthy), Yellow (degraded), Red (critical).
  - Aggregated from metrics, logs, and application performance data.

- **Key Metrics Displayed:**
  - Current uptime (%)
  - Active incidents
  - Mean Time to Resolution (MTTR)

Problem Detection

Step 2: Problem Detection and Anomaly Identification

Enable proactive detection of issues using AI-driven insights and real-time monitoring across applications, services, and infrastructure.

Provides detailed insights into application performance, focusing on the backend microservices for each critical application and service

- **Top 5 Application Metrics:**
  - **Transaction Latency:** Average response time for the most critical applications (e.g., Equipment Monitoring, Helios Cloud Platform).
  - **Error Rate:** Number of errors in key transaction workflows.
  - **Throughput:** Number of transactions or events processed per second.
  - **Dependency Mapping:** Display the status of microservices and their dependencies.

- **Key Visualizations:**
  - Microservices dependency map with color-coding to show performance bottlenecks.
  - Response times for critical applications segmented by users (via RUM).

Diagram 5.3 Guide Client with Industry Best Practices

Together, they adhered to a meticulously structured timeline. By the end of the first week, they had an initial draft of the business strategy ready for internal review. Week two involved collaborative refinement, leading to a comprehensive final review by the third week. By week four, Mimi and her team were fully prepared to present their findings to the client's executive suite.

With the business strategy established, Mimi's team advanced to the second phase: the Partnership Strategy Framework. Here, the emphasis moved toward cultivating long-term collaboration. Mimi led the team in defining shared objectives, outlining joint innovation initiatives, and distributing risks and responsibilities. This phase also adhered to a structured timeline, with weekly milestones ensuring consistent progress and alignment.

The third and final phase was the Investment Strategy Framework. This segment aimed to build a compelling case for the client to invest in transformative technologies. Together, the team crafted projections on technological advancements, mapped out scalable solutions, and proposed phased implementation plans. Mimi, once again, synthesized the team's input into a coherent and persuasive investment narrative, with Ryan, Jay, Ray, and Ingrid each contributing their specialized insights.

MANAGING PROGRAM CADENCE

WIN THEME: **FUTURE-PROOF DIGITIAL RESILENCE**

Committed to Do:	Owner	Client	Due Date	Status
> action 1	Sales	Manufacturing	3.12	completed
> action 2	SE	Dir SOC	3.13	pending
> action 3	BVA	Finance	3.14	delayed
Completed in the Past Two Weeks:	**Owner**	**Client**	**Due Date**	**Status**
> action 4	Services	IT	3.1	completed
> action 5	Exec Sponsor	SVP	3.2	in process
> action 6	Sales	Security	3.3	completed
Outstanding:	**Owner**	**Client**	**Due Date**	**Status**
> action 7	SE	Dir SOC	3.21	pending
> action 8	BVA	Finance	3.22	pending
Milestones:	**Owner**	**Client**	**Due Date**	**Status**
> action 9	Product	CISO	4.2	planned
> action 10	Support	Champion	4.4	planned
Concerns:	**Owner**	**Client**	**Due Date**	**Status**
> action 11	CEO	CEO	4.6	scheduling

Diagram 5.4 Managing Team Engagement

Accountability was central to effective engagement. Each member of the Diamond Team was responsible for delivering their components on time, with Mimi coordinating the process to ensure seamless integration. Internal reviews served as critical checkpoints to uphold quality and alignment, ensuring that by the end of each phase, the team was ready to present to the C-suite with confidence and precision.

By following this structured, milestone-driven approach, Mimi and her team effectively transformed their client relationship. The framework they created not only resolved immediate operational challenges but also established the foundation for a long-term strategic partnership. This story of collaboration, efficiency, and shared vision exemplifies the impact of strategic engagement and collective effort.

CREATING UNBUDGETED PROJECTS

Creating unbudgeted strategic engagements with executives requires a blend of foresight, relationship-building, and demonstrating value through industry use cases. The goal is to initiate high-level conversations that can drive long-term business value, without immediately tying the engagement to an existing budget line. These conversations start by identifying strategic opportunities. Analyze industry trends, business challenges, and technological advancements that align with the executive's goals or pain points. Consider areas like security, observability, or emerging technologies such as generative AI. By understanding your prospect's strategic priorities, you can position the engagement as a solution to a pressing issue or an avenue for innovation.

Next, leverage internal influencers within the organization who have established credibility with the target executives. These individuals can provide insights into executive interests and serve as conduits for initial conversations. This step is crucial in bypassing traditional budgeting constraints by focusing on building trust and relevance.

To gain executive access, you must craft a value-centric narrative that frames the engagement as an exploratory initiative with high potential for return. Highlight case studies, success stories, or proof-of-concept examples that showcase the strategic advantage. Emphasize the low-risk nature of the initial phase while illustrating the long-term impact.

Rather than pitching products, offer exclusive experiences that draw executives to unique opportunities for peer learning from your network. Propose executive briefings with subject-matter experts to have strategic discussions that will naturally evolve without immediate budgetary commitments.

Finally, position an advisory engagement to frame the initiative, which typically requires fewer resources and formal approvals. By positioning it as a learning opportunity or innovation workshop, you can gain executive buy-in without triggering formal budgetary processes.

GENERATING DEMAND

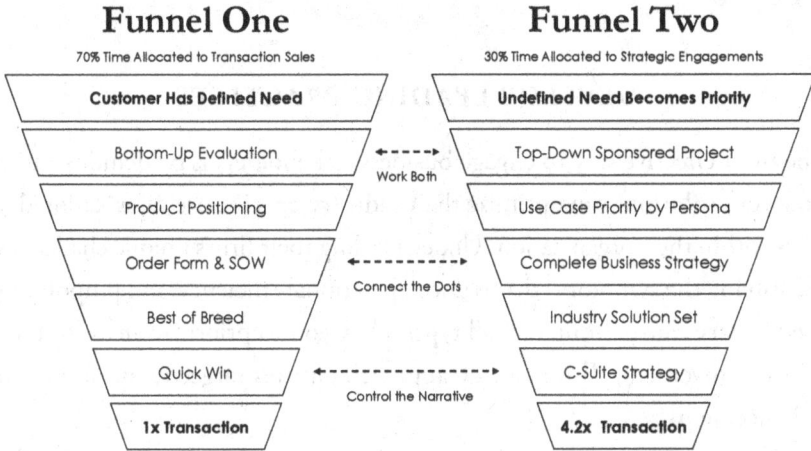

Funnel One	Funnel Two
70% Time Allocated to Transaction Sales	30% Time Allocated to Strategic Engagements
Customer Has Defined Need	Undefined Need Becomes Priority
Bottom-Up Evaluation → ← Work Both →	Top-Down Sponsored Project
Product Positioning	Use Case Priority by Persona
Order Form & SOW ← Connect the Dots →	Complete Business Strategy
Best of Breed	Industry Solution Set
Quick Win ← Control the Narrative →	C-Suite Strategy
1x Transaction	4.2x Transaction

Diagram 5.5 Optimize Both Revenue Funnels

As you move forward, demonstrate your ability to deliver quick, visible wins once the formal engagement begins. Highlight early insights or findings that reinforce the value of the initiative. As we saw in Chapter 4, these quick wins can build momentum and justify future investments, gradually evolving the engagement into a budgeted strategic initiative.

Build for scale as you establish trust and expand the scope of engagement. Don't stop with one deal: Develop a roadmap that aligns with broader organizational objectives and recommend pathways for scaling. This gradual buildup often leads to the creation of dedicated budget allocations for ongoing strategic initiatives.

Unbudgeted strategic engagements hinge on creating perceived value, minimizing initial risk, and fostering relationships that transcend traditional budgetary processes. By aligning engagements with executive priorities and showcasing tangible benefits early, you pave the way for long-term strategic collaboration.

Whenever I have enabled sales professionals to create unbudgeted strategic engagements, I always hear the same response: "I had no idea that you could sell this way!" That's because you're not just selling a product or solution—**you're creating strategic opportunities that the client was not expecting to invest in.**

DEVELOP LEADING PRACTICES

The most effective way to engage business stakeholders is by demonstrating how your solutions can optimize their industry-specific use cases, tailored to roles within their organization. Understanding their firm's unique challenges, identifying the symptoms that reduce operational efficiency, and pinpointing the primary causes from key call types allow you to prioritize areas for business improvement. This strategic approach ensures targeted and impactful enhancements.

Adding business value means leveraging the most relevant recommended use cases to deliver a quick win. This is an excellent payback strategy, as it encourages your client to fund the entire project while reducing the risks of the implementation. Here's an example of customer experience use cases that can be prioritized among executive staff.

- **PRIORITY 1 - MARKETING CAMPAIGNS:** Deliver personalized messages based on customer data and behavior.
- **PRIORITY 2 - SALES ENGAGEMENT:** personalized follow-ups and nurturing leads through email, text, and calls.
- **PRIORITY 3 - CUSTOMER SERVICE:** Automate first-line customer queries using AI-powered chatbots.
- **PRIORITY 4 - FEEDBACK AND COLLABORATION:** Automate post-interaction surveys via email or SMS.
- **PRIORITY 5 - OMNI-CHANNEL:** Connect customers across email, text, chat, social media, and phone from a single platform.

Use this approach to propose swift, high-impact implementations to demonstrate immediate business benefits while developing more intricate processes for cross-channel and cross-unit information sharing. Remember, executives require strategies that foster a competitive edge within their

CALL CENTER BEST PRACTICES

BUSINESS SYMPTOMS	PRIMARY CAUSES FOR KEY SYMPTOMS	PRIMARY CALL TYPES	PRIMARY BUSINESS PROCESS AREAS
Customer Satisfaction Is Low	> Long call wait times		Phase 1
	> First call resolutions		1. Manage Service Inquiry
	> Incomplete information	> Bill Inquires	2. Sales Support
		> Bill Adjustment	3. Explain Bill
	> Limited access to info	> Rate Plan Charges	4. Manage Bill Dispute
	> Can't track escalations		5. Bill Adjustment
Average Call Handling Time High		> Price Inquires	6. Process Payment
	> Limited info access	> Device Management	Phase 2
	> Out-of-date information		7. Campaign Management
	> Inconsistent data	> Fraud Management	8. Manage Device Inquiry
	> Long call wait times		9. Add Phase Two Products
	> Can't target offer	> Usage Inquiries	10. Phase Two Customer Reports
Cross-Sell Rates	> Limited cross-sell data		

Diagram 5.6 Root Cause Analysis

industry, enabling them to effectively measure the business impact and drive sustained growth.

THE TRUTH ABOUT DIAMOND TEAMS

Effective executive selling—especially when your goal is securing significant, unbudgeted transactions—requires specialized competencies, disciplined methodologies, and precise execution. At the core of this approach lies the strategic formation of elite, cross-functional Diamond Teams. These teams leverage diverse expertise from across the organization to maximize effectiveness and impact.

To make this approach work, your sales professionals must master advanced program management and skillfully coordinate various expert resources. Structured frameworks guide these virtual teams, ensuring that every contribution results in impactful, tailored executive deliverables. Aligning resources around these clear frameworks ensures consistent, high-quality outcomes that resonate with executives.

Once these teams are assembled, proactive identification of untapped opportunities is essential. Diamond Teams should consistently uncover significant business challenges within customer organizations and propose compelling, strategic solutions. Aligning these solutions explicitly with customers' stated strategic objectives, as well as the personal goals of individual stakeholders, will increase their relevance and appeal.

Introducing proven, leading practices into engagements further enhances this value. Demonstrating distinctive advantages through industry-best practices helps create a tangible competitive edge that aligns directly with the customer's strategic imperatives. By positioning themselves as strategic advisors, your sales professionals will gain the trust of executive stakeholders by consistently addressing their most challenging problems with insight-driven, innovative solutions.

One of the most critical yet often overlooked elements of successful executive selling is timely follow-up. Teams should establish rigorous follow-up timelines—ideally within eight hours of each customer meeting—to maintain momentum and prevent opportunities from stagnating or being lost. Additionally, deepening financial acumen by understanding CFO confidence levels and related financial indicators will allow your teams to better anticipate and influence timely decision-making processes, particularly as companies often finalize critical decisions in the closing days of financial quarters.

Moreover, empowering stakeholders within customer organizations through stakeholder enablement is pivotal. Providing clear, compelling deliverables that stakeholders can independently utilize enhances internal advocacy and influence. When sales teams proactively assume the role of the customer's proposal team, they significantly reduce the customer's internal workload, allowing stakeholders and champions to advocate for solutions more effectively.

Leveraging advanced tools is equally crucial. Sales professionals must master basic product marketing skills, such as crafting visually appealing and executive-friendly presentations using Excel and PowerPoint. Utilizing advanced AI-powered platforms like **ChatGPT enables rapid, insightful research** into customer accounts and competitors. Furthermore, employing AI-driven content review platforms, like **Anyword, ensures messaging remains clear, concise, and tailored to executive standards**, reinforcing the precision and value of communications. Consistent and disciplined application of these principles and tools will enhance the effectiveness of executive selling efforts, substantially increasing the likelihood of securing high-value, strategic transactions.

AN INSIGHT-DRIVEN MINDSET

Every sales book discusses what to do when you have an opportunity. But what happens if you don't have enough opportunities—how can you develop a higher-value pipeline? You have to change your mindset to invest early, even before there is a defined need, to create new, high-value opportunities long before your competitors think to look for them.

This requires adopting an insight-driven mindset that trades reactive selling for a proactive advisory approach. Position yourself as a market expert who provides valuable insights into trends, risks, and competitive advantages. Dive deep into emerging industry trends and common pain points. Identify areas where your target companies may have blind spots or untapped opportunities. Develop tailored executive deliverables and case studies that spotlight these insights.

This starts by understanding each account's competitive landscape and how they stack up against competitors. Step back and look at your prospect's business in comparison to their peer group, to help you understand their GTM strategy and how they are competing in their marketplace. Conduct a thorough competitor analysis and categorize companies by their market strategy. For example, perhaps they're focused on a lower price point with minimal quality but a high volume of transactions, while their competitors offer different levels of product quality at different price points. In this situation, you might segment their competitors into three categories: 1) price competitors focused on volume and low-cost products, 2) premium competitors who prioritize quality and elite service, and 3) niche innovators that disrupt markets with specialized offerings. Create messaging that aligns with the prospect's competitive pressures and goals. After all, if you don't know what a company is trying to accomplish, landing that first executive meeting will be challenging at best.

Whatever the setting, engage at the leadership level to influence long-term strategy rather than just addressing immediate needs. Frame your engagement as a strategic partnership rather than a sales pitch. Initiate conversations with C-suite executives and key decision-makers, then shape discussions around market shifts and potential disruptions. Provide benchmarking data that compares their performance to peers, then identify unique gaps in their current strategy. Likewise, tailor outreach emails to include industry-specific metrics and case studies, and create interactive tools or reports that demonstrate the value you can deliver immediately.

As you advance the relationship, focus on the end-user's needs by positioning your product as a solution for your customer's customer, driving urgency and relevance. Research the target's end markets and understand evolving customer preferences. Develop use cases and case studies that reflect their customer's pain points. Connect the dots between how your solution impacts their overall customer experience.

More broadly, build long-term relationships across segments and industries by maintaining regular monthly touchpoints and consistently adding value. Keep communication open, even when there's no immediate deal on the table. Build awareness and educate the entire market, not just one client. Host industry-specific webinars, roundtables, and thought leadership events. Share insights through newsletters or exclusive reports. Engage prospects by offering free assessments and readouts. Most of all, offer ongoing support and advice, focusing on being a trusted resource.

Pipeline development isn't about quick wins; it's about fostering strategic partnerships and positioning yourself as indispensable long before the purchase decision is made. Access to information through generative artificial intelligence allows you to do research in 10 percent of the time it used to take.

By investing in insight-driven conversations, understanding the competitive landscape, and consistently adding value, you'll build a robust pipeline of high-value opportunities that drive long-term growth.

TIME KILLS DEALS

At the end of every fiscal quarter, sales teams from virtually every vendor are scrambling to finalize strategic transactions. The prevailing belief is that procurement teams delay buying decisions to secure the best possible price. While price negotiations are indeed a factor, the underlying reason for such delays often lies with the chief financial officer. CFOs' decisions to approve or defer expenditures are significantly influenced by the company's sales attainment as the quarter comes to a close, something you can't control. However, you can use clues from CFO behavior and even body language to evaluate your chances, especially if you're in the room when the CFO reviews your business case. Specifically, strategic transactions typically involve substantial financial commitments, and CFOs must manage cash flow meticulously to ensure their company meets earnings targets. As the quarter end nears, CFOs keep a close watch on their sales teams' performance. If sales surpass expectations, there is more flexibility to invest in strategic initiatives. Conversely, if sales fall short, discretionary spending is postponed to preserve cash flow. This dynamic explains why some deals slip to the next quarter or, for more severe performance concerns, are canceled altogether.

From the CFO's vantage point, every major purchase carries a degree of risk. Committing to a large transaction amidst uncertain revenue can jeopardize the company's financial stability. Even if a project or solution offers long-term value, CFOs may hesitate if the short-term outlook is unclear. By deferring purchases until after the quarter ends, CFOs mitigate risk and safeguard the company's liquidity position. This internal bottleneck means vendors must navigate more than just price objections; they must address broader concerns around timing, ROI, and budget alignment.

For sales teams and vendors, the key to overcoming these delays lies in preparation. Addressing potential objections early in the process— whether related to technical specifications, legal considerations, or budget justification—reduces friction and speeds up deal closure. Sales teams must also build relationships beyond procurement, engaging with finance leaders and understanding their decision-making criteria.

As the saying goes, "Time kills deals." The longer a deal remains open, the more susceptible it becomes to shifting priorities, leadership changes, or budget reallocations. By the next quarter, new initiatives may take precedence, and previously approved projects could lose momentum. This highlights the importance of urgency and meticulous planning in deal-making. By actively aligning with the CFO's priorities and addressing objections proactively, sales teams can enhance their chances of closing deals before time runs out.

SPREAD INFLUENCE THROUGH DELIVERABLES

Equipping internal champions with compelling, client-branded materials is essential for driving investment decisions at the executive level. By providing executive deliverables that clearly articulate the value of an investment from the client's perspective, you empower champions to advocate for your solution more effectively. This positions your team as an extension of the client's internal proposal team, facilitating smoother approvals and faster decision-making.

Client-branded proposals should be written as internal memos that mimic the client's voice, as if authored by their internal teams. Each memo should highlight the strategic rationale, business-case recommendation with an anticipated return on investment for the executive. It should include a concise overview summarizing the problem, solution, and anticipated benefits. Additionally, it should outline existing challenges and opportunities that the investment will address, demonstrate the solution's alignment with the company's strategic goals, and present the value proposition with key metrics, quantifiable benefits, and competitive advantages. Finally, it should detail the projected ROI with a high-level investment breakdown, estimated returns, and time frames, and include a clear call to action outlining the required steps for project initiation.

Adopt an empathetic approach that speaks directly to the client's internal stakeholders and reflects their language and priorities. Frictionless advocacy equips your champions with ready-to-use materials, reducing their effort. Strategic alignment frames the solution within the context of the client's business objectives, enhancing relevance and urgency. By embedding your solutions within their narrative, you transform sales engagements into strategic partnerships, accelerating deal velocity and reinforcing trust.

ENABLE INDIRECT SELLING

Indirect selling likewise empowers internal champions, key stakeholders, and influential team members to **advocate for your value proposition even when you're not directly present**. By utilizing executive deliverables in the form of concise, high-impact materials, you can drive awareness, build momentum, and expand your reach within an organization. This strategy helps overcome the limited retention of live demonstrations and ensures consistent messaging, by leveraging seasoned stakeholders with tenure and influence to create traction and expand internal buy-in.

Develop executive vignettes from sales frameworks targeting relevant assets: one-pagers, executive briefing books, return on investment readouts, and value realization. Ensure that each vignette highlights specific use cases, pain points, and measurable outcomes. Encourage internal champions to distribute these materials during relevant conversations, meetings, or decision-making discussions.

Another useful strategy is to map and activate stakeholders who may not have been able to attend live demos. Engage them asynchronously by providing access to curated deliverables that succinctly explain your value. Position assets to answer common objections, reinforce ROI, and highlight competitive advantages. Focus on continuous engagement to sustain interest and maintain top-of-mind awareness.

As you develop relationships with more stakeholders, iterate and expand by collecting feedback from stakeholders and champions who interact with the deliverables. Refine and expand your asset library of sales frameworks based on emerging needs and evolving stakeholder interests. Consistent and up-to-date messaging ensures stakeholders receive uniform, high-quality information that aligns with your core value proposition. Meanwhile, your internal champions will become strong advocates who feel empowered to represent your solution effectively, fostering stronger buy-in across organizational levels. Behind the scenes, your sales professionals will be their personal strategy consultants, the ones they rely on to make quick updates to their internal documents. This allows you to control the narrative while enabling them to deliver your message internally for you.

Indirect selling through executive deliverables and stakeholder engagement is a powerful method to scale influence and drive adoption. By equipping champions with curated assets, you ensure that your value proposition resonates even in your absence. This strategy not only enhances retention but also accelerates organizational momentum, leading to broader internal buy-in and successful long-term adoption.

In my experience, sales professionals often view executive deliverables as a one-time task. This mindset is deadly to fostering a meaningful, ongoing relationship with an executive. To be seen as a trusted advisor who offers continuous insights, it's crucial to consistently enhance and update your deliverables. To enable that value creation, make sure your sales team is trained in these four tools to create executive deliverables and enable indirect selling.

1. EXCEL should be your paintbrush and primary tool for almost everything. When you build an image in Excel, you can modify it faster than with any other software. For instance, inserting a row or column can be tedious in PowerPoint, but you can do it in seconds in Excel. Everything you build in Excel serves as a reusable framework for an ongoing process. **Clipping images in Excel and pasting them into PowerPoint** allows you to easily control the scale of everything on the page quickly.

2. POWERPOINT is your canvas, allowing you to place images and fonts anywhere on the page without having to be an expert in design software. Sometimes you may also need to build images in PowerPoint, but I suggest limiting this practice because resizing and reusing them is challenging. Keep an eye on your slide orientation as well. Most people are accustomed

to the landscape slide format, which is often used for technical evaluations and can be overwhelming due to the vast quantity of slides shared. But **board members more often present and evaluate data in portrait format**, especially when they're assessing investments and allocating funding. Consider your ultimate goal when choosing your format.

3. CHATGPT is your research engine to uncover insights into your target account and to **research their five closest competitors' business strategies**. While it shouldn't be your only research source, this initial comparison will help you identify gaps in customer performance that you can address for them. As with any AI tool, you should cross-check and personalize the results before you draw conclusions.

4. ANYWORD is your content writing expert that allows you to focus on your narrative without worrying about sentence structure, grammar, and spelling. It **enables you to unleash your thought process** and be creative in solving executive business challenges. When drafting executive deliverables, leverage the advisor tone of voice to provide guidance. When drafting executive outreach emails, use an empathetic tone to be humble with your message, acknowledging that they are the experts on their business, not you.

By utilizing this strategy to create executive deliverables, you can easily update documents after each meeting. I suggest following these four steps in sequence to help you achieve trusted advisor status with the executives you aim to build lasting relationships with.

DIAMOND TEAM THEORY

Effective program management of specialized resources to create tailored content that captivates executive audiences. Accelerating impactful pipeline growth by driving projects that extend beyond current budget constraints, fostering innovation and measurable outcomes.

Why change?

Challenge:	Do you leverage your expert resources to make everyone else better? Have you defined responsibilities to optimize each role's collaboration? Do you have elite resources enabling their peers to introduce change?

How do we differentiate?

Concept 17:	**Insight Driven Mindset** involves proactively identifying and addressing needs before an executive requests them, and providing advance insights that demonstrate your expertise in the industry. This approach enables you to assist clients in assessing your unstructured evaluation effectively.
Concept 18:	**Strategic Oversight** of top-performing teams requires a blend of strategic insight, precise execution, and adept leadership. Assigning high-achieving teams to key roles helps align with broader business goals, providing leadership with actionable reports.
Concept 19:	**Lead with Deliverables** prioritize key decisions without getting bogged down in raw data. Make sure all attendees start the meeting with a clear grasp of the goals, information, and background. Providing materials in advance allows everyone to come prepared, leading to a more efficient meeting and quicker, better-informed choices.
Concept 20:	**Empower Champions** to become internal advocates within an account involves providing them with the necessary tools, knowledge, and confidence to promote your solutions effectively. By identifying seasoned influencers, you can leverage their ability to build consensus.

What do we receive?

Result:	Enable program management skills to effectively lead Diamond Teams. **Increase sales business acumen +36%** to effectively engage executives. Leverage resources to develop content in a fraction of the time.

TIPS AND TRICKS FOR DIAMOND TEAMS

- The Diamond Team Collaboration Framework is strategically designed to leverage organizational excellence through elite cross-functional teams. By carefully selecting highly skilled professionals from various departments, these teams **integrate diverse expertise**, perspectives, and decision-making capabilities. Clear role definitions and effective inter-departmental alignment further reinforce cohesive collaboration, driving strategic impact.
- Diamond Teams are indispensable for **influencing deal outcomes**, leveraging industry best practices, mastering proactive engagement, and prioritizing use case recommendations. By aligning client decisions with overarching business goals, they ensure that every interaction drives measurable success. Armed with data analytics and deep product knowledge, these sales professionals craft compelling narratives that highlight the value of their solutions. Through continuous dialogue and trust-building, they become integral to the client's decision-making process, fostering partnerships that extend far beyond individual transactions.
- Industry best practices serve as the cornerstone of Diamond Teams' guidance. Staying informed about the latest trends and technological advancements allows them to offer your clients cutting-edge insights. By sharing **benchmarks and case studies**, these teams illuminate proven paths to success, reducing uncertainty and increasing confidence in their solutions. Their role as thought leaders enhances their credibility and positions them as essential allies in navigating industry shifts.
- The art of proactive nudges distinguishes Diamond Teams from their peers. Rather than waiting for clients to express their needs or concerns, these professionals **anticipate challenges** and opportunities. They monitor market conditions, track client progress, and intervene at precisely the right moments, ensuring

that clients remain on the path to success. This proactive
mindset extends internally, fostering seamless collaboration
across departments and ensuring that every client interaction is
purposeful and coordinated.

- Recommending use case priorities is another defining practice.
Understanding that clients often face numerous potential
projects, Diamond Teams guide them in **selecting initiatives**
that promise the highest return on investment. Through careful
assessments and strategic roadmapping, they help clients focus on
practical, scalable solutions that align with long-term objectives.
This consultative approach ensures that clients make informed
choices that lead to sustainable growth.

- Ultimately, the strength of Diamond Teams lies in their
ability to act as trusted advisors. Their expertise, foresight, and
commitment to client success drive unparalleled outcomes
and forge lasting relationships. By mastering these four pillars,
they not only enhance client satisfaction but also cement their
reputation as invaluable partners in the client's journey toward
achieving their business aspirations.

- Executive-level deliverables are central to this approach,
meticulously crafted to guide senior executive prospects
through every phase of their **decision-making process**. These
high-quality, tailored deliverables provide clear, actionable
insights aligned closely with prospects' organizational goals.
They also directly address identified executive pain points,
compellingly articulating your unique value propositions.

- To ensure scalability, use past competitive engagements to
establish standardized methodologies and templates. By
maintaining repositories of best practices and facilitating regular
knowledge-sharing sessions, you can consistently refine your
competitive strategies, thereby enhancing productivity and
enabling broad application across diverse customer scenarios.

- Achieving program management excellence is integral to the
framework. Comprehensive, advanced training programs

empower sales professionals with **sophisticated program management** methodologies, resource orchestration capabilities, and refined stakeholder engagement strategies. Continuous skill refinement is encouraged through targeted coaching, constructive feedback, and ongoing professional development.

- Structured frameworks play a pivotal role in coordinating virtual teams, clearly defining roles, responsibilities, collaborative processes, and deliverable creation guidelines. Regular evaluations and updates to these frameworks ensure adaptability to dynamic market conditions and evolving customer demands. Resource alignment is systematically enhanced through detailed communication of deliverable standards, content quality expectations, and strategic messaging guidelines, reinforced by **structured communication** channels and regular alignment meetings.

- Identifying untapped opportunities is another core component of the framework. Through systematic, proactive approaches, Diamond Teams consistently uncover and articulate previously unrecognized business challenges and market opportunities within prospect organizations. Leveraging deep market intelligence and competitive insights, these teams create compelling cases that justify initiating evaluations for significant, strategically advantageous projects previously not budgeted.

- Alignment with customer objectives and stakeholder success criteria is rigorously maintained. Clear processes ensure that solution propositions meticulously align with customers' strategic goals and explicitly address **individual stakeholders' professional success metrics**. Diamond Teams proactively engage stakeholders by demonstrating a deep understanding of their unique challenges and professional drivers.

- The framework emphasizes the introduction and adoption of leading industry practices, distinctly differentiating the organization's solutions from competitors'. By clearly aligning these best-in-class practices with customers' strategic imperatives, the organization creates tangible competitive advantages and measurable improvements in outcomes.

- Finally, cultivating an insight-driven mindset is essential. A culture of continuous curiosity, proactive inquiry, and systematic exploration of customer challenges is fostered throughout the organization. Teams are encouraged to proactively identify, analyze, and solve complex customer challenges, driving innovation and customer-centric value creation. Positioning the team as strategic advisors enhances their credibility and trust with senior executives, consistently delivering impactful, industry-informed solutions that address critical strategic challenges. Regular measurement and documentation of strategic value reinforce credibility and solidify the organization's trusted advisory role.

DIAMOND TEAMS WORKBOOK
CREATE SIGNIFICANT TRANSACTIONS

Diamond Team Frameworks

96 CLIENT SUCCESS FRAMEWORK	Framework that allows customers to share their strategic direction • Allows you to layer best practices based on their projects
97 INDUSTRY BENCHMARKING	Capturing your most successful customers' use cases • Genericise and calculate the thresholds required to compete
98 PROGRAM MANAGEMENT CADENCE	Managing virtual teams requires framework examples • Content development tracking of owners, due dates, and status
99 VALUE EXPANSION TO ELA	Roadmap with options to enable scalable growth • Catalog how your solutions will enable their projects

Diamond Team Sales Plays

100 COLLABORATION	Manage cross-functional team collaboration • Show how each person's work adds to the larger deliverable
101 ENABLEMENT	Development of personable enablement to raise acumen level • Communicate like an executive, simplify the complex
102 PERSONALIZATION	Research allows you to become part of their internal staff • Write internal executive memos, not product data sheets
103 WORK STREAMS	Structure your program management into work streams • Manage the cross-collaboration of teams that don't report to you
104 CONTENT CREATION	Executive-level content creation aligned to business outcomes • Become your customers' proposal team to give them time back
105 ITERATIVE	Everything you develop should be an iterative process • Establish multiple feedback loops to receive unvarnished truth
106 KNOWLEDGE	Centralize knowledge management repository of examples • Industry-specific frameworks with use cases and metrics
107 CUSTOMIZABLE	Customization through strategic workshops • Give to get approach to unlock access to client details
108 ENGAGEMENT METRICS	Engagement metrics to show continuous improvement in accounts • Leverage what works best for your solution offerings

109 EXECUTIVE BRIEFINGS	Provide new ideas in every executive interaction • Share industry thought leadership with client leadership
110 DIAMOND TEAMS	Elite customer-facing resources share their domain expertise • Develop personalized content to become industry solution sets
111 INFLUENCE FUNDING	Deliver complete business strategies based on your expertise • Bring new creative ideas that prioritize your solutions

Diagram 5.7. How Diamond Teams Create Significant Unbudgeted Transactions

EVERYDAY APPLICATIONS

If you aim to successfully lead executives in creating significant, budgeted transactions, it's essential to provide them with a clear, actionable plan to guide their execution. To energize this plan, you need to present a proven example within an industry sales framework. This framework serves as a blueprint, allowing each member of your Diamond Teams to understand their specific responsibilities and optimize their efforts. While content is paramount, it must also be formatted to fit within an appropriate executive document. Having different team members reformat an excessive amount of content can be both time-consuming and challenging, especially when trying to condense a lengthy narrative.

The ultimate aim of a Diamond Team is to foster a close working relationship among its members, where everyone knows who is best suited to execute each section of the executive documents. Team members should volunteer for areas they excel in or recommend the most qualified person on the team. This approach is akin to how Special Forces teams optimize their spacing and lay down excessive amounts of firepower, making them appear as a force of 150 soldiers instead of just six.

Program management is often difficult, particularly when it comes to leading a team of high-performance experts who do not report directly to you. The pinnacle of leadership involves explaining the importance of the mission to the team, providing specific examples of what is required, and offering a clear model to follow. Diagram 5.4, presented earlier in this chapter, offers a straightforward method to assign internal and client-side owners, define required tasks, set due dates, and provide status indicators. During the final weeks of securing a significant transaction, I recommend sending this diagram out to all internal stakeholders and executive approvers, to ensure that everyone is aligned on the plan and accountable to execute.

The Diamond Team model offers precise clarity so that each member can execute as efficiently as possible, delivering the most effective outcome based on their expertise. All team efforts are grounded in prior sales frameworks from a comprehensive sales library, including the forty-eight proven sales frameworks in this book, which can be repurposed to jump-start your Diamond Team engagements and accelerate your results.

DIAMOND TEAM KEY TAKEAWAYS

1. Have you developed a quick win payback strategy for your customers?

   Phase one business impacts should pay the entire project in the first year.

2. Can your GTM teams create unbudgeted projects that are 4.2x larger ACV (Average Contract Value)?

   Creating significant transactions cures all ills delivering 4x pipeline.

3. What does it take for GTM teams to have insight-driven mindset to develop content for the C-suite?

   Every war is won and lost before it's ever fought. —Sun Tzu

4. Why is the CFO the only person who knows if they can fund your project?

Customers' sales forecast in the last five days of the quarter determine investment level.

5. Do the executive deliverables your team puts together influence decision-making?

   Trust is earned when documented in written narrative to support your complete solution.

6. How do elite resources provide accelerated productivity when managed to milestones?

   Sales Frameworks serve as elite examples to apply industry-specific use cases.

7. Why is indirect selling the key to enabling scale and influence in enterprise accounts?

   It's not possible to influence hundreds of stakeholders monthly without deliverables.

8. Do your teams repurpose high-value content from deals they closed?

   Enabling customer value creation at scale requires providing reusable frameworks.

SUMMARY

Diamond Teams operate with precision and rigor, establishing the groundwork for sustained sales success. Their value hinges on a blend of strategic planning, disciplined execution, and continuous improvement. To wrap up this chapter, here is a detailed breakdown of the core operational strategies that drive these teams' effectiveness.

ACCOUNT INTELLIGENCE is a cornerstone for Diamond Teams. They dedicate substantial time to gathering and analyzing data on key accounts, market trends, and competitive landscapes. This deep dive allows them to anticipate customer needs and customize their approach accordingly. Strategic alignment is achieved by collaborating with sales leadership, product teams, and marketing. This ensures their activities are directly linked to overarching business goals and sales priorities.

SCENARIO PLANNING involves engaging in war-room-style preparations, where teams collaborate to simulate customer interactions, anticipate objections, and refine messaging. This rehearsal-based approach builds confidence and adaptability during real-world engagements. The net impact is an increase in business acumen, resulting in higher win rates in complex deals and stronger alignment between customer pain points and solution offerings.

FLAWLESS MEETING EXECUTION is another hallmark of Diamond Teams. They meticulously plan executive engagements, coordinating agendas, briefing participants, and ensuring every stakeholder is aligned on objectives and desired outcomes. Their customer-centric approach to engagements is designed to create value at every touchpoint. By leveraging consultative selling techniques, they focus on problem-solving rather than product pitching.

REAL-TIME ADAPTABILITY is fostered by situational awareness, empowering team members to pivot during meetings, address customer concerns dynamically, and guide the conversation toward mutually beneficial outcomes. One benefit is enhanced credibility and trust with key stakeholders, increasing the likelihood of securing long-term partnerships.

INTEGRATED TEAMWORK is pivotal for Diamond Teams. They operate at the intersection of sales, marketing, product, and customer success. Facilitating cross-functional collaboration, they break down silos and drive cohesive GTM strategies. They provide feedback loops gathered from field teams and customers to refine offerings, messaging, and engagement models. This ensures their strategies remain relevant and aligned with evolving market demands. They optimize resources by acting as a bridge between HQ and the field, ensuring the right resources—whether technical experts, executive sponsors, or marketing collateral—are deployed at the right time. The impact is streamlined sales cycles with faster deal closures and greater internal alignment and coordination.

Finally, KNOWLEDGE SHARING and SCALING SUCCESS extend the value of your Diamond Teams to your entire GTM team. Through playbook development, they document best practices, winning tactics, and lessons learned, compiling them into playbooks distributed across the broader sales organization. Peer coaching and mentoring of less experienced sales reps help foster a culture of continuous learning and knowledge transfer. **Enablement workshops** can upskill your sales force, covering areas such as competitive positioning, objection handling, and storytelling techniques. The end result is an elevated overall sales competency, providing consistency in sales excellence across regions and teams.

The operational strategies employed by Diamond Teams are designed to create a **sustainable competitive advantage by fostering excellence in preparation, execution, and learning**. Their focus on collaboration, adaptability, and customer-centric excellence ensures that the broader sales organization benefits from their expertise, driving growth and enhancing overall performance.

By integrating these strategies, Diamond Teams not only set a high standard for themselves but also elevate the entire sales organization. Their commitment to continuous improvement and strategic alignment ensures that they remain agile and effective in a rapidly changing market landscape. The result is a robust framework that supports long-term success and drives significant value for both the company and its customers. In Chapter 6, you'll learn to engineer the markets for that value, proactively creating space for your new strategic partnerships.

ENGINEER MARKETS

Charter Customer Currency

(Become Top Three Project by 42 Percent)

CHAPTER 6

- ➤ **OUTPERFORM YOUR COMPETITORS:** Industry Leader Influence
- ➤ **PROVING THE PUDDING:** Create Vision for Investment
- ➤ **BUILD AN IDEAL CUSTOMER PROFILE:** Use Cases by Persona
- ➤ **ESTABLISH INNOVATION LEADERSHIP:** Strategic Roadmaps

- ➤ **THE TRUTH ABOUT ENGINEERING MARKETS:** Engagement
- ➤ **GENERATE NEW REVENUE STREAMS:** New Routes to Market
- ➤ **INDUSTRY SOLUTION SETS:** Deliver Complete Solutions
- ➤ **BUSINESS PROCESS LIBRARIES:** Document Use Cases

- ➤ **LEVERAGING A PHASED ROADMAP:** Thought Leadership
- ➤ **ENGINEER MARKET THEORY:** Become a Top Three Project
- ➤ **TIPS AND TRICKS:** Proactively Share Your Best Practices
- ➤ **ENGINEER MARKETS WORKBOOK:** Expand Potential Markets

- ➤ **EVERYDAY APPLICATIONS:** Unfair Competitive Advantage
- ➤ **KEY TAKEAWAYS:** It's Possible to Create Significant Transactions
- ➤ **SUMMARY:** Charter Customer Currency

OUTPERFORM YOUR COMPETITORS

My CEO and I sat down to review the progress of the Customer Engagement Model we had launched twelve months earlier. So far, we had successfully increased our average selling price from $386,000 to $743,000, shortened our sales cycles from nine to four months, and improved our win rates by 43 percent. This transformation was driven by a new sales methodology focused on **customer value creation that leveraged thirty-four newly developed industry solution sets**. These solutions enabled our sales teams to present pre-configured solution offerings, making it nearly impossible for industry leaders to compete.

We had finally reached our most audacious goal: Our strategic investment in providing initial-stage strategy consulting to our customers meant that we now dominated the market. As if on cue, a few minutes after we wrapped up that meeting, my CEO received a call from the CEO of our largest competitor: He wanted to buy our $1.3 billion company for $5.8 billion. It was an incredibly rewarding moment, as we knew we had re-engineered our market in a matter of five months, then dominated that new market by the end of the year. That kind of success only comes when you truly understand what your customers want to buy from you, and you can deliver it in a way that ensures their success.

No matter their industry, successful CEOs develop solutions that create a unique competitive advantage for their customers. Initially, they focus intensely on their main product offerings. However, as their customers shift from small local businesses to industry-leading Fortune 200 companies, they must find more strategic ways to leverage their solutions, fundamentally altering the company's trajectory. It's a crucial decision: Do you stick to the original handful of products that you believed would change the world, or do you realign to meet your largest customers' needs, thereby securing significant investments you hadn't thought possible?

Think of it this way: Product leaders are responsible for developing product offerings with advanced capabilities. If charter customers request a new direction and are willing to fund the development, is that product-led innovation or customer-led? Creating comprehensive solutions—those that not only help end users but also appeal to your clients' mid-level managers and even their executives—is critical to hyperscale success. The sooner you can develop a complete industry solution set, the faster you can validate your ideal customer profile and greatest need for the use cases your solution enables. But the opposite holds true as well: The more you limit your solution's value to a single group, the longer it will take to find that ideal profile—and you may find yourself left behind next time someone else re-engineers your market.

In this chapter, you'll learn how to thrive by not only creating products but also by strategically engineering markets to unlock new revenue streams. Market engineering extends beyond product development, transforming charter customer requirements to create sustainable growth for your company. Here are the key tools you'll need:

1. CATEGORY CREATION is **inventing a new product category that addresses unrecognized problems**. Develop thought leadership around emerging trends. Educate the market with direct engagement from your industry sales teams. Partner with analysts to define and validate the new category.

2. REDEFINING EXISTING MARKETS means **shifting the perception of current products to create new demand**. Develop differentiated messaging. Drive user adoption through viral growth loops. Use brand storytelling to reshape market views.

3. VERTICAL INTEGRATION provides end-to-end solutions that **control multiple layers of the value chain for greater value**. Create industry solution sets that provide complete solutions

to companies that want to accelerate their market leadership. Acquire key players to round out the required capabilities in the ecosystem, develop new industry capabilities, and offer bundled solutions.

4. **FORM STRATEGIC ALLIANCES** by **partnering with companies to co-create solutions and access new markets.** Co-develop integrated solutions. Run joint GTM campaigns. Share sales channels and market access.

PROVING THE PUDDING

Charter customers play a pivotal role in guiding the trajectory of a product, spurring innovation and validating solutions within their fields. By choosing the right partners for these tasks, you can drive long-term strategic growth and carve out a presence in specific market segments.

To pinpoint ideal charter customers, seek those who align closely with your vision, are willing to invest in pilot programs, and hold significant sway within their industry. These customers not only possess the technical acumen to offer valuable feedback on your plans and prototypes but they also have the influence to champion solutions within their networks.

Forging strategic alliances with your charter customers is crucial for building credibility and ensuring successful implementation. As we've already seen, this involves translating intricate technical features into clear business benefits, addressing urgent pain points, and demonstrating measurable outcomes. In particular, creating persona-based case studies that mirror the unique needs of specific industry roles enables potential customers to see the direct relevance and impact of your solution. Additionally, leveraging executive references and testimonials from satisfied charter customers helps to sway others in similar segments.

Establishing footholds in niche industry segments is essential for strategic market engineering. By concentrating on specific sub-industries and prioritizing overlooked pain points, you can quickly showcase transformative value. From there, anchor customers within these segments act as advocates, amplifying the reach and adoption of your solution. Keep in mind that while early adopters are drawn to innovation, they must also manage risk and optimize return on investment. To support these needs, you should offer a structured risk reduction framework that includes phased rollouts, sandbox environments, and dedicated support. Delivering quick wins through proof-of-value initiatives reinforces confidence and speeds up adoption. Ease of use is critical, as end users favor intuitive solutions that boost productivity without requiring extensive training.

Overall, ongoing collaboration with charter customers sustains innovation and ensures continuous alignment with market needs. Regular feedback loops, beta testing programs, and joint innovation sessions facilitate the co-creation of features that provide a competitive edge. Publicly showcasing these innovations at industry events further underscores the value of the partnership. These investments not only help you strengthen your offerings but enable you to cultivate enduring partnerships, secure influential industry positions, and drive sustained growth across market segments.[*]

BUILD AN IDEAL CUSTOMER PROFILE

Defining an Ideal Customer Profile (ICP) ensures that your product development efforts target the organizations and individuals who will benefit most from the product. This alignment maximizes value for both parties: Your customer gains consistent growth and effective adoption, while your team streamlines their marketing, sales, and development strategies.

Start assembling your ICP based on **firmographics**, such as industry verticals, company size, and growth stage. These variables provide insight into the types of organizations that align with your product. Next, **technographics** assess the technology stack and digital maturity of your potential customers, offering a deeper understanding of their readiness to adopt new solutions. In both categories, use **behavioral insights**, including pain points and engagement patterns, to highlight areas where your product can drive the most impact. Finally, understanding each customer's **goals, KPIs, and**

* *Crossing the Chasm*, Geoffry Moore

budget authority ensures that the product development process aligns with their tangible business outcomes.

To ensure objective decision-making, have your product teams apply structured scoring frameworks to evaluate each use case. One commonly used model is RICE (Reach, Impact, Confidence, Effort). This framework measures how many customers a feature will affect, the magnitude of the benefit, the certainty of success, and the resources required for development. Alternatively, teams may use MoSCoW (Must Have, Should Have, Could Have, Won't Have) to categorize initiatives based on their urgency and necessity.

Market and competitive analysis further shape the roadmap. Benchmarking against your competitors highlights opportunities for differentiation, ensuring that your product stands out in a crowded marketplace. Once high-priority use cases are identified, start the development of Minimum Viable Products (MVPs). Collaborating with select ICP customers allows teams to test and refine their solutions, gathering iterative feedback to inform future enhancements. This approach ensures that the final product meets customer expectations while maintaining the flexibility to adapt to evolving needs.

By adhering to this structured process, your product development teams ensure that their resources are allocated to initiatives with the highest potential for impact. This fosters innovation, strengthens customer relationships, and drives sustainable growth across the organization.

ESTABLISH INNOVATION LEADERSHIP

Navigating enterprise technology sales demands a nuanced understanding of two distinct but interconnected audiences—technical buyers and executive leaders. While technical buyers dive into the granular aspects of product functionality and validation, executives focus on how well a solution aligns with the firm's strategic goals and how much immediate business value it offers. Balancing these dynamics ensures that you address both technical feasibility and strategic alignment, leading to faster decision-making and successful enterprise adoption.

The best way forward is a dual-track approach that targets both audiences simultaneously. Let's start with the technical buyers, who require extensive proof of concept, pilot programs, and in-depth technical demonstrations to validate product performance. These buyers play a pivotal role in evaluating product capabilities and ensuring technical feasibility. Their primary focus lies in areas such as reliability, scalability, and seamless integration with existing systems.

However, engaging technical buyers often involves navigating lengthy pilot processes and overcoming decision-making delays. Furthermore, budget constraints for unplanned initiatives can add additional layers of complexity. The key to engaging technical buyers lies in delivering comprehensive technical documentation, providing sandbox environments, and showcasing long-term value through proof of concept. These measures build trust and demonstrate the solution's potential to address their immediate pain points.

Executives, on the other hand, steer the strategic direction of the organization. They are driven by high-level overviews, business impact analysis, and competitive positioning. Unlike technical buyers, executives are less involved in the detailed technical evaluations and instead rely on high-level, actionable insights to make swift decisions. To engage executives effectively, it's critical to present visually compelling executive dashboards, strategic use cases, and outcome-based metrics. Highlighting industry benchmarks and offering new insights that executives may not have previously considered can create a compelling case for immediate investment. Providing case studies and quantifying time-to-value with ROI calculators can justify investment and prompt faster decision-making.

One of the most effective ways to expedite sales is by securing executive sponsorship early in the process. Engaging senior leadership not only secures initial buy-in but also helps expedite the technical validation process by leveraging their influence. From there you can run technical validation concurrently with executive presentations to keep both audiences engaged simultaneously. Regular updates that address technical performance and executive KPIs keep all stakeholders informed and aligned, as well as ensuring continuity across all stages of the sales journey.

THE TRUTH ABOUT ENGINEERING MARKETS

Product evaluations are often seen as a purely technical contest—one where the best product emerges victorious, where innovation speaks for itself, and where technical expertise alone can secure success. Yet, the reality is far more nuanced.

Tech companies excel not just through advanced capabilities but also through deep market understanding, clear problem definition, and effective solution positioning. The true industry leaders build exceptional products and tell compelling stories, leveraging past customer experiences to carve out their competitive niche. Success hinges on the ability to merge innovation with strategic narratives. **How many executive sponsors do you have capable of engineering new markets with Fortune 200 clients today?**

Expertise is more than just knowledge; it's experience that transcends degrees, certifications, and technical proficiency. In the marketplace, expertise represents the accumulation of real-world experience, the ability to discern patterns, and the instinct to anticipate problems before they arise.

A seasoned product owner or business strategist doesn't just know the technology; they understand how it integrates into the broader industry landscape. They grasp the pain points of customers, the inefficiencies that linger, and the trends shaping the future. Their expertise is not merely theoretical, but honed through **hands-on problem-solving**, navigating failures, and seeing projects through from concept to impact. Thus, the most valuable professionals and companies aren't just repositories of technical knowledge; they are interpreters of industry challenges and architects of meaningful solutions.

In short, it's not about the product—it's about the problem. One of the biggest mistakes tech companies make is leading with their solution instead of the problem. They highlight technical specs, patents, and innovations, assuming their superiority will naturally lead to market success. But customers—whether enterprise buyers or individual users—don't start with a solution in mind. They start with a problem, an outcome they need to improve.

The companies that stand out are the ones that frame the problem in a way that resonates. They use real-world stories, data, and industry insights to show the impact of the challenge. They make it clear why the issue matters, how it affects business outcomes, and what opportunities exist for improvement.

A great solution is only valuable if it reflects a clear understanding of the problem. That's why the most effective product leaders and business leaders don't just build—they articulate, they translate, and they connect the dots between technology and real business needs.

Differentiation goes beyond just listing features. In any market, there are competitors, often many, offering similar solutions. So why should a customer choose one over another? The answer isn't solely about having more features or superior performance metrics. True differentiation stems from understanding what customers genuinely value.

Perhaps it's simplicity—addressing a problem in a way that demands less integration or fewer operational hassles. Perhaps it's cost-effectiveness—delivering a more sustainable ROI than the competition. Perhaps it's service—offering a level of responsiveness and expertise that larger competitors simply can't match.

The most elite companies don't just create something new; they engineer a market grounded in differentiation. They identify gaps in the market, listen to unmet needs, and position their solution as not merely an alternative, but a smarter choice.

Success leaves clues from lessons learned in the past. Every business journey is filled with successes and failures. The key is to recognize that every experience—every project, every mistake, every lesson learned—is a valuable asset.

Leading companies take what worked in one industry and adapt it to an adjacent industry. They refine their strategies based on past performance, avoiding pitfalls that once cost them time and resources. They don't reinvent the wheel every time; they improve it, optimize it, and apply it in new ways. Experience isn't just about clocking in years in the industry—it's about leveraging those years effectively. It's about identifying patterns, learning from obstacles, and constantly refining problem-solving techniques.

Harness the power of specialization to find your market. Trying to appeal to everyone is a guaranteed way to get lost in the crowd. The companies that excel are the ones that focus intensely on a specific niche. They choose an industry segment, grasp its unique challenges, and tailor their solutions to meet those needs. They don't just offer a generic product; they provide a specialized solution to a distinct problem.

This strategic targeting not only enhances product-market fit but also bolsters credibility. A company that positions itself as the authority in a particular field gains trust more quickly, attracts more dedicated customers, and builds a reputation that competitors find hard to rival.

Remember, the underdog advantage empowers the third-place contender. The top two companies dominate market share. But history has shown that third place—when approached strategically—can be a powerful position to influence the entire market.

Smaller players possess the agility to innovate rapidly, adapt swiftly, and respond to customer needs in unique ways that larger competitors cannot. They can carve out niche advantages and form strategic partnerships that enhance their offerings. They can focus on personalized customer service, creating a level of engagement that big corporations struggle to achieve.

Being an underdog isn't a weakness—it's an opportunity. Companies that understand this don't attempt to outcompete industry giants on their terms. Instead, they play a different game, emphasizing agility, specialization, and customer experience.

Success in engineering markets isn't just about creating outstanding products; it's about grasping the broader context. It's about understanding that true expertise is forged through experience, that compelling narratives are as critical as cutting-edge technology, and that differentiation is essential to stand out.

It's about realizing that past achievements offer valuable lessons for future victories, that specialization builds credibility, and that even the third-place contender can ascend to dominance with the right strategy. For those who accept this reality, the path ahead is evident. It's not just about engineering the best solution—it's about engineering the best market position.

GENERATE NEW REVENUE STREAMS

In the quest for sustainable growth, businesses often grapple with a pivotal question: Where will the next wave of expansion originate? The answer lies in grasping and leveraging seven distinct routes to market. Each path provides a framework for innovation, empowering companies to evolve, adapt, and excel in competitive landscapes.

The most familiar route involves **increasing market share within existing markets**. By refining their products, enhancing customer experiences, and deploying strategic marketing, companies can outmaneuver competitors to capture larger portions of the same pie. Apple exemplifies this by consistently iterating on the iPhone, which both secures a loyal customer base and increases its share of the smartphone market year after year.

Yet, genuine growth often requires venturing beyond current offerings. Companies can **create new products or services** to meet evolving customer needs. Amazon's journey from an online bookstore to the world's largest e-commerce platform epitomizes this approach. Incremental innovation, driven by customer insights, fueled the company's expansion into new categories, from electronics to groceries.

Growth, however, isn't confined to product innovation. **Expanding into new markets or demographics** can unlock untapped potential. Netflix's global expansion, bringing its streaming services to diverse international audiences, illustrates how scaling across geographies can dramatically increase your reach and revenue.

Sometimes, growth lies just beyond the immediate horizon. By **moving into adjacent spaces**, companies can leverage their existing strengths to venture into new industries. Tesla's foray from electric vehicles to energy storage and solar power reflects how businesses can capitalize on core technologies to diversify.

For the boldest innovators, **disrupting the market** represents the ultimate growth catalyst. This route demands transformative ideas that reshape industries. Uber's revolution of the transportation sector, bypassing traditional taxi services through a simple yet groundbreaking app, underscores the power of disruption to redefine market dynamics.

Finally, companies can seek growth by **integrating vertically and entering new value chains**. By expanding across supply chains, you can control more aspects of production and delivery. Amazon's development of its logistics and delivery network is a testament to how vertical integration can drive efficiency and create competitive advantage.

Together, these seven routes form a map for growth. Whether it's through incremental gains or bold transformations, you can plot your path to sustained success by choosing tactics and strategies that align with your vision, strengths, and market realities.[*]

INDUSTRY SOLUTION SETS

Executives are increasingly seeking ways to implement innovative solutions with minimal disruption and maximum return. An excellent way to meet these goals is by unlocking industry-specific value with preconfigured solution sets. **Industry Solution Sets** provide a transformative approach, enabling leaders to experience tailored, industry-specific solutions before committing to full-scale deployment. These comprehensive packages are designed to accelerate implementation, align with best practices, and offer advanced insights that drive better decision-making.

A complete Industry Solution Set is more than just a toolkit; it's a blueprint for success. At the heart of each solution is a set of executive dashboards, each equipped with leading indicators and key performance metrics tailored to the nuances of the industry. These dashboards provide a clear, real-time view of the organization's performance, empowering leaders to make data-driven decisions that fuel growth and resilience.

To ensure seamless adoption, the rollout of each solution is divided into three carefully structured phases. This phased approach allows organizations to gradually implement the solution, based on their unique readiness and operational capacity. Breaking the process into manageable stages likewise

---

[*] *The Alchemy of Growth*, David White

minimizes the risk of disruption, allowing your clients to focus on the incremental value they receive at each step. This not only accelerates ROI but also ensures that your solution evolves in parallel with your client's business.

INDUSTRY SOLUTION SETS

1. Advertising	17. Institutional Banking	33. Healthcare
2. Entertainment	18. Commercial Banks	34. Medical Equipment
3. Media	19. Data Services	35. Pharmaceutical
4. Wireless	20. Life Insurance	36. Discrete Mfg.
5. Wireline	21. Property & Casualty	37. Process Mfg.
6. Construction	22. Wealth Management	38. Beverage
7. Engineering	23. Public Sector	39. Chemicals
8. Apparel	24. Business Services	40. Food
9. Consumer Goods	25. Cloud Hosting	41. Aerospace
10. Retail	26. Computer Software	42. Aftermarket Parts
11. Wholesale	27. Electronics	43. Airlines
12. Education	28. IT	44. Automotive
13. Engineering	29. Pro Services	45. Hospitality
14. Project Management	30. Household Products	46. Logistics
15. Energy	31. Industrials	47. Transportation
16. Utilities	32. Materials	48. Travel

Diagram 6.0 Preconfigured Solution Offerings

A key differentiator of Industry Solution Sets lies in their focus on persona-based use cases. By prioritizing use cases for different roles—whether executives, managers, or operators—an ISS ensures that every layer of the organization benefits from tailored insights and functionality. This personalization enhances relevance, driving faster adoption and delivering value across the entire enterprise.

Beyond providing tools and workflows, these solutions unlock new avenues of insight. Unique attributes in the data model, previously difficult or impossible to capture, are harnessed to provide executives with a level of analysis they've never had before. What if you went to an executive and shared with them the ten unique attributes you put into your data model that provide unique metrics to create a competitive advantage in your industry, showing how you worked with these three industry leaders to embed them in your solution, and how no one else in our industry has these in their product? This deeper layer of intelligence helps organizations uncover hidden opportunities, mitigate risks, and stay ahead of industry trends.

Ultimately, Industry Solution Sets offer more than just efficiency—they provide a competitive advantage. By combining best practices with advanced technology and strategic foresight, organizations can streamline transformation efforts, enhance their ability to respond to market changes, and position themselves as industry leaders. As industries continue to evolve, the ability to implement solutions quickly and effectively will become a defining factor in long-term success. Industry Solution Sets stand at the forefront of this evolution, equipping executives with the tools they need to lead with confidence and clarity.

INDUSTRY SOLUTION SET COMPONENTS

Industry Sales Briefings

- Pain Points Identified & Addressed

- Target Decision-Makers & Concerns

- Value Proposition & ROI

- Customer Success Stories

Executive Dashboards

- KPIs Prioritized by Customer Role

- Industry Metrics

Prioritized Business Process Flows

- High Value Use Cases by Phase

Demand Creation Content

- Executive Email Library

- Sales Framework Repository

- Industry Segment Use Cases

Discovery Questions

- Functional & Financial Differentiation

- Technical Differentiation

Competitive Positioning

- Competitive Wins by Use Case

Differentiation

- Cost to Develop Comparisons

- Quick Win Benefits by Horizon

- System Dependencies

Reference Architectures

- CIO Application Roadmaps

- Business vs. IT Priorities

- Customer Value Creation

Customer Reference Cards

- Quick Reference on Industry

Competitors

- Industry Initiatives by Operating Unit

Industry Solution Portal

- Industry, Process & Product Content

- Sales Process Mapped to Deliverables

Process Flow Demonstrations

- Storyboards and Demo Scripts

- Persona-Based Use Case Demos

Customer Experience Blueprints

- Implementation Plan Blueprints

Diagram 6.1 Sales Assets for Executive Engagement

BUSINESS PROCESS LIBRARIES

In today's competitive landscape, strategic companies rely heavily on business process libraries to drive efficiency, consistency, and innovation in client engagements. These libraries serve as structured collections of best practices, workflows, frameworks, and methodologies, all of which help consultants analyze, design, and optimize business operations. By drawing from proven approaches, consulting firms can swiftly address client challenges and enhance overall project delivery.

At the heart of these libraries lie key components that shape their effectiveness. **Frameworks and methodologies** form the foundation, encompassing proven strategic tools such as Porter's Five Forces, the BCG Matrix, and SWOT Analysis. **Process optimization techniques** like Six Sigma and Lean further strengthen these frameworks, allowing consultants to map, analyze, and refine processes. **Benchmarking practices** ensure that businesses are continuously compared against industry standards, driving performance improvements.

Beyond general frameworks, business process libraries also feature industry-specific processes. **Tailored workflows** cater to verticals such as healthcare, manufacturing, retail, and finance, maintaining both regulatory compliance and operational excellence. This specialization helps clients navigate sector-specific challenges with confidence. **Functional processes** are another pillar, covering essential business functions like supply chain management, finance, human resources, and sales. Support functions, including IT and customer services, are equally crucial, ensuring smooth internal operations. Meanwhile, innovation processes, such as R&D and new product development frameworks, help clients stay ahead of the curve by fostering continuous growth and creativity.

In the era of digital transformation, these libraries should expand to include **AI and automation roadmaps, cloud adoption frameworks, and data-driven models**. Digital transformation templates guide clients through the integration of cutting-edge technologies, allowing them to streamline workflows and unlock new opportunities. Case studies and playbooks further enrich the libraries by providing real-world success stories and operational guides. These resources serve as blueprints for market entry, mergers and acquisitions, and cost-reduction initiatives, offering valuable insights into practical execution.

Additionally, **tools and metrics** play a vital role. KPI libraries, diagnostic tools for gap analysis, and ROI calculators ensure that performance is consistently measured and optimized. These tools empower consultants to make data-driven decisions that maximize value for clients. Overall, by reducing the need to design processes from scratch, business process libraries accelerate project timelines and enhance scalability across multiple engagements. Their **uniformity and standardization** ensure consistent quality, while **customizable templates** allow for flexibility to meet client-specific needs. Moreover, they **foster knowledge sharing and collaboration** across teams and offices, driving collective growth and continuous improvement.

Building and maintaining these libraries requires a multifaceted approach. Internal development is central, leveraging insights from previous engagements and internal research. Acquiring intellectual property and tools from specialized firms can further expand your capabilities. Solution engineers who are continuously working with customers in the field are in a unique position to repurpose their content with dedicated time once a week to make their inflight-opportunities material generic so the rest of the organization can leverage it in future pursuits. Crowdsourcing insights from consultants across various practice areas ensures that your libraries remain dynamic and relevant—and that you can keep delivering exceptional value to your clients.

LEVERAGING A PHASED ROADMAP

Strategic partnerships play a pivotal role in guiding organizations through intricate transformations. Using them well requires a phased implementation approach that balances immediate wins with longer-term strategic objectives. This strategy not only generates early momentum but also builds stakeholder confidence, expertly aligning organizational efforts with overarching business goals.

To effectively structure implementation, a good first step is evaluating initiatives using an **impact vs. feasibility matrix**. This matrix categorizes initiatives into four distinct areas. *Quick wins*, which are high-impact and low-complexity initiatives, delivering immediate value with minimal effort. *Strategic initiatives*, though complex and resource intensive, drive transformational change and ensure long-term success. *Incremental improvements*, while limited in impact, are easy to implement and contribute to sustained progress. Meanwhile, *low-priority efforts*, characterized by low impact and high complexity, are often deprioritized.

Start with the quick wins to generate early buy-in and build momentum with your new partner. Concurrently, lay the groundwork for strategic initiatives to ensure alignment with both parties' long-term objectives, facilitating a seamless transition from short-term success to sustained transformation. A **phased roadmap** is essential for guiding this process, with each phase tied to specific business outcomes.

In the *foundational phase*, typically spanning the first six months, the focus is on quick wins. These may include automating manual processes, deploying basic data analytics dashboards, or optimizing workflows for cost savings. Next, the *strategic phase*, lasting from six to eighteen months, involves scaling successful pilots across departments. This phase might include expanding AI/machine learning initiatives or introducing system integrations to improve efficiency across the organization. Finally, the *transformation phase*, extending from eighteen to thirty-six months, addresses long-term strategic goals, such as ERP modernization or enterprise-wide digital transformation.

To ensure each phase delivers measurable results, align your initiatives with your client's key performance indicators. Revenue growth, cost optimization, risk mitigation, and innovation serve as guiding benchmarks for evaluating success. By clearly demonstrating ROI at each stage, you can enhance executive sponsorship and secure the necessary funding for continued progress. An agile, iterative approach typically works better here than traditional linear rollouts. By starting with pilot projects, both organizations can validate assumptions and gather valuable feedback. Successful pilots can then be iteratively scaled, with continuous refinement based on stakeholder input. This iterative cycle fosters adaptability and responds to evolving business needs.

Stakeholder engagement remains crucial throughout this process. In the early phases, frontline employees and middle management drive adoption, while cross-functional leaders play a larger role during the scaling phase. Ultimately, of course, long-term transformation requires C-suite sponsorship and enterprise-wide collaboration. Consider the example of AI adoption. In the initial phase, simple workflows, such as chatbots or invoice automation, are deployed. This is followed by the implementation of predictive maintenance models in the scaling phase. Finally, a centralized, AI-driven decision platform is developed to support enterprise-wide analytics, marking the culmination of the transformation journey.

By phasing implementation in a structured, outcome-driven manner, strategic consulting firms enable client organizations to achieve early wins while maintaining focus on long-term goals. This balanced approach not only drives sustained value but also ensures that transformational efforts are both successful and enduring.

ENGINEER MARKETS THEORY

Industry leaders set the bar as charter customers to define unique differentiation for their companies. How many charter customers do you have per industry segment?

Why change?

Challenge:	How do you compete when industry leaders dominate the market? You need to create Significant Transactions that did not exist before. Do you have the right profiles bold enough to create new markets?

How do we differentiate?

Concept 21:	**Ideal Customer Profile** is an individual that would benefit the most from your solution, and in return, provides the highest value to your business. It helps organizations focus their marketing, sales, and product development efforts on the most profitable and strategic prospects.
Concept 22:	**Industry Blueprint** is a preconfigured solution offering with personalized executive dashboards by persona, prioritized use cases to implement by phase, and the unique attributes captured to create a competitive advantage from the advanced insights.
Concept 23:	**Market Awareness** is a level of understanding and recognition that consumers or businesses have about a particular brand, product, service, and how the market is trending. It reflects how well informed a target audience is regarding the offerings and positioning of a company within their industry.
Concept 24:	**Industry Segmentation** is the process of dividing a broad market or industry into smaller, more manageable sub-groups based on shared characteristics. This allows companies to tailor their products, services, and marketing strategies to better meet the needs of specific segments.

What do we receive?

Result:	Confirm Fit secures 4x larger ACVs with no competition. **Ensure you become a top three project +42%** due to its value. Capture new market and move adjacent to your next segment.

TIPS AND TRICKS FOR ENGINEERING MARKETS

- In the competitive arena of enterprise sales, achieving success means mastering the art of market engineering, **influencing high-level decision-makers**, and securing incremental investments. This calls for a proactive, strategic mindset—starting with confidence and culminating in enduring partnerships. By adopting an assumptive close mentality, leveraging cross-functional Diamond Teams, and embedding solutions into account roadmaps, you can drive sustained growth while outmaneuvering your competitors.

- Central to **market engineering** is the concept of assuming progress as a given. Executive discussions should focus on execution, not persuasion. When sellers engage with the belief that their solution is already a strategic fit, they generate a natural momentum that propels their deals forward. For example, imagine a meeting where the conversation shifts from "Would you consider this?" to "How can we ensure the smoothest rollout by Q2?" This change in tone conveys confidence and competence. Executives, who are often time-pressed, tend to favor solutions presented as inevitable extensions of their existing strategies.

- Preparation is crucial. By anchoring proposals in data, aligning with KPIs, and demonstrating tangible value, you can **confidently direct discussions toward next steps**. The assumptive close isn't about ignoring objections—it's about treating them as part of the journey instead of obstacles to progress.

- Enterprise sales are rarely influenced by just one person. Each deal involves a network of stakeholders—executives, technical leads, procurement teams, and so on—with distinct concerns and priorities. Managing this complexity calls for a Diamond Team: a **cross-functional task force** of sales, solutions engineer, marketing, business value, professional service, and product leaders.

- This coordinated effort ensures that every stakeholder receives tailored, relevant content. Technical issues? The product leader steps in. ROI projections? Marketing delivers compelling case studies. By distributing responsibilities and maintaining internal alignment, the Diamond Team provides a seamless experience for the client. Think about the difference between a generic product demo and one that mirrors the client's specific infrastructure. The latter, crafted by engineering and customized by sales, resonates more deeply and accelerates the path to consensus.
- Winning a deal is merely the beginning. To ensure long-term success, sellers must influence account priorities and guide future roadmaps. This requires more than transactional selling—it necessitates thought leadership and a consultative approach.
- By consistently offering insights on market trends and emerging technologies, sellers position themselves as indispensable advisors. Workshops, innovation sessions, and co-created strategies enable clients to envision the future—and place the seller's solution at the core of that vision.
- Picture a scenario where an enterprise is struggling with AI-driven observability. A seller who introduces industry case studies, suggests pilot programs, and ties the solution to broader trends becomes a key architect of the client's future initiatives. This proactive approach not only secures incremental funding but also **solidifies a working relationship for future projects**.
- Large-scale deployments can be daunting—for both seller and client. To reduce risk and drive incremental progress, use phasing strategies for a robust solution. By breaking projects into manageable stages, you can provide clients with flexibility while demonstrating early wins. The phased approach serves a dual purpose: It minimizes up front investment for the client while simultaneously locking out competition.

- By structuring exclusivity into future phases, sellers create pathways for long-term engagement without needing overwhelming initial commitments. Visualize a deployment that starts in a primary data center, with plans to expand to satellite locations. Each phase builds on the last, reinforcing trust and showcasing value. Competitors, left without an entry point, find themselves sidelined as the relationship deepens.
- Market engineering transcends mere sales tactics—it is a **philosophy rooted in confidence**, collaboration, and influence. By assuming the close, orchestrating Diamond Teams, shaping client roadmaps, and phasing strategies, sellers transform from vendors into trusted partners. This playbook provides a blueprint for driving incremental funding, securing long-term deals, and shaping the future of enterprise engagements.

ENGINEER MARKETS WORKBOOK
EXPAND POTENTIAL MARKETS

Engineer Market Frameworks

112 INDUSTRY SOLUTIONS SETS	Pre-configured specific solutions from industry leaders • Jump-start implementation with best practices documented
113 RECOMMEND PHASING	Balance reducing risks with quick win payback to fund project • Break implementation into manageable components with owners
114 BUSINESS PROCESS LIBRARY	Document the leading use cases by industry and person • Collaborate with clients on the order of use case deployment
115 OUTCOMES BY PHASE	Quantify business case benefits by implementation phase • Prioritize use cases by deployment phase

Engineer Market Sales Plays

116 CHARTER CUSTOMERS	Industry-leading customers provide guidance on roadmap • Customer collaboration creates competitive collaboration
117 CO-CREATE	Customer executives recommend solution enhancements • Provide industry expertise that can be a challenge to come by
118 VALUE PROPOSITION	Tailor your value proposition to executives' business outcomes • By industry, account, operating unit, and persona
119 MATURITY	Demonstrate unique capabilities that create competitive advantage • Optimize use cases by maturity level
120 DEFINABLE	Measurable capabilities should define your roadmap • Customer's quantifiable impacts set priorities
121 ACCEPTANCE	Proof of concepts validate user acceptance of use cases • Receiving customer buy-in is critical
122 INFLECTION POINTS	Position your solutions as part of broader industry trend • Attach to solve the largest business challenges
123 EXCLUSIVE	You're in the business of creating exclusive thought leadership • Personalize executive briefings
124 MARKET SUCCESS	Leverage joint marketing with customer success stories • Establish industry credibility at the personal level
125 INNOVATION PARTNERSHIPS	Develop long-term innovation partnerships • Enable end-to-end process flows to remove swivel chair

Diagram 6.2 How to Engineer Markets That Expands Your Market Potential

EVERYDAY APPLICATIONS

Repetition is often undervalued, yet it is the key to unlocking deeper engagement and mastery when working with executives across various industries. The more frequently your GTM team interacts with industry leaders, the more adept they will become at understanding the nuances of communication, the strategic priorities at play, and the inherent challenges executives face. Over time, this repetition builds not only familiarity but also credibility, fostering relationships that can drive transformational projects forward.

Industries have their own distinct languages, each filled with specialized terminology and acronyms. Learning this language is crucial to make an impact at the executive level, but fluency cannot be gained overnight. It comes from repeated exposure—attending meetings, participating in discussions, and immersing yourself in the environment. Regular engagement trains you in the client's vernacular, enabling you to converse more confidently and persuasively. This shared language becomes a bridge to meaningful dialogue, signaling to executives that you truly understand their world.

Beyond language, repetition uncovers the recurring pain points and strategic priorities that define an industry. Whether it's the persistent need to bolster cybersecurity in tech firms or the drive for greater efficiency in supply chains, consistent interaction reveals each client's critical areas of focus. Each conversation adds another layer of insight, sharpening your ability to offer tailored solutions that address executives' most pressing concerns.

Risk management is another domain where repeated exposure proves invaluable. Executives often navigate complex landscapes riddled with regulatory challenges, market fluctuations, and internal resistance to change. By engaging with industry leaders consistently, your team will develop an intuitive sense of these risks and the factors that drive executive decision-making. They will become adept at foreseeing potential objections and crafting strategies that align with your client's appetite for risk.

Not every executive is positioned to lead a large-scale transformation. Through experience, you can learn to recognize the subtle cues that signal an executive's influence and readiness to drive change. Tenure, track record, and internal alliances all serve as valuable barometers. Use them to identify key allies within organizations, ensuring that you target stakeholders with the clout to make meaningful progress.

At its core, repetition in executive engagement is about more than just familiarity—it is about cultivating lasting relationships. Each touchpoint strengthens trust and deepens rapport, gradually shifting the dynamic from transactional to consultative. Over time, your sales team will no longer be seen as external vendors or consultants but as trusted advisors whose insights contribute directly to the company's strategic direction.

Ultimately, the power of repetition lies in its cumulative effect. Through consistent engagement, your Diamond Teams can refine their understanding, sharpen their strategies, and build the relationships necessary to drive transformative initiatives. The process may take time, but the results—greater influence, deeper trust, and successful project outcomes—are well worth the effort.

ENGINEER MARKETS KEY TAKEAWAYS

1. Can your GTM team demonstrate proven customer success within an industry?

   Lead with the answer, that includes a business case by implementation phase to achieve success.

2. Do your sellers have the ability to activate new markets with existing products?

   Provide an industry solution set with content by persona to open new markets.

3. Will customers invest in your innovation to become early adopters?

   Charter customers bet their careers on your ability to deliver a successful project for them.

4. Can sales create 4x ACV transactions with customers who were not looking to invest?

   Collaborative partnerships trust in your account team to deliver.

5. Do your teams know the specific use cases for each ideal customer profile?

Demonstrating vertically specific solutions by persona builds the ultimate confidence.

6. If your teams have industry solution sets, could they double their pipeline?

Leverage pre-configured offerings that have every aspect of an implemented solution.

7. When you win the selection with a customer, do you engage the peers in their segment?

When you implement a proven industry solution, thought leadership influences the market.

8. What actions should GTM teams take to generate momentum and drive hyperscale revenue?

Leveraging customer-facing content is not what GTM teams excel at reusing for others.

SUMMARY

Successfully engineering markets is not for the fainthearted. It demands bold leadership, strategic alliances, and the resilience to tackle both internal and external challenges head-on. Companies in these environments must closely collaborate with strategic accounts, paving pathways and embracing encumbrances that many might avoid. This quest for innovation and market leadership, however, often prompts internal resistance, creating friction that can impede progress.

One of the most significant obstacles comes from internal development teams. These teams are often deeply committed to crafting bespoke solutions, driven by a strong belief in their ability to build everything in-house. While this approach can lead to tailored products, it comes at a cost. The internal development route is typically slow, resource-intensive, and fraught with risks that can jeopardize a company's competitive edge.

Delays in product deployment, unexpected technical hurdles, and resource constraints contribute to longer time-to-market. Additionally, internal-only innovation can lead to stagnation, as teams become entrenched in familiar methodologies and technologies. The result is a plateau in creativity, limiting the organization's ability to stay ahead of evolving industry demands.

To break through these barriers, many forward-thinking companies are turning to external partnerships. Collaborating with specialized external innovators lets you (and your clients) tap into new technologies, gain fresh perspectives, and significantly shorten development cycles. This strategic approach offers numerous benefits:

- Speed to Market. By integrating external solutions, companies can accelerate product launches, ensuring they remain competitive and responsive to market needs.
- Risk Distribution. External collaborations share the developmental load, reducing the likelihood of project failure and allowing internal teams to focus on core competencies.
- Sustained Innovation. External partners bring unique expertise, driving continuous improvement and fostering a steady influx of new ideas and technologies. Companies that can balance internal development and external collaboration are better positioned to overcome resistance and harness the full potential of innovation.
- Cross-Team Collaboration. Involving internal teams in the partnership process from the outset fosters a sense of ownership and minimizes resistance. Collaborative projects create opportunities for knowledge sharing and mutual growth.
- Strategic Goal Communication. Clearly articulating the broader strategic vision behind external partnerships helps internal teams understand the long-term benefits. Emphasizing scalability, efficiency, and market leadership can shift perspectives.
- Effective Scaling. Launching with pilot projects can demonstrate the value of external solutions without a significant initial

investment. As these small wins accumulate, internal trust and confidence grow, paving the way for larger collaborations.

Engineering markets is a challenging task, but it opens up many opportunities for those willing to embrace change. By blending internal ingenuity with external expertise, you can not only overcome resistance but also unlock new levels of innovation and market leadership. The future belongs to those who dare to venture beyond the familiar, forging partnerships that drive progress and redefine industry standards. In Chapter 7, we'll review several sales frameworks that can help you structure and streamline these important processes to become the trusted source to produce proposals for your customers' executive leadership team.

FRAMEWORKS

Executive Deliverables

(Reduce New Hire Ramp Time by 41 Percent)

CHAPTER 7

- ➤ **PLAYING THE INFINITE GAME:** Content Is King
- ➤ **SIMPLIFY THE COMPLEX:** Condense Your Message to One Page
- ➤ **SITUATIONAL AWARENESS:** Deliverables Anticipate Needs
- ➤ **PERSONALIZE YOUR BLUEPRINT:** Define Your Value

- ➤ **THE TRUTH ABOUT FRAMEWORKS:** Good Looks Like
- ➤ **BUILDING GLOBAL BEST PRACTICES:** Provide Frameworks
- ➤ **DEVELOP COMPLETE BUSINESS STRATEGY:** Secure Funding
- ➤ **STRATEGIC ACCOUNT ENGAGEMENT:** Accelerate Conversations

---

- ➤ **CLIENT SUCCESS FRAMEWORK:** Account Management
- ➤ **FRAMEWORK THEORY:** Reduce New Hire Ramp
- ➤ **TIPS AND TRICKS:** Accelerate Executive Engagement
- ➤ **FRAMEWORKS WORKBOOK:** Arrive as the Expert

- ➤ **EVERYDAY APPLICATIONS:** Play the Infinite Game
- ➤ **KEY TAKEAWAYS:** Scale Executive Engagement
- ➤ **SUMMARY:** Executive Deliverables

PLAYING THE INFINITE GAME

My CEO recently had a meeting with a client CIO who'd shown genuine interest in the business strategy we presented. The CIO was considering funding a $12 million unbudgeted project, pending approval from the Board of Directors, so he asked us for a completed executive proposal to secure the necessary funding. Up until that point, we had always left it to our prospects to create their own proposals. Recognizing the missed opportunity, we happily provided an executive proposal for him to use, and the deal closed within two weeks. Within the next month, we established a proposal management team to accelerate our revenue growth, **ultimately shortening our sales cycles by two months** by doing the groundwork for our prospects.

Less than 2 percent of sales professionals have experience working for firms like McKinsey or Accenture, so most are unfamiliar with the design and content of executive deliverables. That's exactly why we created a series of Sales Frameworks: to show our proposal team (and others) the best ways to present decision-relevant information in a succinct and impactful package. You can use a similar process to make your sales teams more self-sufficient and empower them to secure millions in funding for significant, unbudgeted transactions.

Sales Frameworks serve as structured templates that sales professionals can adapt and personalize for their clients, enhancing their efforts throughout the sales process. Knowing what excellence looks like is crucial when creating an executive deliverable that stands out—one that helps your internal champions sell your solution. Because sales professionals play an infinite game, where the real payoff is developing business acumen to drive future transactions, everything you create should expand your ability to create value for your customers.

Let me suggest a few framework design techniques up front, before we move on to consider their content. First, while most salespeople default to landscape orientation (think of a PowerPoint slide), especially for technical evaluations, executives are far more likely to use portrait-style 8.5" by 11" pages. Meeting this expectation can make a big difference when you're pursuing millions in potential funding! Second, brand your frameworks with your customer's logo and color scheme, not your own. This may seem counterintuitive but think of it this way: You are a strategic partner, crafting an internal proposal to secure funding for an unbudgeted project from your client's Board of Directors. Using their own branding creates a beneficial ambiguity about the proposal's origin, prompting further internal discussions. Last, always provide the source file for your frameworks—not just the finished PDF—so your internal champions can tailor their own executive proposals. This approach not only aligns your efforts with their goals but also fosters a deeper partnership, ultimately driving successful outcomes.

Evaluation criteria can change, and decision-makers can come and go, so it's crucial to have fluid and flexible methods for creating value. After all, your goal in enterprise sales is not merely to be selected for one deal but to secure an enterprise license agreement. These frameworks assemble and present valuable industry insights to leverage with that client and in that industry, ideally by focusing on continuous improvement. That success creates momentum, saving time and effort in future strategic engagements.

Shifting your organization to an infinite mindset unlocks the potential for creating enduring success: By connecting your individual team members to something greater than themselves, you will foster innovation and genuine engagement. In a world of constant change and uncertainty, the infinite game provides a roadmap for leaders seeking to build lasting legacies.[*]

---

[*] *The Infinite Game*, Simon Sinek

SIMPLIFY THE COMPLEX

Executives excel at breaking down intricate topics into simple, easy-to-understand explanations that connect with a wide audience. They can cut through the clutter and communicate effectively with stakeholders at all levels—and your sales professionals must do the same thing to influence executive decisions and close deals efficiently.

Fostering this skill starts with **mastering complexity**, since you can't simplify a topic until you understand it deeply. Comprehensive technical training, immersive experiences with engineers and product teams, and regular internal knowledge-sharing sessions help ensure that your sales teams become fluent in the products they represent. By embedding sales professionals within cross-functional teams, you allow them to witness firsthand how solutions are built and deployed, boosting both their confidence and competence.

Once this foundation is established, shift your focus to **creating frameworks for simplification**. Providing sales teams with structured approaches, such as the Problem - Solution - Impact model or the 3x3 Rule, enables them to systematically break down complex concepts. Using analogies further enhances this process, transforming abstract technologies into relatable metaphors. For instance, describing AI as "a GPS for your data" makes the concept more accessible and memorable. Train each salesperson to summarize your products in thirty-second pitches, to reinforce the importance of brevity and clarity.

Storytelling is a powerful tool in this endeavor, as you **craft narratives that emphasize customer outcomes** over technical details. Demonstrating how your products solve real-world problems brings technology to life, making it easier for clients to visualize their own success. Encourage your sales teams to internalize and personalize these stories so they can adapt their messaging to diverse audiences, resonating with both technical and non-technical stakeholders.

As you refine these skills, **practice and feedback loops** are essential drills. Role-play scenarios that simulate executive-level conversations, peer-to-peer reviews, and direct feedback from company leaders to help sharpen your communication. Quarterly pitch sessions likewise help you certify how well your sales professionals can simplify and deliver their messages. These iterative exercises build muscle memory and confidence, ensuring that simplification becomes second nature.

Finally, **continuous learning** is crucial to staying relevant in a rapidly evolving market. By curating and distributing simplified versions of technical documents, organizations help sales professionals stay informed without overwhelming them. Post-pitch debriefs provide an opportunity to reflect on messaging effectiveness, while regular updates on market trends and competitive landscapes ensure that sales teams remain on the cutting edge.

As we'll work through in Chapter 10, generative AI offers a powerful ally in this pursuit. AI tools can assist you and your team members with summarizing complex documents, generating analogies, and refining content for clarity. Real-time coaching platforms that analyze sales calls and provide feedback on simplification further enhance this process. By integrating AI into your sales workflow, you can empower your teams to simplify faster and more effectively.

Ultimately, the ability to simplify complexity helps transform sales professionals into trusted advisors. It accelerates deal velocity, enhances customer trust, and positions sales teams as indispensable partners in the client's decision-making process. By investing in this critical skill, you will not only boost sales performance but also cultivate future leaders capable of navigating and communicating within an increasingly complex world.

SITUATIONAL AWARENESS

Successful sales professionals understand that while standardized methodologies lay the groundwork, situational awareness and the timely delivery of impactful content are often the key factors in earning executive trust and speeding up sales cycles. In fact, proactively identifying and meeting executive needs is the only reliable way to thrive in a dynamic sales environment. By creating a curated library of executive-focused content and utilizing AI-driven tools, your sales teams can demystify complex solutions and effectively address the priorities of decision-makers.

As we've seen, executives expect sales engagements to offer tailored insights that align with their strategic goals—not generic sales materials they can get from your website. An executive-focused content strategy empowers sales teams to respond promptly to executive inquiries, not just by simplifying complex topics but also showcasing thought leadership and expertise. To meet this goal, make sure your content library is relevant, outcome-driven, organized, and easily accessible.

To get started, you'll need white papers, case studies, ROI models, and concise executive summaries. I recommend categorizing these assets based on executive roles and industry verticals. You should also index it according to desired outcomes, such as cost reduction, innovation, or digital transformation, enabling your sales professionals to filter and locate the right asset at the right moment.

The first four chapters of this book delve into the methodologies for initiating strategic engagements with new executives, leveraging outside-in research to generate a hyperscale pipeline. These are sixteen foundational sales frameworks that every sales professional should master to build a 4x pipeline and consistently exceed their quota.

This section, Chapters 5 through 8, explores how product marketing can highlight your solution's unique strengths, empowering strategic sales professionals to create and dominate markets, thereby securing future investments in major deals. As Sun Tzu put it in *The Art of War*, "Every war is won before it is ever fought."

Next up, Chapters 9 through 12 will cover how customer success can quantify measurable value, providing sales professionals with data to engage executives. This data showcases proven industry results and recommends advanced strategies for optimizing business processes, enhancing overall efficiency and effectiveness.

STRATEGIC ENGAGEMENT

| MOMENTUM | ALIGNMENT | CREDIBILITY | OUTCOMES |

1 Partner Summary initiate strategic engagement		**2** CEO Impact Email summarize business strategy	
3 Business Strategy creates Confirm Fit evaluation		**4** Investment Strategy unsolicited proposal	
5 Three-Year Press Release joint value quantified		**6** Relationship Map engagement influence plan	
7 Solution Imaging art of the possible dashboards		**8** Mutual Action Plans gain agreement on next steps	
9 Value Realization quarterly benefit scorecard		**10** Partner Summary roadmap to future projects	
11 Executive Demo Guide identify visual differentiation		**12** Reference Matrix prioritize decision criteria	
13 Executive Decision Document steps completed in process		**14** Procurement Scorecard document success blueprint for procurement	
15 Executive Proposal anticipate & overcome objections		**16** Implementation Plan resources & milestone requirements	

Diagram 7.0 Frameworks to Initiate Engagement

Like a sales sommelier, adopting a persona-centric approach is another vital technique. Different executives prioritize different outcomes—what appeals to a CFO may barely form a blip for a CTO or CISO. Relevant content reflects these distinctions. For instance, CFOs are often focused on cost optimization and ROI, CTOs on scalability and technological advancement, and CISOs on digital resilience. By customizing content to align with these priorities, your sales teams can forge stronger connections and foster deeper engagement.

AI-driven platforms can enable intelligent search capabilities in your library, bringing up the most relevant assets based on keywords, past interactions, and executive profiles. Automated recommendations further streamline the process by suggesting appropriate content aligned with the sales stage and specific executive concerns.

Finally, dynamic and modular templates empower sales teams to swiftly personalize deliverables. Pre-built executive summaries, ROI calculators, and customizable solution briefs make it easy to adapt content efficiently, markedly reducing response times and enhancing the quality of your engagement.

VALUE DIFFERENTIATION

DIAMOND TEAMS	ENGINEER MARKETS	SALES FRAMEWORKS	WRITTEN NARRATIVES
17 Client Success Framework deliver on strategic partnership		18 Industry Benchmarking identify gaps in performance	
19 Program Management guide clients to overcome objections		20 Value Expansion to ELA proven results confirm value	
21 Industry Solution Sets pre-configured recommended solutions		22 Recommended Phasing competitive advantage delivered	
23 Business Process Library use case priority by domain		24 Outcome by Horizon payback by implementation phase	
25 Global Sales Best Practices activity types that move the needle		26 Complete Business Strategy details CEO needs to sponsor	
27 Strategic Account Engagement method to create momentum		28 Client Success Measurement process adoption quantified	
29 Peer Comparison Benchmark identify areas to innovate		30 Problem-Solution Approach industry trend causes an inflection point	
31 Storytelling Approach industry leader outpacing the field		32 Visionary Approach recommend on innovation roadmap	

Diagram 7.1 Frameworks That Articulate Your Differentiation

Situational playbooks are another invaluable resource. These playbooks offer prescriptive guidance for addressing common executive scenarios, such as digital transformation initiatives, cost-cutting measures, or cybersecurity challenges. By bundling relevant case studies and solution briefs within these playbooks, your sales teams can present comprehensive, situationally relevant content that resonates with executives.

CUSTOMER BUY-IN

VALUE REALIZATION		ARTIFICIAL INTELLIGENCE	LAUNCH PLAN		UNIFY AWARENESS
33	Continuous Value Delivery process & metric enhancements		34	Quantify Value by Use Case business case by persona	
35	Total Cost of Ownership identify operational costs		36	Quarterly Realization Readout executive performance scorecard	
37	Personalized Content Creation areas to close the gap		38	Annual Report Insights executive compensation	
39	Industry Assessment innovative use case priority		40	ROI Generation initial outside-in benefit assessment	
41	13-Week Capacity Plan optimize quarterly sales motions		42	Articulate Strategic Narratives audibly ready to engage C-suite	
43	Perfect Executive Meeting anticipate needs prior to meetings		44	Frameworks to Account Plan client verifiable inputs	
45	Strategic Engagement Framework manage multiple sales motions		46	Management Cadence leading indicators	
47	C3 Communication Model client-written confirmation		48	Calendar of Events identify client constraints	

Diagram 7.2 Frameworks That Create Value for Customers

In summary, to implement a useful executive content strategy, begin with an audit of your existing content to assess its relevance and identify gaps. Develop executive personas through collaboration with sales and marketing teams to ensure content aligns with real-world needs. Map existing assets (and newly developed content) to these personas, deploy AI tools for content management, and provide ongoing training to ensure your sales teams effectively leverage the library.

PERSONALIZE YOUR BLUEPRINT

Specialization is undoubtedly valuable, but sellers who become overly reliant on a narrow skill set risk being unprepared for evolving challenges or shifts in the market. For example, a seller who excels at building relationships may struggle in high-pressure, transactional sales environments, while someone focused on product expertise might falter when relationship management becomes critical. This lack of adaptability can limit both individual success and organizational progress. Furthermore, depending too heavily on one or two key sellers for specialized skills can create vulnerabilities if those individuals leave or become unavailable. To safeguard your customers' experience and maintain resilience, it's essential to take deliberate steps to build a team that is versatile and well-rounded.

In any high-performing sales organization, individual sellers carve out their own paths to success by aligning their unique strengths and past experiences with the company's broader sales strategy. One seller might shine in cultivating long-term client relationships, while another thrives by perfecting technical product demonstrations or analyzing data. These distinct approaches offer competitive advantages and contribute to a dynamic, well-balanced team.

A critical aspect of leading a sales team is fostering continuous growth. This involves creating tailored development plans that help sellers strengthen their current capabilities while expanding into new areas. Cross-training programs are particularly effective, as they expose team members to different aspects of the sales process, encouraging empathy and collaboration. A culture of shared learning amplifies this effort. Regular knowledge-sharing sessions allow sellers to exchange insights, blending their specialized expertise with the collective knowledge of the team. When leaders actively recognize and reward individuals who embrace new challenges, it reinforces the idea that growth is a priority and a core value.

Still, the diversity of skills and approaches within a sales team presents a leadership challenge: How do you leverage these strengths while encouraging broader growth? The goal isn't to make everyone sell the same way but rather to create an environment where each seller expands their capabilities, becoming more adaptable and well-equipped for any scenario.

THE TRUTH ABOUT FRAMEWORKS

Sales professionals can no longer rely solely on traditional relationship-building and transactional selling. The most successful GTM teams adopt a comprehensive approach, combining sales acumen with core product marketing skills to deliver highly customized, client-centric solutions. This integration is not just an advantage; it is essential for fostering meaningful engagements with executive stakeholders.

To excel in this environment, sales professionals must thoroughly understand their products' unique differentiators and competitive strengths. But it's the ability to translate these differentiators into meaningful, client-specific benefits that really distinguishes elite sales teams. By aligning value propositions with the specific needs and priorities of each client, these sales professionals position themselves as trusted advisors, rather than merely vendors.

A structured approach to client engagement is crucial. Client-facing frameworks offer a disciplined methodology to validate strategic direction, align proposals with business goals, and refine solutions based on real-time feedback. However, these frameworks are only effective when sales teams are proficient in tools like Excel and PowerPoint. Without these skills, they may struggle to rapidly analyze data, adjust insights, and craft compelling presentations that resonate with decision-makers. Maintaining fluency in these tools enables sales professionals to respond dynamically to client needs, fostering more impactful discussions.

Beyond technical proficiency, the art of consultative selling requires adaptability. Sales teams must not only understand and apply client-facing frameworks but also personalize them to reflect the unique challenges and strategic objectives of each business. Every engagement should be a two-way dialogue, where sales professionals listen intently, adapt their messaging, and continuously refine their approach to align with the client's evolving landscape.

Collaboration between sales and product marketing teams is crucial in this process. Regular knowledge-sharing sessions facilitate cross-functional learning, equipping sales teams with the latest insights on messaging frameworks, competitive positioning, and best practices for client engagement. By working together, these teams ensure that sales professionals have the most relevant, impactful content—enabling them to present their value propositions with clarity and confidence.

The work doesn't end once a client meeting wraps up. Post-meeting adjustments are vital for maintaining momentum and refining proposals based on your client's feedback. Sales professionals should actively integrate client insights into their presentations, showcasing an agile, responsive approach that fosters trust and collaboration. This iterative refinement ensures that proposals stay relevant, compelling, and aligned with the client's strategic vision.

Ultimately, achieving success in modern sales requires a consultative and strategic approach that integrates sales expertise with product marketing intelligence. By utilizing structured client engagement frameworks, encouraging cross-functional collaboration, and continuously refining proposals, sales professionals can cultivate deeper connections with executive stakeholders and drive sustained business growth. Adopting this methodology will not only boost your sales effectiveness but also enhance client relationships, helping you stand out in the market and accelerate revenue growth in an increasingly competitive environment.

BUILDING GLOBAL BEST PRACTICES

Companies with diverse and highly skilled sales teams—chock full of executive sponsors, industry principals, sales professionals, solutions consultants, business value advisors, professional services, subject matter experts, technical experts, and field CTOs—hold a wealth of internal expertise. However, the immense value generated by these experts often remains siloed, making it difficult to distribute their assets across a global sales force. This section outlines a strategic approach to unlock and share that wealth of knowledge, ensuring your sales teams are equipped to engage executives with confidence and precision.

Much like the content library covered earlier, this strategy leverages a centralized knowledge hub—a veritable oracle where all customer-facing content resides. This platform, integrated seamlessly with your existing CRM systems and collaboration tools, will equip sales teams with immediate access to the latest resources. AI-driven search capabilities and metadata tagging will ensure content is easily discoverable by industry, solution, or customer persona. By maintaining strict version control and approval workflows, your tech team can preserve the integrity of these priceless materials, guaranteeing that your sales professionals always operate with the most current and relevant content.

Your hub won't just document recommended sales practices. For example, curated playbooks and verticalized content are foundational assets. These playbooks, tailored to key industries such as Financial Services, Manufacturing, Healthcare, and Telecommunications, should include pitch decks, case studies, ROI calculators, and competitive differentiators. Solution kits, specifically designed around core offerings, will provide technical guides, demo scripts, and customer references. Additionally, persona-driven content will address the specific needs of executives like CIOs, CTOs, and CISOs, aligning with their unique pain points and strategic priorities.

Like any library, these resources don't do much good sitting on the shelf. Instead, use robust field enablement programs to translate them into real skills. Regular webinars featuring subject matter experts and solution architects can provide live training opportunities, while recorded sessions will build a comprehensive on-demand video library for later review. A structured learning management system (LMS) will deliver role-specific learning paths, allowing (for instance) account executives, solutions consultants, and technical specialists to enhance their skills through curated certification programs. This continuous learning environment will not only develop expertise but also normalize a culture of knowledge sharing.

To ensure alignment with executive priorities, use your hub to collate and distribute quarterly executive briefing kits, delivering insights into recent industry trends, customer success stories, and product updates. Of course, your team can customize these materials to reflect their contacts' unique concerns and objectives, positioning your firm's solutions as direct answers to your clients' challenges. Regular competitive intelligence updates will further arm your sales professionals with the knowledge needed to differentiate their offerings.

To stress the value of field-driven insights, encourage your GTM teams to contribute content to this archive. Individual sales teams, for example, can submit successful assets and share best practices, while regional and vertical-specific content committees can identify gaps and co-create materials with your marketing and product teams. The possibilities are endless: Internal communities of practice enable field teams to swap insights and seek advice from their peers, executive circles facilitate high-level discussions and strategy exchanges among senior sales leaders, and innovation labs provide a sandbox for experimenting with new engagement tactics. Whatever form it takes, this collaborative approach ensures that the repository remains dynamic and continuously evolves to meet your firm's needs.

Finally, to drive engagement and adoption, consider adding gamification and formal recognition. Leaderboards and reward systems can track content usage and contributions, providing incentives for active participation. By appointing content champions and recognizing top contributors, you communicate that sharing expertise is not only beneficial but rewarded. By working with and for one another, your team can unlock the full potential of their internal expertise.

DEVELOP COMPLETE BUSINESS STRATEGY

When initially engaging executives, it's essential to present a comprehensive business strategy that you can collaboratively refine. Start with an executive summary that quantifies the business impact your solution will deliver, highlighting the four most significant areas of improvement. To pinpoint these opportunities, an **industry business assessment comparison** can be very useful. From there, propose a detailed implementation plan that **aligns with your client's strategic priorities**. Explain how you will create incremental value for **each of their strategic priorities** throughout each phase of your proposed implementation. But here's the kicker: This complete business strategy should be prepared *before* your initial meeting with the prospect, without leaning on hours and hours of discovery meetings.

A COMPLETE BUSINESS STRATEGY

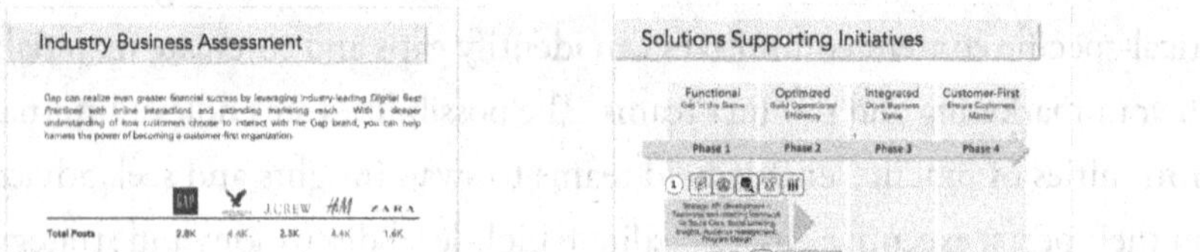

Diagram 7.3 Arrive with a Point of View

STRATEGIC ACCOUNT ENGAGEMENT

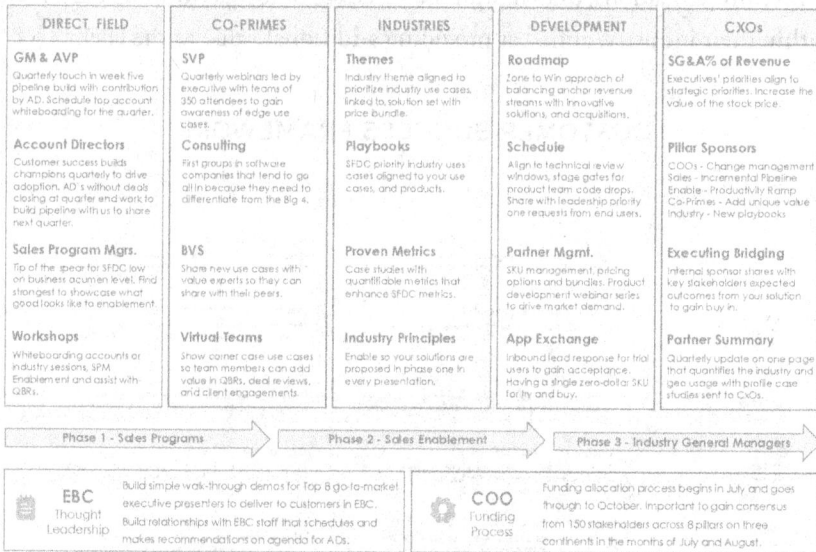

The visual approach shown in Diagram 7.4 engaged a large organization, spread across six distinct groups, to secure funding for a multimillion-dollar transaction. For deals like this, you must first understand how each group collaborates to add value. By leveraging their influence, you can then effectively cascade your sales frameworks and value messages up the four levels of the operating unit. This process influences multiple COOs to increase their annual investment in your solution offerings. It aligns you as a strategic partner, a role that materializes when your customer leadership presents to their customers at executive briefing center sessions.

STRATEGIC ACCOUNT ENGAGEMENT

DIRECT FIELD	CO-PRIMES	INDUSTRIES	DEVELOPMENT	CXOs
GM & AVP Quarterly touch in week five pipeline build with contribution by AD. Schedule top account whiteboarding for the quarter.	**SVP** Quarterly webinars led by executive with teams of 350 attendees to gain awareness of edge use cases.	**Themes** Industry theme aligned to prioritize industry use cases linked to solution set with price bundle.	**Roadmap** Zone to Win approach of balancing anchor revenue streams with innovative solutions, and acquisitions.	**SG&A% of Revenue** Executives' priorities align to strategic priorities. Increase the value of the stock price.
Account Directors Customer success builds champions quarterly to drive adoption. AD's without deals closing at quarter end work to build pipeline with us to share next quarter.	**Consulting** First groups in software companies that tend to go all in because they need to differentiate from the Big 4.	**Playbooks** SFDC priority industry use cases aligned to your use cases, and products.	**Schedule** Align to technical review windows, stage gates for product team code drops. Share with leadership priority one requests from end users.	**Pillar Sponsors** COOs - Change management Sales - Incremental Pipeline Enable - Productivity Ramp Co-Primes - Add unique value Industry - New playbooks
Sales Program Mgrs. Tip of the spear for SFDC low on business acumen level. Find strongest to showcase what good looks like to enablement.	**BVS** Share new use cases with value experts so they can share with their peers.	**Proven Metrics** Case studies with quantifiable metrics that enhance SFDC metrics.	**Partner Mgmt.** SKU management, pricing options and bundles. Product development webinar series to drive market demand.	**Executing Bridging** Internal sponsor shares with key stakeholders expected outcomes from your solution to gain buy in.
Workshops Whiteboarding accounts or industry sessions, SPM Enablement and assist with QBRs.	**Virtual Teams** Show corner case use cases so team members can add value in QBRs, deal reviews, and client engagements.	**Industry Principles** Enable so your solutions are proposed in phase one in every presentation.	**App Exchange** Inbound lead response for trial users to gain acceptance. Having a single zero-dollar SKU for try and buy.	**Partner Summary** Quarterly update on one page that quantifies the industry and geo usage with profile case studies sent to CXOs.

Phase 1 - Sales Programs	Phase 2 - Sales Enablement	Phase 3 - Industry General Managers

EBC Thought Leadership	Build simple walk-through demos for Top 8 go-to-market executive presenters to deliver to customers in EBC. Build relationships with EBC staff that schedules and makes recommendations on agenda for ADs.	COO Funding Process	Funding allocation process begins in July and goes through to October. Important to gain consensus from 150 stakeholders across 8 pillars on three continents in the months of July and August.

Diagram 7.4 Manage Your Value Message Within an Account

So do your GTM teams have a system to manage and demonstrate the impact of your solutions across twenty-four groups within strategic accounts? Can they update each one of those groups on a monthly basis, to ensure sustained engagement and value realization? Do your account teams manage a quarterly engagement cadence to provide personal readouts to each of these groups to create the necessary moment with structured sales frameworks?

CLIENT SUCCESS FRAMEWORK

Once you have secured a global account, concentrate on delivering ongoing value. During quarterly business reviews, it's essential to have a client VP outline the company's business strategy for the next two quarters. This fundamentally transforms the client interaction, fostering greater collaboration and the exchange of ideas at a strategic level reserved for partners. In the diagram below, the first column lists seven distinct work streams to manage throughout the month. The second column categorizes each stream, while the third column details the client's forward-looking strategy. The fourth column features our recommendations, drawn from the successes of top-performing customers within their industry, aimed at providing additional value to the client.

CUSTOMER SUCCESS FRAMEWORK

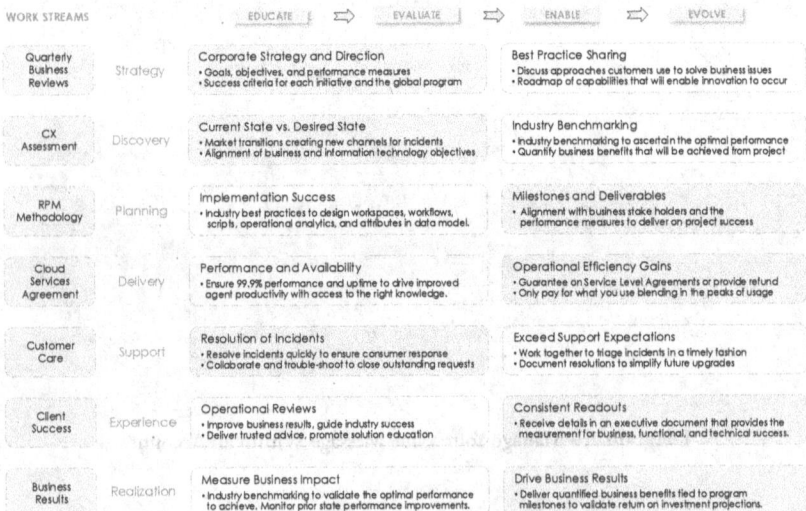

WORK STREAMS		EDUCATE ⇒ EVALUATE	ENABLE ⇒ EVOLVE
Quarterly Business Reviews	Strategy	**Corporate Strategy and Direction** • Goals, objectives, and performance measures • Success criteria for each initiative and the global program	**Best Practice Sharing** • Discuss approaches customers use to solve business issues • Roadmap of capabilities that will enable innovation to occur
CX Assessment	Discovery	**Current State vs. Desired State** • Market transitions creating new channels for incidents • Alignment of business and information technology objectives	**Industry Benchmarking** • Industry benchmarking to ascertain the optimal performance • Quantify business benefits that will be achieved from project
RPM Methodology	Planning	**Implementation Success** • Industry best practices to design workspaces, workflows, scripts, operational analytics, and attributes in data model.	**Milestones and Deliverables** • Alignment with business stake holders and the performance measures to deliver on project success
Cloud Services Agreement	Delivery	**Performance and Availability** • Ensure 99.9% performance and uptime to drive improved agent productivity with access to the right knowledge.	**Operational Efficiency Gains** • Guarantee on Service Level Agreements or provide refund • Only pay for what you use blending in the peaks of usage
Customer Care	Support	**Resolution of Incidents** • Resolve incidents quickly to ensure consumer response • Collaborate and trouble-shoot to close outstanding requests	**Exceed Support Expectations** • Work together to triage incidents in a timely fashion • Document resolutions to simplify future upgrades
Client Success	Experience	**Operational Reviews** • Improve business results, guide industry success • Deliver trusted advice, promote solution education	**Consistent Readouts** • Receive details in an executive document that provides the measurement for business, functional, and technical success.
Business Results	Realization	**Measure Business Impact** • Industry benchmarking to validate the optimal performance to achieve. Monitor prior state performance improvements.	**Drive Business Results** • Deliver quantified business benefits tied to program milestones to validate return on investment projections.

Diagram 7.5 Strategic Account Management

Applying a structured and evidence-based approach to engage with your strategic partners on a quarterly basis is essential. By gaining insight into their priorities and strategic goals for the next two quarters, you can position yourself to address their most pressing challenges and provide tailored support to achieve their objectives. This process enables you to exchange actionable insights and maintain a clear focus on driving the outcomes that matter most to your customer. Collaboratively outlining key milestones for the months ahead creates a shared roadmap for success. Establishing biweekly office hours ensures consistent communication, fosters transparency, and uncovers new opportunities. For instance, regularly presenting strategies to enhance operational efficiency can help optimize your client's current systems, delivering measurable progress over time.

Sales professionals who implement client success frameworks are uniquely positioned to unlock additional value with their customers, even those who initially intended to make a single purchase. A critical factor here is the principle of reciprocity—a deeply ingrained human tendency to respond in kind when someone offers value or support, even without being asked. By consistently demonstrating proactive efforts to benefit your customer, you naturally encourage a reciprocal response. This dynamic can foster deeper trust and collaboration, often leading to expanded opportunities and long-term partnerships.*

FRAMEWORK THEORY

Reduce new hire ramp time by sharing with sales what good executive deliverables look like. The goal is you want to become the customer proposal team during your evaluations to create an unfair advantage.

Why change?

Challenge:	How do we gain executive mindshare when they don't know us? How do teams drive CEO engagements with the same deliverables? Do we have a library of frameworks that have worked previously?

* *Influence*, Robert Cialdini

How do we differentiate?

Concept 25:	**Create a Flywheel of Interest** by establishing a cycle of ongoing interest by consistently delivering value, fostering trust, and using achievements to encourage deeper involvement. Profile peers that are employing comparable tactics to maintain their edge. Facilitate connections among executives to exchange trends and insights.
Concept 26:	**Simplify the Complex** is understanding the root cause of the business challenge by viewing the overall situation. Present the most straightforward solution in a concise written summary. Can you describe it in one sentence?
Concept 27:	**Situation Awareness** involves understanding, interpreting, and predicting events and trends that might influence strategic actions. Recognize when to apply suitable frameworks to proactively handle potential challenges and explore areas for further collaboration.
Concept 28:	**Personalize Your Blueprint** for achievement is crucial since each person's strengths, aspirations, situations, and interpretations of success vary. Customizing your strategy enables you to utilize your distinctive abilities, and consider your personal growth plan.

What do we receive?

Result:	Hyperscale revenue results leveraging proven executive deliverables. Provide CEO frameworks to **reduce new hire ramp time −41%**. Deliver complete business strategies documented to secure funding.

TIPS AND TRICKS FOR FRAMEWORKS

- Modern sales professionals must transcend traditional relationship-building and transactional selling. The most effective GTM teams **blend sales expertise with foundational product marketing skills**. This fusion is crucial for customizing frameworks, tailoring content to each client, and dynamically adjusting strategies based on real-time feedback. In other words, your sales teams must both understand your products' unique differentiators and competitive advantages *and* translate these differentiators into meaningful, client-specific benefits that resonate with executive stakeholders.

- Client-facing frameworks are essential for aligning with client goals, validating direction, and refining proposed strategies. Sales teams should not only understand these frameworks but also personalize and adapt them to reflect the unique needs of each client. This ensures alignment with the client's evolving strategy and objectives.
- Regular collaborative sessions between product marketing and sales teams foster cross-functional knowledge sharing. These sessions equip sales professionals with **deeper insights into messaging frameworks**, positioning strategies, and client engagement best practices. However, without proficiency in tools like Excel and PowerPoint, sales teams may struggle to execute these adjustments swiftly and effectively. This gap can impede their ability to consistently create value for executive-level clients.
- Specifically, sales professionals must be adept at using Excel to analyze data, build dynamic financial models, and quantify ROI for clients. By showcasing tangible value through customized spreadsheets, sales teams can reinforce product benefits with data-driven insights.
- The ability to craft compelling, client-specific presentations is likewise crucial. Beyond basic slide creation, sales professionals should be trained in **visual storytelling**, leveraging PowerPoint to illustrate narratives that align with the client's strategic objectives.
- Practical, hands-on workshops focusing on Excel and PowerPoint skills can empower sales teams to master the tools necessary for personalization and strategy refinement. Micro-learning modules further reinforce these skills in bite-sized, easily digestible formats. Simulated client meetings and role-playing exercises allow sales professionals to practice adapting frameworks and presentations based on real-time feedback. This experiential learning approach enhances confidence and adaptability.

- Post-meeting adjustments are critical for maintaining momentum and refining proposals. Sales professionals should regularly incorporate client feedback into presentations, fostering a collaborative approach that continuously evolves alongside client needs.

FRAMEWORKS WORKBOOK
SCALE EXECUTIVE ENGAGEMENT

Frameworks

126 GLOBAL SALES BEST PRACTICES	Catalog and share best practices from proven wins • Content required to drive acceleration with executives
127 COMPLETE BUSINESS STRATEGY	Provide all the required components for executive decisions • Anticipate needs by solving upcoming business challenges
128 STRATEGIC ACCOUNT ENGAGEMENT	Engagement pillars with unique messaging by level • Phases to drive influence with an enterprise account
129 CLIENT ENABLEMENT FRAMEWORK	Collaboration framework to enable success • Client shares executive project priorities and you recommend best practices

Framework Sales Plays

130 CONSISTENCY	Standardized engagement approaches with seller nuances • Exponential measurable engagement best practices
131 RAMP TIME	• Become an expert on your customer's business model while you're coming up to speed on your solutions

132 SCALABLE	Frameworks allow you to scale within enterprise accounts • Reusable executive content to initiate compelling conversations
133 PRODUCTIVITY	Make the best use of seller's time by providing real-world examples • Frameworks provide 85% of what a seller needs to engage
134 OPTIMIZATION	Focus on business process improvement and optimization • Leverage data-driven insights from customer deployments
135 INTERLEAVING TASKS	Frameworks provide examples to program manage content contributors • GTM teams have very different priorities
136 REPEATABLE	Successful customer engagements determine repeatable success • Leverage content from significant transactions
137 ADAPTABLE	Every seller needs the ability to make frameworks adaptable to what they sell • Each seller creates their own tool kit of asset types
138 COACHING	Framework as the clearer example of coaching acumen • Executives do not attend meetings without agenda and content provided to
139 PERVASIVE	Reusable ease of use the best way to elevate acumen to be pervasive • Leading with best practice to be compelling with executives
140 CONTINUOUS	Ongoing value delivery requires implementation success • Value realization to measure process improvement
141 BLUEPRINT	Enable every GTM team member to create their own blueprint • Everyone has their own creative style to selling

Diagram 7.6 How Frameworks Empower Executives to Communicate Your Message

EVERYDAY APPLICATIONS

Organizations that rapidly deliver tailored solutions to their clients not only secure a strategic advantage but also cultivate deeper, more enduring relationships. One critical, yet often neglected, aspect of this process is empowering sales professionals to take ownership of customizing and adapting sales frameworks. By giving sales teams the skills and tools to edit and simplify these documents directly, companies can eliminate unnecessary layers of complexity, fostering quicker decision-making and more effective engagement with executives.

Executives are perpetually inundated with information and must navigate through myriad reports, presentations, and data points to make informed decisions. In this maelstrom of information, presenting clear, concise, and relevant insights is crucial. However, relying on virtual or external resources to customize or even access frameworks squanders valuable time—and misses the opportunity to create additional value. By empowering your sales professionals to manage these tasks independently, you can streamline processes, enhance agility, and significantly accelerate outcomes.

At the heart of this empowerment is key productivity tools such as Microsoft Excel and PowerPoint. Building these skills enables sales professionals to edit financial models, craft compelling presentations, and distill complex information into digestible formats that resonate with executive audiences. When sales professionals can adjust documents in real-time, they can respond dynamically to evolving customer needs, cultivating a more responsive and adaptable organization.

Faster turnaround times for customized solutions lead to increased efficiency and a more proactive sales force. Executives receive more targeted, relevant content that directly addresses their concerns, boosting the likelihood of gaining buy-in and advancing sales opportunities. Additionally, when sales teams are responsible for customizing their own materials, their messaging remains consistent and closely aligned with the insights they have gathered from direct customer interactions.

To achieve these benefits, adopt a structured approach to skill development. Training programs focused on Excel and PowerPoint fundamentals provide a robust foundation, while practical exercises grounded in real-world sales scenarios reinforce learning. Supplementing these efforts with hands-on resource development—such as templates and guides—further simplifies the process of framework customization. Continuous learning opportunities, including workshops and online courses, ensure that sales teams stay current and capable of leveraging the latest tools effectively. Leadership must advocate for these initiatives, emphasizing their importance and fostering a culture that values self-sufficiency and innovation within the sales organization.

Ultimately, empowering sales professionals to edit and simplify frameworks independently is a strategic investment that drives tangible results. By removing barriers, enhancing communication, and accelerating the delivery of customer value, organizations position themselves for sustained growth and success. In a world where speed and precision are critical, this proactive approach to sales empowerment can make all the difference.

FRAMEWORKS KEY TAKEAWAYS

1. How many of your GTM team members have worked for Accenture or McKinsey?

   Create executive deliverables to enable indirect selling and reduce sales cycles.

2. Can your team simplify their message to engage executives in a compelling way?

   Frameworks condense everything an executive needs on one page to make a decision.

3. Have your Diamond Teams created thirty frameworks for global sales to modify?

   Strategy consulting best practices are required to enable change management.

4. How does each seller craft their own personalized frameworks to achieve their success?

Program management skills are missing and required to engage at an elite level.

5. Do you have a systematic way to capture success and share with your field sales force?

Hyperscale global sales best practices to guarantee revenue performance.

6. Can your teams deliver predictable revenue results quarterly?

Outpace revenue targets with consistent monthly linearity closing 50 percent in the first two months.

7. Do you have a process to up level the business acumen of GTM team members?

Document how your elite team members leverage executive presence to scale engagement.

8. Can you reduce ramp time of new hires by four months by enabling executive engagement?

Reduce new hire ramp time 41 percent to accelerate revenue contribution in the first two quarters.

SUMMARY

Orchestrating customer value creation necessitates frameworks to initiate new executive engagements and continually personalize them over time. These client-facing frameworks are crucial for aligning with client goals, validating direction, and refining proposed strategies to enable consultative strategic selling. The essence lies in how these frameworks are tailored to capture the executive's strategic direction, ensuring alignment.

The most valuable client feedback emerges in the field during competitive evaluations. In these high-stakes situations, potential customers rigorously assess various solutions, providing candid insights into their expectations and concerns. Their unfiltered perspectives often stand in stark contrast to the more tempered feedback from long-standing customers who visit your corporate office periodically. To drive meaningful enhancements, you must seek out customers willing to challenge your solutions. These individuals offer constructive criticism that reveals hidden gaps and unmet needs. Sales frameworks serve as an effective method to expedite this feedback process. Embracing this feedback unlocks opportunities for growth, refining offerings to better meet evolving market demands.

Harnessing customer feedback requires a proactive and structured approach. Engaging with a diverse array of stakeholders, as illustrated in Diagram 7.5, ensures a rich variety of perspectives, while fostering open channels of communication encourages honest and transparent dialogue. Providing swift feedback to your product management teams keeps them informed of requirements, strengthening the relationships you aim to build. Embedding a culture of continuous improvement positions an organization to remain competitive and responsive in a rapidly changing landscape.

Ultimately, the true value of customer feedback lies in its potential to drive innovation and long-term success. By listening not only to voices that affirm but also to those that challenge, you can shape more impactful, customer-centric strategies. This approach propels your business to take a leadership role in each industry segment, one step at a time.

NARRATIVES

Cascade Differentiation

(Increase Sales Participation by 37 Percent)

CHAPTER 8

> **SHAPING CEO CONVERSATIONS:** Sent to Who You Sound Like

> **SAILING THE SEVEN C'S:** Guardrails to Define Your Style

> **PATTERN MATCHING:** Rule of Three

> **COMPETITIVE BENCHMARKING:** Outperforming Peer Group

> **THE TRUTH ABOUT NARRATIVES:** Focus on the Customer Needs

> **THE PROBLEM-SOLUTION APPROACH:** Cost of Inaction

> **STORYTELLING WITH IMPACT:** Real-World Scenario

> **A VISIONARY APPROACH:** Big Picture Strategy

> **HANDLING CEO REFERRALS:** Identify the Problem-Solver

> **NARRATIVE THEORY:** Improve Sales Participation 37 Percent

> **TIPS AND TRICKS:** Accelerate Executive Engagement

> **NARRATIVES WORKBOOK:** Arrive as the Expert

> **EVERYDAY APPLICATIONS:** Play the Infinite Game

> **KEY TAKEAWAYS:** Expected Outcomes Drive Feedback

> **SUMMARY:** Cascade Differentiation

> **DEFINE FRAMEWORK:** Product Marketing in the Field

SHAPING CEO CONVERSATIONS

Effectively engaging CEOs requires precision and strategic clarity, especially in writing. CEOs work in fast-paced environments and make high-level decisions for their firms—so any narrative worth their time must deliver concise, impactful insights. The challenge is to condense complex information into compelling formats that align with the company's broader goals. To master that process, you must first understand the purpose of different narrative forms in this engagement process.

First and foremost, **executive summaries** are critical for decision-making, offering concise overviews that present the *bottom line up front* (BLUF). These summaries prioritize brevity and clarity, distilling essential insights and next steps into a format that CEOs can read and understand in a few minutes. Keep the tone direct and action-oriented, to help streamline the decision-making process.

For CEOs needing more analytical engagement, **data-driven reports** provide the necessary depth. These reports complement visual representations with narrative summaries, emphasizing key performance indicators and return on investment. An objective tone keeps the focus on your data-backed insights, enabling informed evaluation of trends and performance.

Keeping CEOs informed of emerging industry shifts requires **trend analyses**. These forward-looking narratives offer high-level overviews of relevant trends, assessing the associated risks and opportunities. By incorporating competitive landscape evaluations, such analyses provide the strategic foresight needed to maintain a competitive edge.

Scenario-planning narratives are especially crucial in risk management. By outlining plausible future scenarios and their potential impacts, these documents equip CEOs to anticipate challenges and prepare mitigation strategies. Their balanced, analytical tone fosters confidence in navigating uncertain futures.

When your goal is to inspire and align the CEO with a vision, **narrative briefs** become essential. Using storytelling approaches, these briefs tie success stories or case studies directly to organizational goals, presenting a persuasive and motivational call to action. A conversational yet inspirational style not only fosters engagement but also reinforces long-term strategic alignment.

Whatever the genre, building successful narratives starts with understanding your audience. Use their priorities to **structure** your messages, **simplify** complex data with visual aids, then **summarize** the key points and action items at the end of the document. This is not just courteous communication but a strategic imperative—by tailoring content to the CEO's perspective and focusing on high-impact insights, you can drive favorable decision-making, foster strategic alignment, and enhance executive engagement.

SAILING THE SEVEN C'S

To craft strategic and thoughtful communication, apply the Seven C's of Communication—guiding principles that bolster your message and build the trust and credibility you need for meaningful relationships.

Clarity is paramount when addressing CEOs. Their time is incredibly valuable, and any ambiguity can lead to misinterpretations or even missed opportunities. Crafting clear and straightforward messages, free of unnecessary jargon or complexity, allows your core ideas to shine. When communication is transparent and logical, CEOs can quickly grasp the essence, enabling informed decisions without unnecessary back-and-forth.

Equally important is **conciseness**. CEOs must process a lot of information, so make your case efficiently. Distilling messages to their most vital insights shows respect for their time and attention. A concise, well-structured message commands focus, reflecting both confidence and expertise.

Correctness underpins all forms of communication with CEOs. Inaccuracies, whether in data, language, or presentation, can erode their trust and damage your reputation. Every element of your message must be factually accurate and grammatically sound, signaling seriousness and professionalism. CEOs expect nothing less.

Completeness is another vital aspect, as CEOs require comprehensive insights to make informed decisions. Omitting key information can mislead them, even inadvertently, about your value and its alignment. A complete message addresses all pertinent aspects of the case, offering a holistic view that enables CEOs to assess the full picture. This thoroughness reflects diligence and attention to detail, qualities that resonate with senior leaders.

Courtesy plays a crucial role in establishing and maintaining positive rapport. CEOs appreciate respectful and considerate communication that acknowledges their position and time constraints. Politeness, empathy, and a tone that aligns with their priorities can foster goodwill and strengthen relationships. Courtesy also reflects an understanding of the CEO's perspective, reinforcing the value of mutual respect.

Concreteness bridges the gap between abstract ideas and actionable outcomes. By grounding communication in specific data, examples, and real-world references, your message gains weight and credibility. Vague statements seldom inspire confidence, whereas concrete facts and figures provide a solid foundation grounded in reality.

Finally, **consideration** ties all these elements together by focusing on the CEO's unique perspective. Tailoring your communication to align with their strategic vision, operational challenges, and leadership style ensures greater receptivity. This effort demonstrates empathy and foresight, both essential for fostering collaboration and trust.

PATTERN MATCHING

Effective messages not only communicate but resonate, even long after you've left the figurative stage. To avoid losing your audience halfway through, condense your message into three simple, yet powerful ideas. This is the magic of the Rule of Three—a principle that has shaped rhetoric, storytelling, marketing, and even the way we communicate daily.

The Rule of Three isn't just a stylistic choice; it's deeply ingrained in the way our brains process information. Our minds crave patterns, and three is the smallest number of elements that can form a complete and satisfying structure. A single point feels incomplete, two can create a sense of conflict, but the third provides resolution. It's this natural rhythm that makes triads memorable and compelling.

Can you imagine Julius Caesar stopping after "I came, I saw," the Declaration of Independence merely promising "life and liberty," or Abraham Lincoln musing on "government of the people and by the people"? And where would poor Goldilocks be if she couldn't find the porridge that was just right? The Rule of Three gives your message a narrative arc—beginning, middle, and end—that ensures a coherent and satisfying journey.

Marketers understand this power well, especially when it comes to catchy slogans. "Just Do It." "Finger-Lickin' Good." "The Few. The Proud. The Marines." These succinct phrases, each composed of three key elements, linger in our collective memory long after the advertisement fades. They work because the Rule of Three sharpens communication and enhances persuasion, distilling complex ideas into three main points that drive decisions and inspire action.

So, how can you apply the Rule of Three in your own communication? I'm sure you've guessed that there are three steps! Start by breaking down your message until three core ideas emerge. Next, organize them in a logical progression, guiding your audience step-by-step based on their priorities. Finally, reinforce these points through repetition, ensuring they leave a lasting impression.

The Rule of Three isn't just a technique—it's a gateway to more powerful, persuasive, and memorable communication. Whether you're telling a story, delivering a speech, or designing a brand, embracing the Rule of Three will ensure your message not only reaches your audience but stays with them long after the conversation ends.

COMPETITIVE BENCHMARKING

For CEOs, a competitor's rise to industry leadership is more than just a milestone—it's a wake-up call. This shift in competitive dynamics signals potential threats that can disrupt market share, stall growth, and impede long-term relevance. Ignoring these signals can lead to market erosion, operational inefficiencies, and a decline in investor confidence.

Capturing a larger market share typically requires superior products and services, based on unique technology. Customers, especially those drawn by innovation and value, naturally gravitate toward these leaders, leaving less proactive companies behind. The longer a CEO hesitates to respond, the more challenging it becomes to reclaim lost ground and retain loyal customers. This is not simply a game of cat and mouse; it is a race for professional survival. CEOs who recognize the risk of stagnation understand that the failure to innovate is akin to falling behind permanently.

Talent is another crucial resource here. Industry leaders become magnets for the best minds, offering a forward-thinking environment where growth and learning thrive. Companies that fail to lead struggle to attract and retain top-tier talent, falling further behind. The financial repercussions cannot be overstated. Because investors pay close attention to market trends and leadership shifts, a company that lags behind risks diminishing stock performance, crumbling investor trust, and reduced valuations. On the contrary, a CEO who responds decisively can reignite investor interest and bolster confidence through strategic realignment and bold initiatives. The market rewards companies that demonstrate resilience and proactive vision.

Beyond investors and talent, customer expectations evolve alongside industry advancements. Those who fail to meet these evolving demands risk losing their audience and their reputation, no matter how strong their product line is. In an age of instant feedback and rapid shifts in consumer loyalty, no organization can afford to ignore warning signals. That's where **competitive benchmarking** comes in—analyzing data that compares your client's performance against industry leaders. This process unveils critical areas for growth and highlights achievable goals that can restore competitiveness.

Understanding the voice of the customer through market research can shed light on why their competitors have gained ground, providing insights that inform strategic pivots.

Case studies also serve as powerful reminders of the cost of inaction. The corporate landscape is littered with examples of once-dominant companies that ignored competitive threats (or worse, overlooked opportunities) and ultimately faded into irrelevance. Balance these warnings by showcasing organizations that embraced change and thrived, offering both reassurance and proof of the transformative power of strategic shifts.

A **visionary roadmap** acts as the guiding light for the organization, outlining key milestones and innovative projects. CEOs who clearly articulate their vision foster alignment and enthusiasm, rallying their teams around a shared future. This alignment becomes the foundation for collective success, ensuring that every level of the organization is engaged in the pursuit of renewed leadership.

In a market red in tooth and claw, responding proactively to the emergence of new industry leaders is imperative for survival and growth. CEOs who embrace innovation, adaptability, and strategic change will not only close competitive gaps but often surpass their rivals. No matter the field, urgency, vision, and decisive leadership separate the leaders of the pack from those left behind to rot.

THE TRUTH ABOUT NARRATIVES

CEOs operate in a high-pressure, fast-paced environment where time is their most valuable resource. They are inundated with information daily, so any written communication must be concise, solution-oriented, and strategically insightful. A well-crafted narrative can capture their attention, drive decision-making, and influence business outcomes.

A CEO's focus is always on high-impact issues. Therefore, your communication should frame the conversation around solving urgent business challenges. Define the problem clearly, align it with industry trends, and highlight the risks of inaction. Use data-driven insights to support your points, ensuring readers see the financial and operational implications. Most importantly, present a clear solution—CEOs do not want problems without a proposed course of action.

Sharing compelling facts and figures is helpful, but stories make them unforgettable. Craft a narrative that demonstrates a real-world challenge and how your proposed approach can resolve it. Use relatable business outcomes, a clear structure, and straightforward language to enhance clarity. Avoid unnecessary jargon—simplicity and precision are essential.

Take a visionary approach: Executives are forward-thinkers, always looking for competitive advantages and long-term growth. Link your message with strategic initiatives such as digital transformation, market expansion, or operational efficiency. Highlight emerging trends and innovations that justify immediate action. A well-articulated vision, especially one emphasizing scalability and ROI, will resonate deeply.

Handle C-suite referrals with precision. When an executive directs you to another executive, it's a test of your execution skills. Acknowledge the referral swiftly and follow up with diligence. Keep the C-suite informed about key milestones and decisions but avoid overwhelming them with details. Re-engage them as needed to ensure alignment on critical decisions. Managing their referrals with professionalism and accountability builds trust.

Provide guidance every six weeks, with regular updates to demonstrate progress and maintain engagement. Executives need structured, high-level insights, not extensive reports. Focus on key achievements, roadblocks, and next steps. Utilize measurable KPIs and highlight business impact. Proactively address challenges, showing foresight and adaptability in execution.

Understand that executives are inherently analytical and naturally inclined to inspect. Expect rigorous scrutiny of your proposals, including some tough questions, and be prepared with data-backed responses. Confidence and clarity are essential; ambiguity will weaken your credibility. That includes clarity about project execution—present a clear plan, timeline, and expected results. Most importantly, show tangible ROI—whether in revenue growth, cost reduction, or efficiency improvements.

Engaging C-suite audiences effectively requires a strategic and structured approach. A well-crafted written narrative must be precise, relevant, and solutions focused. By framing discussions around business challenges, telling compelling stories, and maintaining a visionary outlook, you can capture their attention and drive meaningful decisions. Executives expect insights, efficiency, and impact—so ensure that every word delivers value.

THE PROBLEM-SOLUTION APPROACH

CEOs face a variety of challenges that demand quick responses and strategic pivots to secure (or regain) industry dominance. The key to prompting executive action is **articulating the urgency** of an issue, quantifying the **consequences of inaction**, and presenting **clear, actionable** solutions that integrate seamlessly with the company's long-term objectives.

To address a problem, you must first articulate its root cause. Whether it arises from operational inefficiencies, revenue leakage, or competitive pressures, simply stating that a problem exists is insufficient. Likewise, your narrative must demonstrate how the problem directly impacts growth, disrupts operations, or threatens market standing. Grounding your analysis in concrete data—percentages, cost implications, and measurable impacts—reinforces the seriousness of the situation and ensures the challenge is taken seriously.

However, recognizing urgency is just the beginning. Because CEOs steer organizations toward long-term growth and sustainability, you must highlight the cost of inaction. The greatest enemy of every proposal is the status quo! Build a compelling case by forecasting potential losses in revenue, productivity disruptions, and competitive disadvantages. Executives need to visualize the cascading effects that could unfold if a challenge is left unaddressed, from financial repercussions to regulatory risks to reputational damage.

Now it's time to present your solution. Simplicity and clarity are key here: The C-suite values clear roadmaps with tangible results, not overly technical explanations. Your proposed solution must be scalable, actionable, and seamlessly integrated into existing frameworks. Emphasize benefits such as cost savings, enhanced operational efficiency, and increased market share to align your solution with their overarching business goals.

The final piece of this narrative ties the solution to the company's strategic objectives. CEOs are visionaries, and your proposed strategy must fit into that vision. Whether it positions the company for market leadership, strengthens innovation capabilities, or reinforces the brand's core mission, aligning the solution with strategic aspirations moves your proposal from catchy to compelling.

Ultimately, driving C-suite action hinges on crafting a story that underscores the urgency of the challenge while painting a clear path to resolution. Through a structured and persuasive narrative—one that methodically addresses the problem, quantifies the risks of inaction, and offers strategic, goal-aligned solutions—you empower your client executive team to make transformative decisions that not only address immediate concerns but also fortify their company's position in the marketplace.

STORYTELLING WITH IMPACT

CEOs are constantly bombarded with data, reports, and proposals. With so many competing priorities, getting your new business strategy noticed requires more than just six slides of statistics. What truly resonates is a personalized, engaging message, wrapped in real-world storytelling and supported by **clear evidence of broader business implications**.

Imagine a CEO receiving yet *another* email pitching a strategy to enhance their firm's operational efficiency through AI-driven analytics. Yawn. Now picture that same email, but instead of a sales pitch, it starts with a story about another company that was struggling to keep pace with market demands. Recognizing that their status quo was no longer an option, they implemented this very strategy. Within months, they achieved remarkable results—reducing costs, streamlining operations, and boosting productivity. Suddenly, the strategy isn't just theoretical—it's real, it's relatable, and it's proven to work.

CEOs operate under immense pressure, managing a delicate balance of risk and reward. A personalized narrative that speaks directly to their company's challenges and aspirations cuts through the noise, both by demonstrating an understanding of their unique situation and by creating a sense of urgency. This emotional connection makes the story stick, even if ten of your competitors offer a superficially similar solution.

But the story isn't just about one customer's success—it's about how their experience reflects a larger trend or industry shift. Perhaps it suggests a way to drive market leadership, unlock new revenue streams, or outpace competitors. After all, a business strategy is not about solving one problem; it's about transforming the organization on a larger scale. Alignment is critical here: CEOs are more likely to champion initiatives that seamlessly fit into their vision for the future. By framing the new strategy as a natural progression of their roadmap, your recommendation will feel less like a disruption and more like an opportunity waiting to be seized.

Of course, even the most compelling story needs data to anchor it—stories may capture our hearts, but data drives our decisions. CEOs need evidence to present to stakeholders and justify the investment: Complement the narrative with clear metrics and performance indicators, striking the perfect balance between inspiration and rational analysis. This will give your client the confidence that pursuing this strategy is not only exciting but also a sound business decision.

CEO STORYTELLING EMAIL

Subject: Vehicle Manufacture Best Practice

Hi John,

My team has identified an exciting partnership opportunity to invest in your company, drawing on the impactful projects we've successfully executed with Tesla, Volvo, Daimler, Ford, and Paccar. These initiatives have delivered each client a distinct and measurable competitive advantage. I'd like to propose that three of our vehicle manufacturing implementation experts present advanced use cases that enhance production line efficiencies. By predicting 34 percent of failures up to eight days in advance, we've saved an estimated 180,000 hours of downtime, equating to $8 million per part each month. In the spirit of collaboration, let's schedule an executive briefing with your team in the coming weeks, aligning with everyone's availability.

Warm regards,

Mimi

Diagram 8.0 Predicting Part Failures

In essence, the combination of **personalized messaging, relatable storytelling, broader strategic framing, and data-driven recommendations** creates a powerful case for action. By appealing to both the emotional and logical facets of decision-making, you boost your chances of CEO buy-in. In a landscape where attention is scarce and decisions are high stakes, mastering this form of communication is an essential driver of business success.

A VISIONARY APPROACH

CEOs' strategic responsibilities go beyond managing day-to-day operations; they must also clarify the company's vision, future-proof the business, and steer it toward long-term success. This is where **visionary proposals** come in. When aligned with strategic objectives, these forward-looking strategies enable organizations to lead markets, outpace competitors, and navigate future disruptions.

As we've seen, CEOs are drawn to initiatives that resonate with the broader company vision. A proposal that reflects and reinforces strategic goals is more than just an idea—it transforms into a necessity for growth. It speaks directly to the core of the leadership's agenda, addressing their desire for expansion, technological advancement, and operational efficiency.

In a world where industry shifts can redefine market leaders overnight, proactive innovation is non-negotiable. Visionary proposals should not only anticipate these shifts but position your client to capitalize on them, reinforcing their place at the forefront of industry developments. However, even bold ideas must balance risk and reward. CEOs understand that risk is part of innovation, but they are more inclined to act when those risks are calculated and controllable. Strategies that offer high potential rewards while mitigating potential downsides through phased implementation resonate deeply. They reflect thoughtful planning and a clear understanding of the business landscape.

CEO VISIONARY EMAIL

Subject: World-Class Customer Experience

Hi Robert,

Every consumer will soon have the ability to resolve their own service requests within minutes directly from their phone—this transformation is achievable in just five months. This approach, which has been effectively implemented for Comcast and Apple, positions you to move from number eight to number three in customer service rankings within the next ten months. By empowering consumers to access and verify solutions independently, data shows that 62 percent of customers prefer this method, leading to a substantial reduction in call center volume—108 million fewer calls annually—resulting in a cost savings of $823 million. I'd like to schedule a briefing with your executive team to outline the pathway to this transformation.

Warm regards,

Todd

Diagram 8.1 Customer Self-Service Cost Savings

Ultimately, the most effective proposals craft a narrative of innovation and resilience. They tell a story of a company that remains agile, adaptive, and prepared to lead in the face of market evolution. By presenting these visionary, data-driven, and strategically aligned proposals, leaders can inspire decisive action, fostering the growth and innovation that secures their place at the helm of tomorrow's industries.

HANDLING CEO REFERRALS

CEOs often serve as the gatekeepers of a firm's strategic priorities and long-term vision. When a sales professional reaches out with a promising business proposal, they might expect direct engagement from the CEO, but in most cases the CEO will refer such inquiries to one of their direct reports. This referral is rarely a dismissal—instead, it reflects a nuanced approach to organizational efficiency, leadership empowerment, and strategic alignment.

When a CEO passes a sales proposal to a direct report, such as a VP of sales, chief operating officer, or head of business development, they are ensuring that the opportunity is evaluated by the person best equipped to handle it. These professionals are typically closer to the operational aspects of vendor relationships and partnership opportunities. Their specialized expertise also allows them to assess the proposal with greater precision, ensuring the CEO's time is reserved for the highest-level decision-making.

By delegating such interactions, CEOs preserve their bandwidth while ensuring the proposal still receives the necessary consideration. This delegation is also a powerful tool for leadership development. By entrusting senior executives to evaluate potential partnerships, CEOs foster a culture of empowerment and accountability. This reinforces their trust in their teams and encourages direct reports to take ownership of business development efforts.

In many cases, a referral to a direct report also serves as a vetting mechanism. Even if the CEO finds your proposal intriguing, they may prefer to have a trusted executive review it first. This preliminary evaluation filters out less relevant opportunities while allowing promising proposals to rise to the surface. If the direct report finds significant value in the proposition, the CEO can re-engage at a later stage, armed with insights and validation from their team.

Finally, a CEO's direct involvement in a sales pitch can unintentionally signal a strong interest or premature commitment. By routing the conversation through a direct report, the CEO introduces a level of measured engagement that tempers expectations and ensures a more deliberate exploration process. This incremental approach prevents misunderstandings while allowing the company to assess the proposal at its own pace.

In fact, delegation enables the CEO to engage at pivotal moments rather than sitting through the initial discussions. This selective involvement marks the significance of the partnership for the firm, and signals to the sales professional that the proposal is progressing through the proper channels and being seriously considered. In short, a referral to a direct report indicates a thoughtful, strategic response rather than a brush-off. It reflects a commitment to operational efficiency, leadership development, and prudent decision-making. Treat it as an opportunity, not a demotion!

NARRATIVE THEORY

Craft tailored messages for each persona to clearly communicate your distinct advantages to important influencers. Has senior leadership been informed on the progression you're making with their team this month?

Why change?

Challenge:	Why are you relevant for an executive to engage with you at this time? Can your sellers condense their value down to a single page? Do you communicate your business value in just a few sentences?

How do we differentiate?

Concept 29:	**CEO Conversation** requires precision and strategic clarity. Making high-level decisions that demand narratives respecting their limited time while delivering impactful insights. Condense complex information that drives action, aligning with broader organizational objectives.

Concept 30:	**Seven C's of Communication** involve articulating the message clearly, using concise language, offering detailed information to prevent ambiguity, making the message easy to understand, and communicating with respect, empathy, and courtesy.
Concept 31:	**Pattern Matching** pinpoints the recurring trends observable in nearly every sales process. It involves anticipating needs and crafting a message that continues to resonate well beyond your departure from the executive meeting, effectively addressing the customer's business challenges.
Concept 32:	**CEO Referral** emphasizes the importance and urgency, indicating that it should be treated as a high priority. The direct report of the CEO feels assured in collaborating with you to speed up the process of assessing your solution.

What do we receive?

Result:	GTM Team members know how to create value for executives. Executive narratives **increase sales participation +37% quarterly**. Expand relationships with monthly narratives and quarterly scorecards.

TIPS AND TRICKS FOR CREATING NARRATIVES

- Crafting an email to a CEO can feel intimidating. These individuals are often under significant time constraints, manage numerous priorities, and deal with a constant influx of messages. To break through the noise and **capture their attention**, your email must be concise, well-structured, and directly aligned with their objectives. The key to an impactful message is delivering clear value in the shortest time possible.
- Your first tool for getting a CEO's attention is the subject line. CEOs, like anyone else, make quick judgments based on the subject line, deciding within seconds whether to open the email or move on. To maximize your chances, the subject line should be brief—ideally between five and seven words—and **convey**

urgency or potential benefits. It should hint at the core value your email offers without using generic phrases.

- Personalization plays a critical role in maintaining interest. Addressing the CEO by name and referencing a recent company initiative, public appearance, or relevant achievement shows that your outreach is intentional, not mass-produced or AI-generated. CEOs are much more likely to engage with messages that reflect **genuine interest in their work** rather than broad, impersonal pitches. Even a single line demonstrating familiarity with their goals or company strategy can set your email apart.

- Time is the most valuable asset a CEO has, meaning every second they spend reading an email needs to feel worthwhile. Therefore, the opening lines must get to the point immediately. Clearly state why you are reaching out and how your message benefits them or their organization. Avoid lengthy introductions or excessive background details. A CEO should be able to **grasp the essence of your proposal** within the first two sentences.

- When discussing your offering, focus less on the specifics of the product or service and more on the results it delivers. CEOs think in terms of outcomes, whether that means increased revenue, enhanced efficiency, or mitigated risk. Frame your message around how your solution addresses key pain points or creates new opportunities. By **emphasizing measurable results** and high-level impact, you appeal to the strategic mindset of your executive audience.

- Credibility is another vital component of an effective email. CEOs are naturally skeptical of cold outreach, making it essential to establish trust quickly. Citing reputable clients, awards, or case studies can prove your ability to deliver results. When possible, **draw parallels** between their company and others you've worked with, reinforcing the relevance of your solution. Demonstrating prior success adds weight to your message and reduces perceived risk.

- Executive emails should be concise. A good target is 100 to 150 words, with bullet points used sparingly to highlight specific outcomes or benefits. This brevity respects the CEO's time and ensures your message can be read in under a minute. Replace large blocks of text with impactful summaries, making the content easy to digest.
- Every email should end with a clear and **simple call to action**. CEOs are unlikely to take the next step if the path forward is ambiguous. Whether you are requesting a short call, a meeting, or a brief review of materials, say so plainly. Remember, you are trading value for the CEO's time and attention.
- No matter how compelling your content may be, errors or clumsy phrasing can undermine the entire effort. Even small mistakes can create doubt about your professionalism. Before sending the email, carefully proofread the content for accuracy and flow.
- Read your message aloud to identify awkward phrasing or overly complex sentences. Then read it again! By crafting a message that is concise, **outcome-driven**, and professionally polished, you significantly increase your chances of not only receiving a response but also sparking meaningful engagement.

NARRATIVES WORKBOOK
EXECUTIVE PRESENCE

Narrative Frameworks

142 PEER COMPARISON BENCHMARK	Awareness of account's competitive advantage in their segment • Develop business strategies that enhance competitive advantage
143 PROBLEM SOLUTION APPROACH	Identify and solve known business challenges for customers • Creative approach to create an even greater competitive advantage

144 STORYTELLING WITH IMPACT	Presenting an idea an executive has not considered previously • Be compelling with a new creative approach
145 VISIONARY APPROACH	Deliver a three-year strategic roadmap approach • Shows your commitment to the executive's ongoing success

Narrative Sales Plays

146 EXECUTIVE PRIORITIES	Continually reprioritize each executive's top project needs • Iterative approach based on the changing business climate
147 ENDGAME	Start with endgame in mind to solve business challenges • What needs to be accomplished prior to reduce the risk profile
148 EVIDENCE	Show proven results from solving similar business challenges • Guide client to ensure their success
149 CONCISE	Executives excel at simplifying the complex • Net out value concisely to make the best use of time
150 BUSINESS IMPACTS	Deliver the highest value business impacts with lowest risk • Prioritize use cases that fund entire project in phase one
151 SOLUTION VALUE	What solution value map delivers measurable benefit? • Begin with high impact area with low resource impacts
152 STORYTELLING	Become a strategic storyteller to provide context • Protagonist challenges faced and how they overcame them
153 ANTICIPATE	Anticipate needs by overcoming every objection prior • Guide clients on a path to success and avoid pitfalls

154 DIRECT ASK	Important questions put in writing and ask directly for answers • Test your relationships with uncomfortable conversations
155 OBJECTIONS	Address and overcome objections directly with executives • Document how you will resolve in a framework that can be shared
156 FRAMES	Grab attention in a frame of the opportunity to improve processes • Balance with the risks associate with each opportunity
157 FLEXIBILITY	Leading with point of view requires you to be flexible to adapt to executive direction • Having the confidence to adjust based on executive feedback
158 REVISIT	Continually revisit strategies during quarterly executive reviews • Ongoing process to reprioritize use cases
159 REPEATABLE	Offer repeatable templates that have proven to create attention • Make the best use of sales professionals' time

Diagram 8.2 Narratives Allow You to Communicate Like an Executive

EVERYDAY APPLICATIONS

Mastering CEO-level communication is crucial for influencing decision-makers and crafting persuasive messages that align with corporate strategies. It demands precision, strategic insight, and a relentless focus on results—as well as a careful eye for effective writing. Developing this proficiency involves continuous learning and immersion in executive environments.

Engaging with executive publications is a critical starting point. Subscribe to sources like the *Harvard Business Review*, *McKinsey Quarterly*, and *Forbes*

Executive Insights to keep updated on leadership trends, economic forecasts, and case studies reflecting senior executives' priorities. As a bonus, this ongoing exposure sharpens your grasp of the language and frameworks commonly used by CEOs.

Attending leadership seminars and conferences further refines this skill set. Events like the World Economic Forum (Davos) and CES offer firsthand insights into how top executives articulate their visions and tackle pressing challenges. These experiences provide valuable lessons in framing messages with clarity and authority.

Additionally, quarterly reports and shareholder letters from industry giants like Amazon, Microsoft, and Tesla offer a blueprint for effective executive communication. These documents demonstrate how CEOs distill complex information into concise, outcome-driven narratives that resonate with stakeholders.

Central to CEO-level writing is clarity and precision. CEOs have little tolerance for ambiguity or lengthy explanations. The objective is to be succinct yet comprehensive—distilling information to its core while maintaining all of your message's critical elements. Simplifying jargon and removing unnecessary complexity helps you reach a broad audience, aiding understanding across various departments and stakeholders.

Equally important is focusing on outcomes and results. CEOs seek proposals that align with growth, operational efficiency, or innovation. Likewise, they prioritize measurable achievements, so every communication should highlight KPIs, ROI, and the broader impact of your initiatives. By quantifying success and emphasizing scalability, you illustrate alignment with executive priorities and enhance your document's relevance.

Adopting a leadership voice is essential to exuding confidence and decisiveness. Assertive language, free from hesitation or tentative phrasing, inspires trust and mirrors the qualities your executive readers value. By consistently communicating vision and emphasizing transformative outcomes, professionals position themselves as forward-thinking leaders who belong in the conversation.

NARRATIVE KEY TAKEAWAYS

1. If you're sent to who you sound like, how will sales effectively engage executives?

   Communication framework to converse with your client's executive leadership team.

2. How can you be compelling with executives so they will engage with you?

   Understand their top priorities and bring a unique competitive advantage.

3. How should your GTM team initiate customer value creation at scale?

   Deliver multiple levels of value in every interaction with executives.

4. What does it take to master the Seven C's of Communication to be compelling with executives?

   Everyone should create their own collaboration approach that aligns to their style.

5. Do you make it easy for executives to refer you to their direct reports?

   Condense complex concepts down to the Rule of Three and simplify them.

6. Can you initiate collaboration within an account to sell on your behalf?

   The art of cascade communication cadence of messaging to create momentum.

7. Do you have a complete business strategy for an executive to bet their career on it?

   Provocative strategy will win over personal relationships every time.

8. How do you enable everyone to engage executives while removing their trepidation?

Improved sales participation increased 37 percent quarterly by creating unbudgeted transactions.

SUMMARY

CEOs are driven by a need to stay ahead of market trends and refine their leadership strategies. The content they consume often centers on growth, innovation, operational efficiency, and competitive positioning. Consuming the same content will help you understand the strategic frameworks CEOs use to guide decision-making. As you read, identify recurring themes that influence executives' priorities, such as digital transformation or market expansion. Speak directly to your clients' concerns by framing proposals in the context of industry challenges and growth opportunities.

CEOs value communication that is clear, concise, and results oriented. Executive-focused publications reflect this style, favoring brevity and impactful language that cuts through complexity. By getting to the point quickly, you demonstrate respect for their time, and by clarifying value you increase the likelihood that your ideas will be considered and acted upon.

Position yourself as a strategic thinker who understands the executive's perspective. Start your communications with a summary of key takeaways or ROI projections, followed by supporting details. Use bullet points and data-driven insights to make your case succinctly and quantify the benefits of your recommendations. Focus on outcomes such as increased revenue, reduced downtime, or enhanced customer satisfaction. Tie initiatives directly to the company's overarching strategic objectives.

The CEO will refer you to a direct report 92 percent of the time. Once you engage and start the work, it's crucial to loop back with a tangible update every six weeks, thanking the CEO for the referral and providing an update on the progress made so far. Executives are inherently inclined to inspect, and you've just given the CEO the necessary details to follow up with his leadership team during an executive staff meeting. This creates a flywheel of interest in your project at the highest level. This is the pinnacle of strategic selling—providing the CEO with a meaningful update on a recommendation he has made to his team.

Reading CEO-level content helps you develop the ability to view challenges and opportunities through the same lens as an executive. By understanding their strategic focus, adopting their language, and aligning your proposals with emerging trends and measurable outcomes, you enhance your ability to influence decision-making at the highest levels.

DEFINE FRAMEWORK (JOIN CHAPTERS 5 TO 8)

By dedicating your top-tier resources to work together regularly, you can develop advanced executive deliverables that drive substantial, unforeseen transitions. Organizing a select few **Diamond Teams** yields two distinct benefits that cash in on consistent exposure to high-stakes evaluations. First, operating at this level, much like a Special Forces unit, significantly boosts your win rate in the most competitive evaluations. Second, the resulting content can be generalized to form the foundation for industry solution sets, which can then be utilized by your global sales force to propagate your company's best practices across an entire industry segment.

This approach necessitates an insight-driven mindset to anticipate needs and develop recommendations that the customer has not yet identified. Your sales professionals will learn to program-manage multiple resources, who do not report directly to them, to create account-specific deliverables tailored for each executive persona. The ultimate objective is to empower new influential champions to advocate for your solution, staking their careers on its potential impact because they believe in your ability to drive competitive advantage for their company.

To create a unique competitive advantage in your market, it's essential to **engineer markets** with charter customers. These specific accounts are uniquely positioned as ideal customer profiles for your solution and are highly interested in collaborating with you on your future roadmap. This partnership allows you to incorporate specific industry nuances that your product team typically cannot access, especially advanced use cases. Such close collaboration accelerates your market engagement, enabling you to develop comprehensive industry solution sets that include executive dashboards, prioritize use cases by persona, and capture unique attributes in the data model.

This market awareness distinguishes your company from competitors who do not adopt an industry-first approach. Consequently, you can speak directly to industry segments in a personalized manner. Executives, who have spent the past twenty-five years immersed in their specific industries, understand key performance indicators and unique use cases. To use their time (and your own) effectively and demonstrate excellence, you must communicate in their specific language, addressing business outcomes by implementation horizon to create consistent value.

Frameworks play a major role in this strategy. As the success of McKinsey and Accenture demonstrates, proficiency in planning and executing various executive frameworks is essential to engage C-suite audiences. Over the past twenty-five years, I have developed templates for forty-eight different frameworks covering nearly every GTM motion, which I share in this book. Frameworks enable sales professionals to generate a flywheel of interest with both new and existing executives, ensuring relevance and efficient interactions.

The primary objective of executive frameworks is to distill complex information into as few pages as possible, clearly articulating the value of your partnership. By combining these proven templates with account knowledge and situational awareness, your GTM teams can respond swiftly and coherently, a quality everyone values. But it's not just about condensing thirty slides into one page. Access to these forty-eight executive frameworks allows each GTM team member to customize their own engagement blueprint, whether in sales, marketing, or customer success, thereby elevating their conversations at the executive level.

Finally, mastering the art of written **narratives** is essential for successfully engaging new executives. The key to a CEO conversation is to be impactful with the fewest words possible, introducing a novel idea that can be executed to unlock meaningful improvements. While many aim to negotiate solely with a C-suite executive, another effective approach is to provide unique value and request a referral to the appropriate person on their executive staff.

This strategy allows you to gain sponsorship from the correct stakeholder who owns the business challenge, enabling you to loop back later with your C-suite contact.

To reach this goal, your narrative must be clear and concise. CEOs' time is incredibly valuable, and any ambiguity can lead to misinterpretations or missed opportunities. Crafting clear and straightforward messages, free of unnecessary jargon or complexity, allows your core ideas to shine. Transparent and logical communication enables CEOs to quickly grasp the essence of your idea, facilitating informed decisions without unnecessary back-and-forth. They require concrete next steps that drive actionable outcomes with their teams.

Defining your value differential empowers your sales professionals to lead with proven answers when engaging executives. By prescribing solutions from case studies of their industry peers, you provide a roadmap that resonates with each client's specific challenges and opportunities.

VALUE REALIZATION

Quantify Measurable Benefits

(Reduce Discounting by 21 Percent)

CHAPTER 9

> **IMPACT DELIVERED:** Quantify Business Outcomes

> **MOVE THE NEEDLE:** Executive Compensation Drives Priorities

> **PERFORMANCE SCORECARDS:** Value Expansion

> **JUSTIFICATION BY TIME HORIZON:** Benefits by Phase

> **THE TRUTH ABOUT VALUE REALIZATION:** Quantifiable Value

> **RETURN ON INVESTMENT:** Differentiated Value

> **TOTAL COST OF OWNERSHIP:** Top Resources to Engage

> **CUSTOMER EXPERIENCE METRICS:** Customer Resolution

> **SUPPLY CHAIN METRICS:** Optimize Production

> **VALUE REALIZATION THEORY:** Reduce Discounts 21 Percent

> **TIPS AND TRICKS:** Accountable for Projects Delivered

> **VALUE REALIZATION WORKBOOK:** Impact Delivered

> **EVERYDAY APPLICATIONS:** Monetize Your Value

> **KEY TAKEAWAYS:** Method to Engage New Accounts

> **SUMMARY:** Quantify Measurable Benefits

IMPACT DELIVERED

One hundred and eighty executives at my firm's largest customer each receive a two-page value realization readout in the third week of every quarter, precisely detailing the business outcomes our solution has delivered. A week after we deliver those readouts, I host an eighteen-minute webinar to brief them on these results. About 35 percent of the invitees typically attend the webinar live, and dozens of others watch the recordings soon afterward. This analysis provides significant opportunities to expand our value to those customers, which raises an important question: Why don't we get a similar scorecard from our other strategic partners? Quantifying value is not a one-time process—at least once a year, your clients' CFOs need to understand the value your solutions provide and assess how they should invest in the value you provide moving forward. This is the difference between a significant value expansion or a down renewal without warning.

Perhaps you already do something like this, but chances are it only reaches four or five internal champions in the account at the director level—the faithful supporters who are well-versed in the value you bring, but also incredibly busy with their day jobs. Why leave out the hundreds of other influencers in their company who also need your solution and may not even be aware of how much your solutions are benefiting their business? In most cases, those benefits are attributed to your champions' internal projects or their individual prowess, not to your company at all. If you want to build on that success, you have to be responsible for capturing and sharing a value realization readout with the top executives in *each* of your accounts on a quarterly basis. You wouldn't sign over your paycheck to a coworker, so why sign over your value to your internal champion?

Every CEO must clearly measure the benefits their solutions deliver to their customers. Without the ability to quantify impact, their future potential is nebulous at best, introducing risks that could obstruct growth and market acceptance. Your customers, and their customers in turn, have to justify their purchases in a competitive landscape, which means demonstrating a clear return on investment. Solid data showing your value can be the tipping point in a buying decision, especially when **expanding your relationship from *vendor* to *strategic partner*.**

As we've seen, success stories supported by data resonate more profoundly with prospective clients. Performance metrics, case studies, and testimonials rooted in quantifiable benefits serve as compelling proof points that distinguish your company from competitors. This evidence-based approach bolsters your authority and credibility, fostering trust among your audiences. Beyond sales, though, measurable outcomes propel continuous improvement and customer retention. When clients can perceive the tangible value of your solution, they are more inclined to continue using it and broaden its application within their organizations.

This visibility not only mitigates the risk of churn but also paves the way for upselling and cross-selling, nurturing deeper, more resilient relationships. And you benefit too: By comprehending how users interact with your product and the results they achieve, you can refine your offerings to better cater to customer needs. This iterative process not only enhances your solution but also future proofs your company's competitiveness.

However, not all solutions are amenable to straightforward measurement. Some products or services deliver intangible benefits, such as boosting employee morale, enhancing brand perception, or fostering innovation. In these scenarios, methods like collecting qualitative feedback, compiling anecdotal evidence, or using proxy metrics can yield valuable insights into your solution's indirect value.

Ultimately, long-term success hinges on the ability to track and demonstrate the benefits you deliver. As you expand your accounts, be sure you're building frameworks that enable you to quantify impact and clearly articulate it to your customers. In doing so, you lay the groundwork for sustainable growth, customer satisfaction, and enduring success.

MOVE THE NEEDLE

Monthly value realization has become an essential tool for measuring progress, enabling organizations to stay agile, optimize their resources, and maintain a competitive edge. By homing in on specific quantifiable metrics, both you and your clients can gain deep insight into the value of your solutions and make informed decisions to guide the company forward.

Financial metrics often start this conversation. **Revenue growth** is the most straightforward indicator of success, reflecting increased customer demand and the direct impact of new solutions on profitability. CEOs meticulously track this growth month over month to ensure continuous upward momentum. Simultaneously, **cost savings** are a critical component of value realization. By streamlining operations and reducing waste, businesses can significantly cut operational and capital expenses.

Similarly, **enhancements in gross margin** further highlight operational efficiency, while a reduction in **Customer Acquisition Cost** (CAC) indicates more effective customer targeting and acquisition strategies. But it's **Return on Investment** (ROI) that often serves as the most pivotal metric, encapsulating the firm's net financial gain relative to the cost of a solution. A steady improvement in ROI reassures CEOs that their investments are yielding sustainable returns.

Operational efficiency is another cornerstone of CEO oversight. When evaluating the **impact of automation**, CEOs assess how well solutions reduce manual processes, enhance productivity, and lower error rates. **Time savings**, measured by hours freed up through improved workflows, directly translate to increased organizational capacity. CEOs are particularly mindful of **system uptime and downtime**, as even minor disruptions can lead to significant financial losses. **Resource utilization**, which involves optimizing staff and assets, ensures that no part of the organization operates below its potential.

Customer experience and retention metrics provide CEOs with crucial insights into the long-term viability of their business. **Customer Satisfaction**

(CSAT) and **Net Promoter Scores** (NPS) take the pulse of customer sentiment, guiding service and product improvements. A declining **churn rate** reflects enhanced customer loyalty, while growth in **Customer Lifetime Value** (CLTV) underscores the enduring revenue potential of existing clients.

Innovation and growth metrics are likewise vital for sustaining momentum. CEOs track reductions in **time to market**, ensuring that their firm remains responsive to evolving consumer needs. **Research and Development (R&D) efficiency** highlights the balance between input and output in innovation cycles, while successful **market penetration** demonstrates the effectiveness of expansion strategies. A growing sales pipeline offers evidence of future business development opportunities.

Fifth, in an increasingly volatile digital landscape, security and risk metrics have become non-negotiable for CEOs. **Incident response times** are closely monitored, as swift action is critical to mitigating potential threats. **Compliance rates** act as another safeguard against regulatory risks, ensuring the company operates within industry standards. CEOs also focus on **overall risk reduction** to protect the organization from operational, financial, and technological vulnerabilities.

Employee productivity and engagement round out the framework of value realization. High **employee engagement** directly correlates with enhanced morale, increased motivation, and reduced turnover. By tracking **attrition rates**, CEOs gain insight into workforce stability, while measuring **productivity gains per employee** reveals the tangible impact of implemented solutions.

By tailoring these metrics to align with specific industry goals, CEOs can elevate their leadership, foster innovation, and drive sustainable success. Ultimately, by systematically tracking these diverse yet interconnected metrics, you can ensure that your strategies consistently deliver measurable value. This structured approach allows for agile adjustments, ensuring your partnership not only grows but thrives in a constantly shifting market.

PERFORMANCE SCORECARDS

You must continuously demonstrate the value of your technological solutions to secure your clients' executive support and drive ongoing investment. Quarterly performance scorecards not only quantify the impact of technological initiatives but also foster transparency, trust, and data-driven decision-making at the highest levels of the organization.

By tracking key performance indicators such as return on investment, revenue growth, cost reduction, operational efficiency, and risk mitigation, you create concrete evidence of the value you've delivered, making it easier for your clients to justify continued investment and expansion. But you also have to align these technology initiatives with overarching business objectives. Scorecards are ideal for this process, showing how innovations and solutions support and enhance the company's vision. This connection ensures that your client's technology investments are seen not as isolated efforts, but as critical components of the organization's long-term strategy.

Beyond highlighting achievements, quarterly scorecards also uncover risks and opportunities. By analyzing performance trends, executives can identify potential bottlenecks and vulnerabilities before they escalate into larger issues. Simultaneously, these scorecards can reveal untapped opportunities for innovation and expansion, helping the organization stay ahead of the competition and seize new market possibilities.

Transparency and trust are fundamental to any successful relationship between technology teams and executive leadership. Regular performance reporting through quarterly scorecards builds this trust by demonstrating accountability and a commitment to results. By openly communicating progress, challenges, and areas for growth, technology teams reinforce their dedication to delivering measurable value, fostering a collaborative and trusting environment. Here's a sample scorecard you can use as a model.

PERFORMANCE SCORECARD

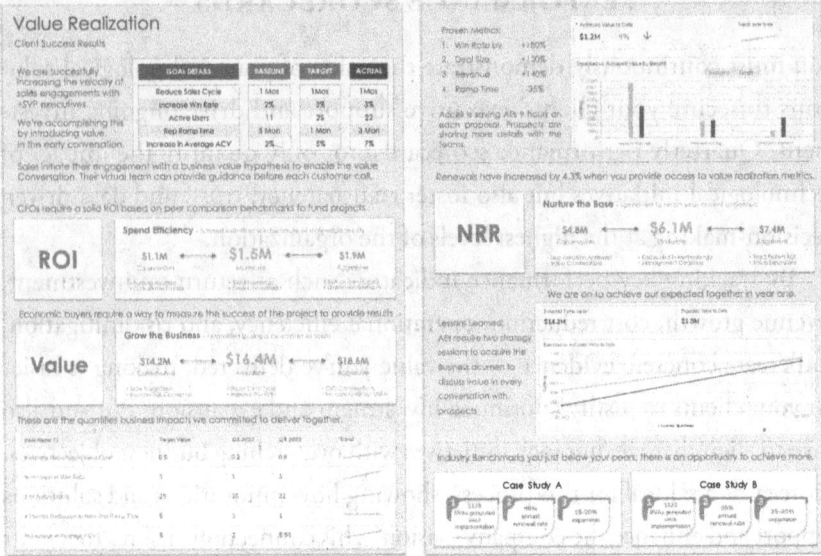

Diagram 9.0 Quantify Value Delivered Quarterly

Demonstrating present value makes your client executives stronger advocates for future projects. This advocacy is instrumental in securing larger budgets, exploring new technologies, and expanding into new markets, laying the foundation for continued innovation and growth. As you navigate an increasingly dynamic and competitive landscape, the consistent use of quarterly scorecards will be crucial for ensuring sustained executive support and long-term technological advancement.

JUSTIFICATION BY TIME HORIZON

Financial justification across different time horizons plays a critical role in implementing projects successfully. By structuring the evaluation into short, medium, and long-term phases, organizations can ensure that investments are aligned with measurable outcomes at each stage of deployment, fostering sustainable growth and operational excellence.

In the short-term, spanning the initial six months, the focus is on achieving immediate impact through rapid deployment and **securing a quick return on investment**. During this phase, costs typically include initial setup and deployment expenses, licensing fees, and minimal consulting or training costs. The benefits lie in automating routine tasks, preventing system failures, and delivering quick wins such as faster data processing or anomaly detection. To justify these expenditures, businesses should prioritize low-risk, high-reward initiatives, often through pilot projects or proof-of-concept implementations. Key performance indicators, like a reduction in incident response time, provide tangible evidence of success.

As the implementation progresses into the medium-term, spanning six to twelve months, the emphasis shifts to scaling and optimizing performance across the organization. This period involves expanding the initial deployment, integrating with existing enterprise systems, and providing ongoing training and support. The benefits become more pronounced as operational efficiencies scale across multiple departments, fostering collaboration and reducing incident detection and resolution times. Financial justification at this stage highlights process optimization, growing ROI, and cost consolidation through unified platforms, which streamlines workflows and enhances data visibility.

In the long term, covering the twelve-to-eighteen-month horizon, strategic outcomes and transformative growth take center stage. This phase requires investment in system enhancements, AI/ML integration, and advanced analytics. Organizations may also allocate resources toward system upgrades, R&D, and partnerships that drive innovation. The benefits include competitive differentiation through predictive analytics, reduced system downtime, and overall cost reductions driven by comprehensive automation. Long-term financial justification underscores the importance of market leadership, lifetime value projections, and profitability assessments. Scenario planning ensures resilience and adaptability, safeguarding the organization's future position.

Ultimately, a structured approach to financial justification across different time horizons ensures that organizations continuously evaluate their investments for both immediate impact and long-term sustainability. By aligning project phases with strategic objectives, companies can achieve consistent growth, operational efficiency, and innovation, reinforcing their competitive standing in the marketplace.

THE TRUTH ABOUT VALUE REALIZATION

To achieve sustainable hyperscale revenue growth, an innovative solution is not enough—you also need a quantifiable framework for measuring value. Without a clear methodology for assessing your solution's impact, you risk losing credibility with stakeholders and will struggle to scale effectively. A well-defined framework also ensures alignment with industry-specific needs, financial decision-making, and credible benchmarks. This section explores the essential components of value quantification that drive business case validation and revenue scalability.

Industry-specific value is the cornerstone of effective measurement. Every sector operates under distinct KPIs that define success for firms and customers alike. For technology development and observability, for instance, reducing Mean Time to Resolution (MTTR) and improving system uptime are critical metrics. Financial services and security firms focus on fraud detection rates and risk mitigation savings, while healthcare organizations emphasize patient outcomes and regulatory compliance. Manufacturing, on the other hand, prioritizes supply chain efficiency and predictive maintenance.

By customizing your value propositions to align with industry-specific benchmarks, it's far easier to establish credibility and enhance stakeholder engagement. Without this alignment, even the most advanced solutions may struggle to gain traction within your target markets. Similarly, you must tailor your value differently for business-to-business (B2B) versus business-to-consumer (B2C) markets. Their respective perceptions and realizations of value differ significantly. B2B companies seek solutions that drive cost efficiency, regulatory compliance, and scalability. Decision-makers in these organizations prioritize measurable impacts on revenue, operational streamlining, and automation.

In contrast, B2C businesses focus on customer experience, brand trust, and behavioral loyalty. The emphasis is on convenience, personalization, and sustained engagement rather than direct financial savings. Understanding these distinctions ensures that value propositions are appropriately structured and communicated to decision-makers in each sector. A company that fails to differentiate between these models risks misaligning its messaging and underestimating the needs of its audience.

Hard dollar savings serve as the cornerstone of business justifications. CFOs and financial stakeholders place a high value on tangible financial benefits. Prioritizing hard dollar savings is essential in any business case. Reductions in operational costs, such as lowering OPEX and CAPEX through automation, optimized infrastructure, and enhanced security, provide an immediate justification for investment. Efficiency-driven revenue growth, like speeding up GTM strategies, improving conversion rates, and expanding market reach through AI-driven insights, further solidifies the case. Workforce automation is also pivotal, reducing reliance on human labor for repetitive tasks and freeing teams to focus on strategic initiatives. Demonstrating a product's contribution to financial efficiency fortifies the argument for widespread adoption.

While tangible savings are critical, intangible benefits bolster the business case. Enhanced productivity, driven by automation and AI tools, liberates valuable employee time and boosts overall efficiency. Brand loyalty and customer loyalty, tracked through positive Net Promoter Scores (NPS) and customer retention rates, are vital indicators of long-term success. Employee satisfaction and retention are also key, as companies that invest in tools to enhance the employee experience often see reduced turnover and increased engagement. Although these factors may not yield immediate financial returns, their long-term impact contributes to overall business stability and growth. Organizations that overlook these benefits may struggle to demonstrate the full range of their products' value.

To effectively gauge success, organizations must establish precise "move the needle" thresholds for value realization. A well-constructed framework should incorporate low-impact scenarios, providing conservative estimates of minimal adoption effects, alongside midpoint-impact scenarios, which reflect realistic expectations of standard implementation outcomes. High-impact scenarios highlight the best-case potential of the solution. For example, an

AI-driven threat detection system might reduce breach probability by 10 percent in a low-impact scenario, 30 percent at the midpoint, and 50 percent in a high-impact situation. This structured approach sets attainable targets while allowing room for aspirational growth.

CFOs assess investments by weighing risk against potential returns. A robust business case should illustrate a spectrum of possible outcomes to align with CFO expectations. The conservative benefit offers a cautious estimate to ensure initial approval. The midpoint benefit presents the anticipated return that warrants financial backing. Finally, the stretch goal sets a high-reaching yet achievable target that highlights the maximum potential value. By framing expectations within these tiers, you can balance risk while highlighting opportunities for higher returns. This method provides decision-makers with a comprehensive view of the investment's potential impact.

Finance executives depend on industry case studies to evaluate a product's viability. These real-world examples offer solid evidence of measurable impact in similar environments, provide benchmarking data for anticipated ROI, and enhance credibility when presenting to enterprise buyers. Without documented success stories, achieving widespread adoption—particularly at the enterprise level—becomes considerably more challenging.

Organizations that invest in compiling and presenting case studies can significantly enhance their ability to persuade stakeholders and drive adoption. Creating a Business Process Library with established industry benchmarks is a crucial step. Your library should feature industry-specific benchmarks for common process improvements. Historical data that standardizes projected value realization, along with automated tools and calculators that help customers quantify expected benefits, can likewise be invaluable resources. By utilizing these assets, sales teams and decision-makers can validate assumptions, speed up time-to-value (TTV), and build confidence in prospective buyers. Companies that develop these repositories position themselves as leaders, offering not just solutions but also trusted expertise.

Achieving sustainable hyperscale revenue growth demands a meticulously crafted framework for value quantification. By strategically measuring value, you can ensure your innovations yield tangible business impact, enabling you to scale up with confidence and credibility. If you focus on industry-specific

KPIs, distinguish between B2B and B2C needs, emphasize hard dollar savings, and substantiate their business cases with benchmarks and case studies, you'll set the stage for long-term success. Without these core elements, achieving enterprise adoption and scalable growth remains an uphill battle.

RETURN ON INVESTMENT

Return on Investment (ROI) is one of the most fundamental financial metrics: Businesses in every industry rely on it to evaluate how effectively they are utilizing their resources. Whether you're launching a new product, streamlining operations, or investing in emerging technologies, ROI plays a critical role in tracking your success. By measuring the profitability and efficiency of their investments in your services, your clients gain invaluable insights that guide strategic decision-making and resource allocation.

To understand ROI, one must start with its basic formula: Divide the net profit of an investment by the initial cost, then multiply the result by 100 to express it as a percentage. A positive ROI signals a profitable investment while a negative ROI indicates a loss. This simple yet powerful metric allows businesses to easily compare different projects and gauge their relative effectiveness. This makes it an essential tool for comparing projects, acquisitions, and other business endeavors—and for ensuring that ongoing initiatives justify continued investment.

Differentiation is key to standing out in competitive markets, and ROI is essential in quantifying the value of these differentiation strategies. When companies innovate, streamline operations, or invest in customer retention, they must measure the returns to validate the effectiveness of their efforts. If an innovation attracts higher demand or enhances customer loyalty, the resulting ROI serves as a testament to the product's uniqueness and market appeal. Companies that introduce products with distinct features or superior performance often achieve higher returns, reinforcing the importance of innovation.

Operational efficiency is another area where ROI plays a significant role. Companies that invest in advanced technologies, such as AI-driven analytics or observability tools, often experience reduced operational costs and increased productivity. ROI can demonstrate how these investments drive down expenses while boosting efficiency, highlighting the competitive advantage gained through superior operational practices. For example, a marketing strategy that reduces acquisition costs while increasing revenue is a clear indicator of success, further justifying continued investment in these areas.

ROI is also helpful for less tangible outcomes. Sustainability and Environmental, Social, and Governance (ESG) initiatives are increasingly recognized as vital differentiators in modern business. Companies committed to sustainability often calculate ROI by analyzing long-term cost savings, regulatory benefits, and enhanced customer loyalty. By quantifying how an initiative reduces energy consumption and waste, for instance, a company can attract more environmentally conscious consumers, resulting in higher returns and reinforcing brand reputation.

Ultimately, ROI demonstrates the effectiveness of differentiation strategies. Whether through innovation, operational improvements, or sustainability, companies that consistently measure and communicate their ROI position themselves for long-term success. By leveraging ROI, businesses validate their market leadership, attract investors, and solidify their competitive edge in an ever-evolving landscape.

TOTAL COST OF OWNERSHIP

Total Cost of Ownership is a powerful financial tool to capture the full scope of expenses associated with acquiring, deploying, and maintaining a product, service, or system. Unlike simple price comparisons, TCO looks beyond the initial purchase to account for all direct and indirect costs over the entire life cycle. This comprehensive approach enables organizations to make more informed decisions and justify investments with greater confidence.

Acquisition costs form the first pillar of TCO, encompassing the initial purchase price, implementation, and deployment expenses. This includes not only the price tag of the asset but also the costs involved in integrating it into existing workflows and infrastructure. Procurement costs, though sometimes overlooked, also contribute to the overall acquisition expenses.

Once an asset is in place, operational costs begin to accumulate. These include maintenance, repairs, and ongoing technical support. For technology solutions, licensing and subscription fees are significant contributors to operational expenses, as are energy consumption and resource usage. Personnel costs add to the equation, with expenditures tied to employee training, onboarding, and ongoing management of the system. Salaries for staff dedicated to system oversight and maintenance represent an often-underestimated portion of long-term ownership costs.

Risks and downtime present another dimension of TCO. Periods of system inefficiency or failure can lead to productivity losses, negatively impacting revenue. In industries where data security is paramount, the potential costs of breaches, compliance violations, and reputational damage must also be factored into the overall calculation. Finally, at the end of an asset's life, businesses must consider decommissioning and disposal expenses. Whether they're recycling, reselling, or safely disposing of equipment, these costs can add up. Additionally, replacement costs for transitioning to newer solutions further extend the life cycle analysis.

One of the most common applications of TCO is comparative analysis between competing solutions. While one option may appear more expensive up front, a deeper TCO evaluation might reveal lower long-term operational costs, making it a more cost-effective choice. TCO also plays a critical role in demonstrating long-term value. Projects with significant initial costs, such as cloud migrations or automation initiatives, often result in substantial operational savings over time. By emphasizing these long-term benefits, organizations can make a compelling case for investing in innovations that lead to faster returns on investment.

Risk mitigation is another area where TCO proves invaluable. By identifying hidden costs related to system downtime or vulnerabilities, businesses can prioritize investments in more reliable, secure solutions. This proactive approach not only protects against unforeseen disruptions but also enhances overall operational resilience. Accordingly, effective budgeting and forecasting both rely heavily on TCO analysis. By accounting for all foreseeable costs, organizations can avoid unexpected budget overruns and ensure that future expenses are accurately anticipated. This level of foresight contributes to more strategic financial planning.

More strategically, TCO helps businesses align specific projects with broader organizational goals. Whether they're pursuing sustainability, scalability, or digital transformation, businesses can demonstrate how specific investments contribute to these objectives. For instance, TCO calculations highlighting energy savings or resource efficiencies can reinforce sustainability initiatives. This can make TCO a valuable bargaining tool: With a clear understanding of the total life cycle costs, businesses are better equipped to negotiate favorable pricing, extended warranties, or enhanced service-level agreements.

Consider the case of cloud migration. A company evaluating whether to maintain on-premises infrastructure or transition to the cloud might initially perceive cloud services as more expensive. However, when TCO is fully assessed, the benefits of reduced IT overhead, automatic updates, and minimized downtime often justify the switch. The ability to reallocate personnel to more strategic initiatives further strengthens the case for cloud adoption.

Ultimately, Total Cost of Ownership is more than just a financial metric—it is a strategic asset that enables organizations to make well-rounded decisions. By providing a comprehensive view of costs, TCO empowers businesses to compare options, forecast expenses, and pursue solutions that deliver the best long-term value. This approach not only strengthens project justification but also ensures that investments align with broader organizational strategies and risk management frameworks.

CUSTOMER EXPERIENCE METRICS

Customer experience companies often leverage quarterly value realization scorecards to showcase the tangible business impacts of their solutions. These scorecards serve as essential tools for communicating ROI and quantifying the effectiveness of deployed technologies. By highlighting improvements across various domains, you can help your clients visualize performance enhancements, operational efficiencies, and overall business growth. Familiarize yourself with the categories and specific metrics defined next.

REVENUE GROWTH AND SALES PERFORMANCE is the first category to track, since one of the primary objectives of customer experience solutions is to drive revenue growth. Scorecards frequently focus on sales performance metrics that reveal how solutions contribute to enhanced revenue streams.

- Pipeline Growth – Tracks the increase in sales pipeline volume, reflecting greater opportunities for conversion.
- Deal Win Rate – Measures the percentage of closed deals against the total number of opportunities, demonstrating sales effectiveness.
- Average Deal Size – Monitors growth in Average Contract Value (ACV), indicating larger deals and stronger client relationships.
- Cross-Sell/Upsell Rates – Highlights revenue generated from selling additional products or services to existing customers.
- Sales Cycle Length – Measures reductions in the time required to close deals, reflecting improved efficiency in sales processes.

OPERATIONAL EFFICIENCY metrics reflect how well customer experience solutions streamline internal processes and reduce costs.

- Lead Conversion Rates – Indicates improvements in the conversion of leads to customers, a critical metric for assessing marketing and sales alignment.
- Cost per Lead/Acquisition – Demonstrates reductions in marketing and sales expenses per lead or acquired customer.
- Automated Workflows – Tracks the number of manual processes automated, highlighting operational scalability.
- Time Savings – Quantifies hours saved by automating workflows and eliminating manual tasks.

CUSTOMER ENGAGEMENT AND SATISFACTION are key drivers of long-term success. Value realization scorecards often prioritize metrics that showcase specific improvements in customer experience.

- Net Promoter Score – Measures customer loyalty and satisfaction by evaluating their likelihood of recommending the company.
- Customer Retention/Churn Rates – Tracks retention improvements and churn reductions, demonstrating long-term client relationship success.
- Customer Lifetime Value (CLV) – Reflects the projected revenue generated from customers over their relationship life cycle.
- Support Ticket Resolution Time – Measures reductions in the time taken to resolve customer issues, indicating enhanced support efficiency.
- Case Deflection Rate – Tracks the percentage of issues resolved by self-service tools, reducing the need for human intervention.

EMPLOYEE PRODUCTIVITY AND COLLABORATION metrics are critical indicators of a successful solution implementation.

- Sales Productivity – Measures the amount of time sales teams spend on selling versus administrative tasks.
- Training Completion and Adoption Rates – Tracks the adoption and completion rates of training programs, reflecting solution usability.
- Employee Satisfaction – Measures employee engagement and satisfaction post-solution implementation.
- Quota Attainment – Evaluates the percentage of sales representatives meeting or exceeding targets.

MARKETING IMPACT is a direct indicator of how well customer experience solutions enhance lead generation and campaign success.

- Marketing ROI – Reflects the return on investment from marketing campaigns and initiatives.
- Campaign Engagement – Measures email open rates, click-through rates (CTR), and lead quality, indicating campaign effectiveness.
- Event/Content Performance – Tracks leads generated from events, webinars, and content marketing activities.

AI AND AUTOMATION METRICS play a growing role in customer experience solutions, requiring specific metrics to highlight their value.

- AI Prediction Accuracy – Reflects the effectiveness of predictive analytics in forecasting business outcomes.
- Reduction in Errors – Measures the decrease in manual errors through automation.
- AI-Driven Insights Adoption – Tracks the percentage of decisions influenced by AI-driven recommendations.

SECURITY AND COMPLIANCE provide valuable insights into risk mitigation and adherence, especially for industries with stringent regulatory requirements.

- Incident Response Time – Measures the time taken to detect and respond to security incidents.
- Compliance Adherence – Tracks improvements in regulatory compliance, ensuring alignment with industry standards.

To enhance the impact of these metrics, quarterly value realization score-cards are often presented using visual tools and dashboards. Here are some of the most popular options.

- Heatmaps – Identify performance gaps and areas of concern.
- Trend Lines – Showcase progress across multiple quarters, illustrating improvements over time.
- Benchmarks – Compare performance against industry peers, offering context and goal-setting opportunities.

Incorporating these metrics into your quarterly value realization score-cards allows you to consistently demonstrate value, foster stronger client relationships, and drive continuous improvement across various business functions.

SUPPLY CHAIN METRICS

Businesses continuously seek ways to enhance efficiency, minimize costs, and drive performance. Leading supply chain software providers have emerged as pivotal players in this pursuit, delivering tools that not only streamline operations but also quantify success. Their scorecards reflect the tangible outcomes of supply chain solutions and guide organizations toward greater return on investment. Think of them as *narratives of progress*, broken down into critical operational focus areas. Each section sheds light on essential performance indicators, providing your stakeholders with a clear view of how your technology influences their supply chain's heartbeat.

OPERATIONAL EFFICIENCY: This cornerstone of success efficiency stands at the core of supply chain excellence.

- Order Fulfillment Rates – reveal the percentage of orders delivered punctually and completely, a direct testament to supply chain reliability.
- Production Downtime – highlights reductions in unforeseen interruptions, ensuring that manufacturing lines remain fluid and productive.
- Inventory Turnover – showcases the frequency of inventory cycling, signaling effective stock management.
- Cycle Times – encapsulate the entire journey from order placement to delivery, providing insight into critical processes like Order-to-Cash and Procure-to-Pay.

COST MANAGEMENT: In an environment where margins are razor-thin, cost containment is paramount.

- Cost per Order/Shipment – reflects operational efficiency in fulfilling and shipping customer orders.
- Supply Chain Costs as a Percentage of Revenue – a vital gauge of expenditure in relation to earnings.
- Reduction in Expedited Freight Costs – underscores the value of optimized logistics strategies.

- Warehouse Space Utilization – ensures that every square meter is maximized to reduce overhead.

RISK AND RESILIENCE: In an unpredictable world, resilience is a defining trait of a successful supply chain, tracking how organizations manage disruptions.

- Supplier On-Time Performance – captures supplier reliability, safeguarding against input delays.
- Supply Chain Disruption Response Time – measures the agility of response mechanisms.
- Risk Mitigation Savings – quantifies the financial benefits of proactive risk management.

SUSTAINABILITY AND COMPLIANCE: Modern supply chains are measured not just by speed and cost but by their environmental and ethical footprint.

- CO_2 Emissions Reduction – an indicator of efforts to minimize carbon output.
- Waste Reduction – illustrates how supply chains manage surplus and returns.
- Sourcing Compliance Rates – ensures adherence to responsible sourcing practices.

CUSTOMER SATISFACTION AND EXPERIENCE: Supply chains are ultimately judged by the experiences they deliver.

- Customer Order Accuracy – demonstrates precision in order fulfillment.
- Net Promoter Score (NPS) – reflects customer sentiment and loyalty.
- Return Rates – shed light on areas where quality or delivery may require refinement.

REVENUE GROWTH AND MARKET RESPONSIVENESS: A thriving supply chain is not just efficient but also growth-oriented.

- Revenue from New Products – highlights the role of supply chains in innovation.
- Demand Forecast Accuracy – crucial for balancing supply with market demand.
- Service Level Improvements – captures enhancements in delivery performance and service quality.

In essence, the quarterly value realization scorecard is more than a performance review; it is a testament to the symbiotic relationship between technology and supply chain excellence. For businesses striving to unlock continuous improvement, enhance resilience, and achieve sustainable growth, these scorecards serve as indispensable roadmaps to success.

VALUE REALIZATION THEORY

Provide quarterly performance scorecards to executives to measure the impact of their investment choices in your solution. Make sure you are recognized for the outstanding efforts your team contributes each week to create value.

Why change?

Challenge:	How can you acquire customers without measuring prior success? Are customers with a two-year subscription willing to collaborate? Which metrics amplify your solution to become the industry standard?

How do we differentiate?

Concept 33:	**Quantify Business Outcomes** using clear metrics to empower leaders with informed decision-making based on performance data. This approach aids in prioritizing investments in areas that offer the greatest returns. Monitor outcomes so you can adapt quickly to innovate.

Concept 34:	**Executive Quarterly Scorecards** offer executives the assurance they need to confirm the value of their investment in your solution. By presenting a shared mission statement and highlighting the business areas that have shown improvement you reinforce the positive impacts.
Concept 35:	**Measurable Benefits** emphasize the tangible advantages every three months and are a distinct strength, possibly making this the sole option that provides such comprehensive insights to the leadership team. Present this as a key differentiator to enhance your connection and boost value growth.
Concept 36:	**Scorecard for Expansion** is necessary to present to the executive team in order to secure increased investment in your partnership. Assessing the improvement that users experience from your solution is essential to gaining the full advantage of what you offer.

What do we receive?

Result:	Verify investment decision quarterly across the entire leadership team. Empower sales with value measured to **reduce discounting −21%**. Consistent updates to the executive team that makes the decisions.

TIPS AND TRICKS FOR VALUE REALIZATION

- Quantifying customer value starts with a fundamental truth: You must understand your customer's objectives. It all begins with collaboration. Engaging stakeholders early allows for a deeper understanding of their pain points and aspirations. Success isn't one size fits all, and defining the right success metrics is crucial to developing the right solution. **Establishing a clear baseline**—whether it's reduced downtime, enhanced performance, or cost savings—sets the stage for meaningful measurement.

- Continue that collaboration by co-developing value metrics. By involving the customer in joint value assessments, you ensure alignment and shared responsibility in defining what success looks like. Segmenting value into operational efficiency, risk reduction, and innovation acceleration paints a clearer picture, while accounting for intangible benefits like improved satisfaction and faster decision-making provides a holistic view of value.

- Tracking value over time reveals the true transformation your solution enables. Establish a benchmark early on, to **capture your customer's initial state** before implementation. From there, use continuous monitoring through real-time data tools, both to measure improvements and reassure your customers that their investment is yielding tangible results. Regular check-ins reinforce this, offering both parties opportunities to adapt and refine.

- Both numbers and narratives are needed to convey value. Quantitative data, such as revenue growth or latency reduction, speaks to the tangible aspects of value, while qualitative insights gathered through surveys and interviews add context and depth. Together, they form a compelling case for your solution's impact.

- To further solidify that case, implement real-world examples and industry benchmarks. Customers need to **see themselves in success stories**. Highlighting performance benchmarks and weaving together case studies showcases how others have achieved significant gains. Scenario modeling takes this one step further, projecting potential value based on real success.

- In today's digital age, the ability to provide real-time insights through dashboards and AI-powered analytics has become a game changer. Customers appreciate visibility into ongoing value generation. Dashboards displaying live data allow them to track KPIs in real time, while AI analytics offer predictive insights and optimization recommendations, reinforcing the solution's continuous value.

- Quantifying value often culminates in the form of ROI calculations. A simple yet powerful formula—subtracting investment from the value realized and dividing by the initial investment—lays it out clearly. Factoring in avoided costs, reduced risks, and future scalability adds layers of depth, demonstrating long-term gains that extend beyond the immediate return.

- Remember, the process of measuring value isn't static. Direct feedback loops ensure that the value you measure aligns with customer perceptions. Surveys, interviews, and Net Promoter Scores provide **invaluable qualitative insights**, while Voice of the Customer (VoC) programs establish continuous channels for capturing feedback.

- Risk reduction and scalability are often the unsung heroes in value conversations. Beyond immediate benefits, showing how your solution mitigates vulnerabilities and scales to meet future growth adds to its appeal. Customers need to know that the solution will evolve alongside their business, ready to address emerging challenges.

- Regular reporting and iteration form the backbone of ongoing value measurement. Quarterly Business Reviews (QBRs) offer structured opportunities to present data, demonstrate progress, and **highlight evolving needs**. This iterative approach ensures that the value story never stagnates but grows in tandem with the customer's journey.

- Ultimately, quantifying customer value is about building a lasting partnership grounded in data and trust. By aligning with customer objectives, harnessing real-time insights, and continuously iterating, businesses not only demonstrate the value of their solutions but also secure a foundation for sustained growth and competitive advantage. The process isn't just about measuring impact; it's about creating it, nurturing it, and ensuring that it endures.

VALUE REALIZATION WORKBOOK
QUANTIFY MEASURABLE BENEFITS

Value Realization Frameworks

160 CONTINUOUS VALUE DELIVERY	Continually uncovering new areas of benefit and efficiency • Quantify and present to executive staff quarterly
161 QUANTIFY VALUE BY USE CASE	Measuring the impacts by use case and persona • Efficiency gains captured for your economic buyer
162 TOTAL COST OF OWNERSHIP	Complete cost to acquire, operate, and maintain solution over its entire life cycle • Facilitate transparent purchase decisions
163 REALIZATION READOUT	One-page realization readout for the executive staff • Quarterly scorecard to validate ongoing investment decision

Value Realization Sales Plays

164 QUANTIFY IMPACT	Quantify the impact to the business compared to other solutions • Profile your solution's unique capabilities
165 KEY OBJECTIVES	Identify key business objectives and metrics early • Deliver your value proposition aligned to key objectives
166 VALUE FRAMEWORK	Develop a value framework that can be leveraged for your solutions • Quantifiable measures that can be captured and compared
167 RETURN ON INVESTMENT	Evaluate the profitability of an investment • Performance measurement for decision-making
168 VALIDATE	Collect validated measurement from similar customers • Industry, company size, use case deployment

169 KEY PERFORMANCE INDICATORS	Quantifiable metrics used to evaluate progress to achieve a goal • Clear units of measure that can be compared
170 HORIZONS	Three distinct time horizons and phases of implementation • Quick win, 3 months; medium term, 9 months; transformation, 12 months
171 EXECUTIVE DASHBOARDS	Visual reporting tool that provides leaders with a clear view • Real-time view of KPIs and critical business metrics
172 SUCCESS PLANS	Customer-centric strategy that defines the goals and outcomes • Ensure client achieves desired objectives with solution
173 SHOWCASE	Showcase your competitive advantage compared to alternatives • Outcomes achieved by use cases by persona
174 LONG RANGE	Create a long-term value narrative jointly with the customer • Path to continually adding value on your foundation
175 CONTIGENCY PLAN	Strategic plan to address potential risks, disruptions, or unexpected events • Proactive measure to ensure the organization can respond
176 ECONOMIC BENEFIT	Measurable financial advantages gained by a project • Increased revenue, cost savings, or improved productivity
177 IMPROVEMENT	Process of enhancing an organization's financial health • Profitability through strategic initiatives, cost management, or revenue growth

Diagram 9.1 How to Justify Business Cases to Fund Unbudgeted Projects

EVERYDAY APPLICATIONS

Establishing market leadership in any industry often starts with securing a key partnership that validates the solution and sets the stage for wider adoption. This strategy involves cultivating a flagship customer willing to engage in a long-term partnership, capturing baseline performance data, and developing a compelling case study to drive further market penetration.

This anchor client plays a crucial role in demonstrating the value of your solution. The ideal candidate is an early adopter—a company or organization eager to innovate and address pressing operational challenges. To encourage participation, consider offering attractive incentives such as discounted pricing, extended support, or value-added services. The goal is to secure at least two 2-year subscriptions, ensuring a stable foundation for collaboration and success.

Once the partnership is established, the focus shifts to understanding your anchor client's existing performance. A thorough baseline assessment is conducted, involving close collaboration to gather data on current inefficiencies, costs, and operational challenges. Together, with the client, define KPIs that will measure the success of your solution. This baseline serves as a benchmark for tracking improvements over time, ensuring that progress can be clearly demonstrated.

With baseline data in hand, begin your implementation in a phased manner. This strategy prioritizes high-impact areas where the solution can deliver the most immediate and noticeable benefits. A pilot deployment allows for fine-tuning, followed by broader scaling across the client's operations. Throughout the process, continuous monitoring and reporting are essential to capture incremental improvements and ensure alignment with the defined KPIs.

As the solution takes hold and delivers measurable results, the benefits are carefully documented. Performance improvements are quantified, and a comprehensive ROI analysis is conducted. Client testimonials play a key role in this phase, providing authentic, firsthand accounts of the positive impact they've experienced. Weave these elements together into a structured case study that highlights the initial challenges, the implemented solution, and the achieved results.

The resulting case study will be a powerful tool for market expansion. It serves as a testament to the solution's effectiveness, providing prospective clients with concrete evidence of its value. Sales and marketing teams leverage this narrative in pitches, while thought leadership initiatives ensure visibility across industry platforms. Webinars, conferences, and publications further amplify the message, positioning your company as a trusted authority.

Through this methodical process, securing one key client paves the way for broader market adoption. By documenting success and demonstrating reproducible results, you can more easily attract new clients, accelerate growth, and establish yourself as a leader in your industry.

VALUE REALIZATION KEY TAKEAWAYS

1. Can you quantify business outcomes quarterly to achieve hyperscale revenue?

   Business requires you to measure results to achieve success and provide recommendations.

2. Do you know each executive's compensation that will drive monetary results for them?

   Highlight how you impact metrics that move the needle for the executive leadership team.

3. Without providing success metrics to expand clients, will they reduce their spending with you?

   Quarterly scorecards shared with executives quarterly validates your differentiation.

4. Why are business outcomes the best way to define your competitive differentiation?

   Outcomes are hard to come by. Your project will be the only one with measurable results.

5. How will you measure the end-to-end customer journey for your clients?

Managing the client success framework to collaborate as a strategic partner.

6. Can you explain the value in business terms to differentiate your quantify value by use case?

Profile the highest value use cases by persona to share in your most competitive evaluations.

7. Are the clients' top resources available to engage on your project to make decisions?

The limiting factor is top resource availability to implement your solution, not the cost.

8. Can you quantify customer value creation by segment to provide industry benchmarks?

Positioning value to reduce discounting by 21 percent providing proven industry results.

SUMMARY

You must consistently demonstrate the value of your solutions to secure your clients' executive backing and drive ongoing investment. One of the most effective tools for achieving this buy-in is quarterly performance scorecards. These scorecards not only quantify the impact of technological initiatives but also foster transparency, trust, and data-driven decision-making at the highest levels of the organization.

At the core of these scorecards is the ability to measure and clearly present your solution's return on investment. By tracking KPIs such as revenue growth, cost reduction, operational efficiency, and risk mitigation, you can provide executives with concrete evidence of the value you've delivered. This spotlights the direct contributions of technology initiatives to their overall business performance, making it easier to justify continued investment and expansion.

In addition to highlighting success, performance scorecards also play a pivotal role in facilitating data-driven decision-making. By presenting complex data in a structured and digestible format, they empower executives to make informed choices regarding resource allocation, project prioritization, and risk assessment. This approach enhances the efficiency and effectiveness of decision-making, ensuring that resources are directed toward initiatives that yield the highest returns.

In the next chapter, we'll consider how an emerging tool—AI—can help you prepare insights and create targeted value propositions, freeing up your time to work more efficiently and effectively.

ARTIFICIAL INTELLIGENCE

Acquire Industry Expertise

(Increase Seller Productivity by 41 Percent)

CHAPTER 10

> **UNPARALLELED EXECUTIVE INSIGHTS:** 100 Meter Speed

> **EXECUTIVE RESEARCH:** How to Be Compelling

> **CONTENT WRITING REVIEW:** Provide Depth from Your Insights

> **OUTREACH VISIBILITY:** Consistent Feedback Loop

> **THE TRUTH ABOUT ARTIFICIAL INTELLIGENCE:** Velocity

> **PERSONALIZED CONTENT CREATION:** Value Creation

> **ANNUAL REPORT INSIGHTS:** Financial Intelligence

> **COMPETITIVE BENCHMARKING:** Game-Changing Use Cases

> **AI-GENERATED RETURN ON INVESTMENT:** Economic Benefit

> **ARTIFICIAL INTELLIGENCE THEORY:** Increase Seller Productivity

> **TIPS AND TRICKS:** Elite Efficiency to Compelling Insights

> **ARTIFICIAL INTELLIGENCE WORKBOOK:** Pace of Innovation

> **EVERYDAY APPLICATIONS:** Answer Every Outstanding Question

> **KEY TAKEAWAYS:** Become Well Informed

> **SUMMARY:** Acquire Industry Expertise

UNPARALLELED EXECUTIVE INSIGHTS

T ime is our most valuable asset, and how we choose to use it defines our productivity. In today's data-driven world, however, artificial intelligence (AI) is reshaping the landscape of sales, offering sales professionals the tools they need to engage with executives at a strategic level. Preparing for an executive meeting once took me three days, not to mention the collaboration of three cross-functional experts. By leveraging AI tools, it now takes just two hours on my own—a 93 percent time savings. It's like signing up for a footrace and letting Usain Bolt do all the running!

AI-driven productivity is quickly becoming the norm for high-performing professionals. For instance, a prospect at a Fortune 100 company once tasked my account manager Trevor with creating six detailed company profiles for accounts in six different industries, so their Group Vice Presidents could evaluate the revenue impact on their sales teams' strategic pursuits. Trevor's colleagues, including the head of his business advisor team, insisted that it was too much effort for a mere prospect. Undeterred, Trevor dedicated two days to utilizing AI to generate these comprehensive account profiles. The client was thoroughly impressed with the depth of detail provided, resulting in an $11.4 million transaction three months later.

In the realm of enterprise sales, time is a luxury you rarely have, and rising to the occasion means using the best tool for the job. As organizations increasingly turn to digital transformation, the ability to harness AI effectively throughout your sales process can make the difference between surface-level interactions and meaningful, value-driven engagements. Among other things, sales teams can leverage AI to gather insights, personalize outreach, and anticipate executive needs, ultimately driving stronger business outcomes. Here are just a handful of exciting AI applications in enterprise sales.

- Building strong executive relationships requires a thorough understanding of an organization's structure and key players. AI facilitates this by **mapping out account hierarchies and identifying decision-makers, influencers, and key stakeholders**. This approach, often referred to as multi-threaded engagement, ensures that sales professionals engage with the right individuals at various levels of influence within the organization. Platforms like **ZoomInfo** and **LinkedIn Sales Navigator** leverage machine learning, natural language processing (NLP), and big data analytics to gather and structure organizational intelligence.

- Predictive analytics play a crucial role in identifying opportunities before they surface. AI tools equipped with lead scoring capabilities assess behavioral data to highlight the most promising prospects. Platforms like **6sense** and **Gong** specialize in intent analysis, detecting signals that executives are actively seeking solutions. This insight allows sales professionals to engage at precisely the right moment, ensuring their outreach aligns with the executive's buying journey.

- The most effective sales professionals craft highly personalized engagements. AI can streamline that process: Through AI-driven tools like **Crystal Knows** and **Humantic AI**, sales teams can analyze communication styles, behavioral patterns, and preferences. By pulling insights from publicly available data, these platforms allow sales professionals to tailor their messaging in a way that resonates on a personal and professional level.

- Beyond personalization, AI **facilitates data analysis** for custom reports and insights. By aggregating data from earnings calls, social media activity, press releases, and interviews, AI will help your sales teams develop a comprehensive understanding of your prospect's pain points and strategic goals. This level of detail not only captures attention but also establishes credibility from the outset.

- The value of AI extends into the realm of conversations. **Gong** and **Chorus** analyze sales calls, extracting patterns that reveal what works and what doesn't. By studying these insights, sales professionals can refine their approach, enhancing their ability to connect with executives. Furthermore, AI-powered sentiment analysis evaluates tone and language, offering real-time feedback during phone calls or virtual meetings. This not only improves the quality of engagement but also strengthens rapport by allowing sales professionals to adjust their messaging dynamically.

- Executives value concrete demonstrations of potential ROI and strategic fit. AI enhances this by generating customized demos and proposals that reflect each executive's KPIs and organizational needs. **Scenario modeling**, powered by generative AI, allows sales teams to showcase the impact of their solutions across different business scenarios, reinforcing the value proposition with data-driven insights. Likewise, AI can continuously **monitor competitor activities** and industry trends, arming sales teams with valuable competitive intelligence. By staying informed about the movements of rival organizations, sales professionals can position their solutions as unique and indispensable, aligning with the executive's broader strategic vision. Solutions like **Salesforce Einstein** predict sales opportunities and deal influence while **People.ai** maps buying committees and decision-makers.

- Trust is the cornerstone of executive engagement, and AI helps sales professionals build it by consistently delivering **relevant and insightful content**. As you build executive relationships, generative AI can help you produce tailored thought leadership content, reports, white papers, social media content, and even personalized video messages, all designed to reflect the executive's unique challenges. Platforms like **ChatGPT** enable you to perform efficient research while **Anyword** allows you to have AI edit your content with a specific tone.

- AI-powered networking platforms such as **Affinity** further enhance trust-building by identifying mutual connections and suggesting strategic touchpoints. These platforms provide valuable insights into relationship dynamics, allowing sales professionals to cultivate deeper and more meaningful connections with executive stakeholders. **LinkedIn Sales Navigator** allows you to see which connections you have in common, and **UserGems** highlights which executives have changed companies because 90 percent of their decisions will be made in the first ninety days.

- Executives operate in fast-paced environments where real-time data is critical. **AI-driven dashboards** aggregate and present market intelligence, competitor performance, and organizational updates, enabling sales teams to provide executives with timely and relevant insights. This ability to deliver up-to-date information further solidifies the sales professional's role as a valuable resource and partner. The solutions that provide AI-powered reporting dashboards are **HubSpot** for predictive sales analytics and deal prioritization or **Tableau** for AI recommendations.

In short, AI is not just a tool—it is a strategic enabler that transforms how sales professionals engage with executives. By harnessing AI's capabilities for personalization, predictive engagement, and strategic account planning, your sales teams can build trust, demonstrate value, and drive meaningful business outcomes. As AI technology continues to evolve, it will become an even more integral component of successful executive engagement strategies, setting the stage for deeper connections and long-term partnerships.

EXECUTIVE RESEARCH

Preparing for executive meetings requires a meticulous blend of research, content creation, and strategic planning. These gatherings play a pivotal role in shaping organizational direction, aligning leadership, and fostering impactful decision-making. To ensure executives are well-equipped for these high-stakes discussions, consider leveraging tools like **ChatGPT** to significantly enhance your preparation process.

The first step in preparation is thorough research and information gathering. Executives must remain informed about the latest industry developments, technological trends, and competitive movements. AI streamlines this process by distilling complex industry reports, summarizing white papers, and providing concise analyses of emerging innovations. Additionally, it can offer regular updates on shifting market landscapes, ensuring leaders stay ahead of the curve.

Understanding competitors is equally crucial. AI can compile detailed competitor profiles, juxtapose product offerings, and highlight strategic differentiators. By monitoring competitor announcements and tracking partnerships, AI helps executives anticipate market moves and position their organizations effectively. Financial health is often at the forefront of these discussions. AI assists by summarizing earnings reports, highlighting growth metrics, and analyzing market valuations. This financial insight offers executives a holistic view of their organization's standing, as well as that of their competitors.

Internal readiness is another cornerstone of executive preparation. AI aggregates relevant news, press releases, and financial disclosures to provide clear snapshots of ongoing initiatives, partnerships, and performance metrics. It simplifies complex technical concepts, providing summaries and glossaries that break down difficult subjects and foster a deeper understanding across diverse topics. Strategic planning is likewise enhanced by AI's ability to generate thought-provoking questions, simulate various business scenarios, and outline SWOT analysis. These elements enable executives to explore different strategic avenues, weighing the pros and cons of each path forward.

Effective communication is paramount, and AI simplifies the drafting of emails, speeches, and position papers. It tailors messages to diverse audiences, refines tone and language, and ensures alignment with organizational goals. AI also excels at crafting executive summaries, extracting key points from lengthy documents, and highlighting actionable insights. Whether you're developing presentation outlines, suggesting slide content, or drafting briefing notes, AI ensures that every element of your communication is polished and impactful. For more comprehensive deliverables like reports or white papers, AI aids in structuring, drafting, and visualizing data. It ensures coherence across sections and provides references and citations to strengthen credibility.

As meetings approach, AI continues to provide real-time updates. By gathering live information and monitoring competitor activities, it ensures executives have the most current insights at their fingertips. This constant stream of information allows for agile adjustments to strategy and enhances preparedness. In essence, AI serves as a comprehensive assistant for executive meeting preparation. From research and content development to strategy and communication, it empowers leaders to make informed decisions, engage stakeholders effectively, and drive organizational success.

CONTENT WRITING REVIEW

In the fast-paced world of sales, where competition grows fiercer by the day, success often hinges on your ability to connect, communicate, and convert. For sales professionals striving to stay ahead, AI emerges as a crucial ally. For example, the copywriting platform **Anyword** equips sales teams with the tools to craft personalized messages, optimize outreach strategies, and ultimately drive more meaningful engagement with potential clients.

The magic begins by crafting tailored messages. Imagine stepping into a meeting already knowing what your client wants to hear. AI makes this possible by analyzing audience demographics and behavioral data, allowing sales professionals to produce content that resonates deeply. Whether it's a LinkedIn message that directly addresses a client's pain points or an email that strikes just the right chord, AI ensures that communication feels personal, not generic.

What sets AI apart, though, is its predictive performance scoring. Picture a world where you no longer need to guess which version of your pitch will perform best. AI evaluates each variation and assigns a score, highlighting the most promising option based on its audience analysis. This not only saves time but also eliminates the uncertainty that often clouds sales communications. Sales teams can move forward with confidence, knowing they're sending messages with the highest likelihood of success.

Time is a precious commodity in sales, and AI recognizes this by automating content creation. Drafting cold emails, follow-ups, and product descriptions no longer needs to consume hours of your valuable time. With just a few clicks, AI generates high-quality copy for your review, freeing sales professionals to focus on what matters most—building relationships and closing deals. This automation extends to A/B testing—two options to test which resonates best with prospects—enabling your teams to compare multiple message variations and quickly identify what works best.

Consistency in brand messaging is another cornerstone of effective sales communication. Prospects need to feel a seamless experience across every touchpoint, from the initial email to the final pitch. AI platforms automatically align your message tone and content across social media, emails, or landing pages, helping you reinforce brand identity and create a cohesive and trustworthy image that resonates with potential clients.

Of course, even the most experienced sales professionals encounter writer's block. Crafting compelling, persuasive messages day after day can be challenging. AI acts as a creative partner, offering suggestions for recasting your message in different tones and styles. Need a formal pitch? AI delivers. Looking for a more casual, friendly tone? The platform can handle that too. With endless possibilities at their fingertips, sales teams can keep their messaging fresh, innovative, and engaging.

Nurturing leads is an essential part of the sales process, and AI excels in this area as well. AI platforms generate compelling content for drip campaigns and follow-ups, ensuring leads remain engaged over time. Personalized follow-ups keep communication relevant, reflecting the evolving needs of clients and gently guiding them toward conversion. By maintaining consistent, valuable touchpoints, sales professionals can increase their chances of turning prospects into loyal customers.

In conclusion, AI stands out as more than just a copywriting tool; it's a strategic partner for sales teams aiming to elevate their communication and achieve greater success. By leveraging AI for personalized messaging, predictive scoring, and automation, AI empowers sales professionals to optimize their outreach efforts, enhance engagement, and drive stronger results. As the sales landscape evolves, those equipped with curated AI tools will be best positioned to thrive and lead in an ever-changing market.

OUTREACH VISIBILITY

Outreach software has transformed how sales teams approach demand creation by automating engagement, tracking performance, and delivering valuable insights on executive open rates, all to help ensure your value proposition hits the mark. This transformation allows your sales teams to maintain a consistent feedback loop, a crucial component in refining strategies and driving better outcomes.

One of the primary advantages of outreach software lies in its ability to automate engagement and track every interaction. Sales teams can deploy automated email sequences, call scripts, and LinkedIn messages that ensure prospects receive timely and personalized communication. As these campaigns unfold, the software monitors key engagement metrics, such as email opens, responses, and link clicks, providing instant feedback on outreach performance.

Beyond engagement, outreach platforms offer robust analytics that guide sales teams in making data-driven decisions. Real-time analytics provide immediate insights into what works and what doesn't, allowing teams to adjust their strategies quickly. With A/B testing capabilities, sales representatives can experiment with different messaging approaches, gradually honing their outreach to maximize engagement and response rates.

An essential element of demand creation is the ability to prioritize leads effectively. Here, outreach software leverages AI-driven lead scoring to rank prospects based on their likelihood to convert. By analyzing engagement data, the platform highlights high-potential leads, ensuring that sales teams focus their efforts where they are most likely to succeed. Meanwhile, predictive analytics forecasts which leads are likely to move through the sales funnel, enabling more accurate resource allocation.

Outreach platforms don't operate in isolation; they seamlessly integrate with CRM systems, ensuring that every touchpoint with a prospect is recorded and accessible. This integration creates a closed-loop feedback system, where data flows between outreach campaigns and the CRM, offering a comprehensive view of lead progression. Sales teams can track the entire journey of a lead, from the initial point of contact to deal closure, identifying successful touchpoints and areas for improvement.

Coaching and continuous improvement are fundamental to sales success, and outreach software plays a pivotal role in this process. Features like call recording and analysis allow managers to review interactions, providing constructive feedback to refine techniques and improve communication. Performance dashboards further enhance workflow by offering visibility into individual and team performance, enabling targeted coaching based on concrete data.

Collaboration across sales teams is another key aspect supported by outreach platforms. Successful outreach strategies and playbooks can be shared across teams, ensuring that best practices are consistently applied. Automated follow-ups help maintain engagement, ensuring no lead falls through the cracks, and keep the momentum of outreach efforts alive.

The benefits of a **consistent feedback loop in outreach** are substantial. Sales teams can iterate faster, refining their approach based on real-time data. As outreach becomes more personalized and targeted, engagement rates improve, leading to higher conversion rates. Automation enables outreach at scale, allowing teams to expand their reach while maintaining the quality of interactions.

By automating communication, providing real-time insights, and fostering collaboration, these platforms establish a continuous feedback loop that propels growth and enhances sales performance. As outreach software continues to evolve, its impact on demand generation will only deepen, solidifying its role as a cornerstone of successful sales strategies.

THE TRUTH ABOUT ARTIFICIAL INTELLIGENCE

Leveraging strategic information is the key to securing new executive meetings, the first step toward business growth, strategic partnerships, and achieving organizational goals. Studies show that organizations using strategic information and targeted processes can dramatically boost their success rate in securing executive meetings—from as low as 1 percent to as high as 41 percent. This approach also reduces research time from ninety hours to just two hours. Despite this compelling evidence, many organizations still fail to effectively utilize the strategic resources available to them.

Organizations often face several barriers that hinder the adoption of proven strategies. Teams frequently view processes such as personalized content creation, executive and competitive benchmarking, and detailed executive research as overly complicated. This perceived complexity creates hesitation, ultimately deterring teams from fully integrating these powerful strategies into their routine operations.

Furthermore, the widespread lack of essential skills and comprehensive understanding exacerbates the issue. Without targeted training programs and clear guidance, tasks like researching companies and executives, crafting personalized content, and analyzing competitive intelligence can feel overwhelming. Consequently, teams might resort to simpler but less effective methods.

Time constraints also play a significant role. Effective personalization and thorough research require substantial investments of time and resources. Under pressure to deliver quick results, teams often choose generalized outreach, sacrificing the increased effectiveness and potential long-term benefits of personalized strategies.

Misaligned incentives are another critical factor. Organizations frequently prioritize and reward outreach volume over the quality and depth of interactions. This misalignment discourages team members from dedicating time and effort to the strategic personalization that is proven to deliver superior outcomes.

Additionally, resistance to change remains a persistent barrier. Organizational inertia and deeply ingrained routines create resistance to adopting new methodologies, even when their effectiveness is clear. This cultural resistance can significantly hinder progress, causing organizations to miss critical opportunities.

Lack of adequate resources or specialized tools further complicates matters. Without robust systems for tracking outreach visibility, conducting comprehensive executive and competitive research, or generating tailored ROI analyses, teams struggle to execute effectively, even when they understand the importance of these strategic practices.

Organizations also frequently suffer from data overload, grappling with the challenge of converting vast amounts of available information into actionable insights. Without structured processes to distill annual reports, competitive analyses, and executive profiles, teams can quickly become overwhelmed and revert to ineffective, generalized methods.

Underestimating the impact of strategic processes is a common oversight among organizational leaders. Decision-makers often fail to recognize the substantial difference that personalized outreach, targeted content creation, and comprehensive research can make in securing executive meetings and driving overall organizational success.

To overcome these challenges, your GTM teams must adopt a structured approach. Simplifying workflows through clearly defined frameworks and providing targeted skill-development training will encourage team adoption. Allocating sufficient resources, realigning incentives to reward quality over quantity, and fostering organizational agility through proactive change management will further enhance effectiveness.

Moreover, consider investing in advanced analytical tools and resources to ensure effective execution. Building structured frameworks to convert data into actionable insights is equally vital. Finally, educating your stakeholders about the quantifiable impacts of strategic processes will ensure ongoing organizational commitment. By systematically addressing these barriers, you can effectively leverage strategic information, significantly enhancing your ability to secure valuable executive meetings and driving sustained business growth and success.

PERSONALIZED CONTENT CREATION

Engaging with executives calls for more than a generic pitch. It's a nuanced art that combines research, empathy, and tailored messaging to cut through the barrage of daily solicitations. The essence of standing out lies in showcasing a profound understanding of their business and presenting value that aligns with their strategic objectives. This guide delineates the critical components for crafting outreach that captivates executives and fosters meaningful connections.

Establishing a foundation with research enables effective personalization, beginning with an in-depth exploration of the executive's environment. From company strategy to individual interests, uncovering relevant insights provides the context required to formulate compelling messages. Start with the organizational landscape, using annual reports, interviews, news articles, third-party analyses, and press releases to enrich your knowledge. What major initiatives, acquisitions, or growth plans are shaping their agenda? Where might your solution align with their ambitions?

Understanding each leader's personal journey offers more clues to their priorities. Review LinkedIn profiles, articles, and keynote addresses to comprehend your prospect's career path and leadership philosophy. Have they championed innovation or led major transformation projects? Do you share professional or personal interests that can help you draw connections and establish common ground?

Next, broaden your understanding of the industry landscape by researching industry trends and competitor activities. Reference industry reports or studies during your interactions to demonstrate an awareness of market shifts. By showcasing how your prospect's competitors are addressing these challenges, you position yourself as a strategic partner capable of guiding the executive toward differentiated solutions.

Crafting value-creation messaging translates insights into messaging that speaks directly to the executive's priorities. This alignment enhances the relevance of your outreach, boosting the likelihood of engagement. Likewise, connecting your solutions to their strategic goals frames your work as a direct enabler of their future success. Whether it's driving revenue growth, reducing costs, or improving customer experience, ensure your solution fits seamlessly into their broader strategy. Reference specific projects or initiatives to illustrate alignment.

Quantifying your solution's impact is crucial since executives are driven by results. Use data to emphasize its tangible benefits, such as ROI, operational efficiency, or market-share gains. Customer case studies from similar industries provide credibility and showcase real-world applications. The more specific and measurable your value proposition, the more compelling your outreach becomes.

Personalizing by persona entails tailoring your message to the executive's functional role:

- CEOs/COOs care about market expansion and competitive positioning. Address growth, market trends, and long-term vision.
- CFOs prioritize cost control, financial risk, and ROI. Frame your pitch around financial efficiency and cost reduction.
- CTOs/CIOs focus on scalability, innovation, and technological advancement. Highlight technical differentiators and scalability potential.

Remember, a **human-centered approach builds trust** and differentiates your outreach from impersonal sales pitches. Executives value authenticity, empathy, and meaningful connections. That means acknowledging the challenges your audience faces and positioning yourself as a problem-solver, not just a vendor. Use empathetic language that resonates with their experience. Keep communication clear, concise, and free from unnecessary jargon.

Telling a story is a powerful way to apply these standards. Frame your solution within a broader story of transformation and success—how have similar organizations overcome similar challenges with your help? By painting a vivid picture, you create an emotional connection that complements the logical appeal of your offering. You also guide executives toward streamlined action, ensuring their path forward is clear and frictionless.

The right call to action typically includes low-commitment options, such as a brief call, demo, or industry insight session. Position these actions as mutually beneficial, but emphasize the value the executive will gain, whether it's benchmarking their performance or exploring new strategies.

Multi-touch engagement is rarely achieved through a single interaction. Utilize a mix of channels—emails, LinkedIn messages, and phone calls—to maintain visibility. Personalize each touchpoint to reinforce your understanding of your audience's needs. Plan your follow-up cadence carefully to stay top-of-mind without being intrusive.

Delivering the message effectively is as important as the message itself. Timing is key. Identify optimal moments for outreach, such as post-earnings calls, leadership changes, or milestone announcements. Aligning your message with these events enhances relevance.

Finally, simplifying communication helps convey your value with brevity. Summarize key points in one-pagers or executive briefs that can be easily shared internally. Where applicable, incorporate visuals and data to distill complex information into digestible formats.

Personalized outreach to executives demands a blend of insight, empathy, and strategic communication. By investing time in research, crafting value-aligned messages, and humanizing your approach, you can build lasting relationships that drive business growth. The journey begins with understanding—and the rewards lie in the partnerships you cultivate along the way.

ANNUAL REPORT INSIGHTS

The 10-K filing, a cornerstone of corporate transparency, offers investors and analysts a window into a company's operations, risks, and financial standing. Yet the dense and extensive nature of these documents often makes them challenging to dissect manually. AI is a clear ally here, as it can streamline the analysis process, uncover hidden patterns, and surface critical insights with unprecedented efficiency. This section explores how AI can unlock the full potential of key sections within the 10-K, turning static reports into dynamic sources of actionable intelligence.

THE STORY OF THE BUSINESS. Our task begins, of course, in the "Business" section. This segment paints a picture of the company's operations, products, services, and market positioning. AI can serve as a storyteller, distilling complex narratives into concise summaries that capture the essence of a company's core functions.

By applying market analysis algorithms, AI sifts through multiple filings to identify common threads, competitive differentiators, and emerging industry trends. Furthermore, opportunity detection models can highlight mentions of expansion plans, innovation initiatives, and strategic pivots, enabling investors to stay ahead of the curve.

CONFRONTING UNCERTAINTY. Risk factors lurk in every corner of corporate life, and companies devote entire sections of their 10-K filings to cataloging these threats. AI acts as a risk navigator, categorizing and ranking risks based on severity and frequency. It can also analyze language shifts over time, flagging emerging risks and evolving challenges.

By benchmarking risk factors across competitors, AI provides a broader view of the risk landscape, empowering stakeholders to make more informed decisions and anticipate potential headwinds.

DECODING THE DISCUSSION. The Management Discussion and Analysis (MD&A) section offers a candid glimpse into how firm leadership interprets past performance and envisions the future. AI transforms this qualitative section into quantifiable insights. Sentiment analysis tools dissect management's tone, revealing subtle cues of optimism or caution.

Meanwhile, strategic tracking algorithms follow recurring themes, allowing for comparisons across different reporting periods. This not only highlights performance indicators but also sheds light on shifting strategic priorities.

UNVEILING THE BOOKS. Financial statements are the bedrock of the 10-K, but they can be dense and intimidating. AI simplifies this complexity by automating ratio analysis, profitability assessments, and liquidity evaluations. Machine learning algorithms can spot anomalies or inconsistencies, serving as an early warning system for potential financial misstatements. Moreover, predictive models harness historical data to forecast future performance, providing stakeholders with forward-looking insights that extend beyond the current fiscal year.

READING BETWEEN THE LINES. Notes to the financial statements are where accounting policies, contingencies, and hidden risks reside. AI meticulously combs through these notes, extracting policy shifts and flagging off-balance-sheet activities that might otherwise go unnoticed.

THE LEGAL LANDSCAPE. Litigation and regulatory actions can pose significant threats to a company's stability. AI steps in as a legal analyst, classifying ongoing cases and tracking their progression. By benchmarking legal disclosures across industry peers, AI highlights companies that may be facing disproportionate legal risks.

MAPPING MARKET RISKS. Market volatility is a given, and companies outline their exposure in the Market Risk Disclosures section. AI quantifies these exposures, modeling different scenarios to predict how shifts in interest rates, currency fluctuations, or commodity prices could impact the bottom line.

EXECUTIVE COMPENSATION often reflects a company's performance priorities. AI delves into this section to benchmark pay structures, correlate compensation with financial outcomes, and analyze the incentives driving executive behavior. This can reveal alignment—or misalignment—between leadership incentives and shareholder interests.

UNLOCKING STRATEGIC DOCUMENTS. The exhibits section houses material contracts and agreements that shape corporate strategy. AI acts as a digital archivist, extracting key terms from contracts and identifying strategic partnerships or obligations. This provides valuable insights into a company's operational dependencies and future commitments.

ANNUAL REPORT SEARCH TERMS

1. Financial Performance	**4. Operational Efficiency**
Revenue	New Office Space
Net Income/Profit	Cost Reduction
Operating Margin	Automation
EBITDA	Efficiency Gains
Cash Flow	Process Optimization
Expenses/Cost	**5. Technology and Innovation**
Gross Margins	Artificial Intelligence
2. Strategic Outlook	Machine Learning
New Products	Cloud Adoption
CEO Blog	Digital Platforms
Growth Strategy	Cybersecurity Investments
Market Expansion	Technology Roadmap
Innovation	**6. Customer and Market Focus**
Research and Development	Customer Experience
Partnerships	User Engagement
Digital Transformation	Market Share
3. Risk and Compliance	Competitive Advantage
Risk Factors	Brand Strength
Cybersecurity	**7. Human Capital**
Regulatory Compliance	Job Posts
Litigation	Leadership Promotions
Supply Chain Disruption	Employee Retention
Market Volatility	Training and Development
Geopolitical Risks	

Diagram 10.0 Speed Up Your Research

AI employs a diverse toolkit to unlock insights from 10-K filings. Natural Language Processing (NLP) distills complex text, sentiment analysis reveals hidden tones, and machine learning predicts financial trajectories. Clustering algorithms group companies by shared risks or strategies, painting a clearer picture of industry dynamics.

By integrating AI into the 10-K research process, your analysts can transform raw data into actionable intelligence, unlocking new dimensions of understanding and fostering more confident, data-driven decisions.

COMPETITIVE BENCHMARKING

Staying ahead of the competition requires a profound grasp of industry dynamics. Industry benchmarking serves as a potent tool, enabling businesses to measure their performance against peers and market leaders. Through benchmarking, organizations can unearth valuable insights, pinpoint areas for growth, and refine their strategic direction. AI technology is a transformative asset in this process, providing businesses with the means to analyze vast amounts of data, uncover trends, and generate actionable insights with unparalleled efficiency.

Gaining market insights through benchmarking begins by immersing yourself in the competitive landscape. As a comprehensive research assistant, AI software is capable of sifting through countless reports, news articles, and financial disclosures. By distilling this wealth of information, you and your clients can obtain clear insights into competitor strengths, weaknesses, and strategic initiatives. Additionally, tracking industry trends ensures that you remain informed about emerging technologies, regulatory changes, and evolving market dynamics. This constant flow of information is vital for maintaining a pulse on the industry and ensuring benchmarking efforts reflect current realities.

Financial metrics form the backbone of benchmarking. Your analysis should extract and compare key performance indicators such as revenue growth, profit margins, and R&D investments. By juxtaposing these figures with those of competitors, prospects and clients gain a clearer picture of their standing in the industry and identify areas for financial optimization. Another critical component of data analysis is identifying gaps. By comparing internal performance metrics against industry leaders, AI technology highlights discrepancies and pinpoints areas where businesses can enhance efficiency, improve productivity, or capture greater market share.

Custom data-driven analysis goes beyond external market data; AI technology thrives on processing large internal datasets to reveal hidden patterns and insights. This capability allows businesses to evaluate year-over-year growth, operational efficiency, and market share directly from their own data sources. Visualization adds another layer to this analysis: Transforming raw data into compelling charts and graphs paints a visual narrative of industry benchmarks. These visual aids not only facilitate internal discussions but also enhance presentations to stakeholders, making complex data more digestible and actionable.

Understanding qualitative benchmarks involves studying the numbers that tell part of the story, but qualitative insights often reveal the full picture. Software is adept at summarizing customer reviews, online feedback, and competitor product descriptions. Additionally, technology can conduct detailed product feature comparisons, allowing businesses to understand how their offerings stack up against competitors. This insight proves invaluable when refining products or crafting new value propositions. By synthesizing these sources, businesses can gauge public perception, customer satisfaction, and areas where competitors excel or fall short.

Sentiment analysis further deepens qualitative benchmarking. By analyzing social media mentions, reviews, and online discussions, technology identifies prevailing attitudes and sentiments toward competitors. This not only helps businesses stay attuned to market perception but also reveals opportunities to address unmet customer needs or capitalize on competitor shortcomings.

Automating the benchmarking process ensures sustained competitiveness. Benchmarking must be continuous, and technology facilitates this by automating the generation of regular benchmarking reports. Whether on a weekly, monthly, or quarterly basis, the right software can compile up-to-date reports, allowing businesses to track performance trends over time. In addition to routine reports, AI technology can create SWOT (Strengths, Weaknesses,

Opportunities, Threats) analyses that offer structured insights into the company's position relative to competitors. This ongoing assessment empowers businesses to adapt to changing market conditions swiftly and strategically.

Keep in mind, however, that benchmarking without follow-through yields limited value. Technology bridges the gap between insight and action by providing strategic recommendations tailored to your client's benchmarking data. Whether suggesting operational improvements, recommending product enhancements, or identifying new market opportunities, technology transforms benchmarking results into tangible growth strategies. Scenario planning represents another strategic advantage. By simulating various market scenarios, technology helps businesses anticipate competitor moves, prepare for industry shifts, and stress-test their strategies against potential future developments.

The integration of advanced technology into the benchmarking process marks a new era of efficiency and insight. By leveraging its ability to analyze data, track trends, and generate strategic recommendations, businesses not only stay competitive but also cultivate long-term growth.

AI-GENERATED RETURN ON INVESTMENT

Calculating the return on investment is a crucial step in assessing the profitability and effectiveness of any solution. Whether deploying new technology, launching a product, or implementing a service, understanding ROI provides the insight needed to make informed decisions, allocate resources efficiently, and predict long-term performance.

The first step in this process is defining the scope of the solution. This involves identifying the exact nature of the product, service, or technology being introduced. By clearly outlining the purpose and goals of the solution, as well as the departments or teams affected, organizations can set the foundation for accurate cost and benefit estimates.

Next, you must gather key metrics to break down the financial aspects of the project. This can be done by categorizing costs and returns. On the cost side, initial implementation expenses, ongoing operational costs, personnel and training, and indirect costs like downtime or productivity losses should all be considered. Benefits, on the other hand, may include productivity gains, operational cost savings, increased revenue, and risk mitigation through improved security and error prevention.

Once the necessary data is collected, applying the ROI formula becomes straightforward. By calculating total costs and estimating projected benefits, the net return can be determined. Subtracting total costs from total benefits and dividing by the total investment provides the ROI percentage, offering a clear view of the solution's financial viability.

To refine this calculation, it is important to incorporate specific scenarios and time horizons. Performing ROI calculations over varying periods, such as six months, twelve months, or eighteen months, helps capture the evolving nature of investments. Developing multiple scenarios—including best-case, worst-case, and most likely outcomes—further enhances analytical reliability. Additionally, adjustments for inflation, market shifts, and operational changes ensure that the ROI reflects real-world conditions.

Automating the ROI calculation process can significantly improve accuracy and efficiency. Tools like ChatGPT, Excel, and Python scripts can assist in building tailored ROI models, simulating different scenarios, and generating detailed reports and visualizations. This automation not only saves time but also reduces the margin for error, providing decision-makers with reliable data to drive strategic planning.

Ultimately, calculating ROI is a critical component of project planning and evaluation. By clearly defining the project scope, gathering comprehensive data, and applying structured analysis, your clients can ensure sound investment decisions and justify expenditures with confidence. Should you require assistance in creating a detailed ROI model or calculator, expert help is available to customize the process to fit your unique needs.

For example, ChatGPT can create a complete ROI analysis for SIEM and Observability deployment at Panasonic with only knowing the target investment of $1 million. In this exercise, the AI knows that Panasonic is aiming to enhance security, system uptime, and operational efficiency.

Assumptions:

- Deal Value: $1 million (up-front investment)
- Deployment Time: 4 months
- Operational Lifetime: 4 years
- Reduction in Downtime: 25 percent
- Average Cost of Downtime per Hour: $300,000
- Annual Downtime Hours (pre-deployment): 40 hours
- Incident Reduction: 30 percent
- Average Cost per Security Incident: $400,000
- Annual Number of Incidents (pre-deployment): 15
- Efficiency Gain in IT Operations: 20 percent
- Labor Cost Savings: $250,000/year
- Compliance and Regulatory Penalty Avoidance: $600,000 over 4 years

ROI Components:

1. Downtime Reduction and Cost Savings:
   - Pre-Deployment Downtime: 40 hours/year
   - Post-Deployment Downtime: 30 hours/year (25 percent reduction)
   - Cost Savings per Year: 10 hours × $300,000 = $3 million/year
   - Four-Year Savings: $3 million × 4 = $12 million
2. Incident Reduction and Cost Savings:
   - Pre-Deployment Incidents: 15/year
   - Post-Deployment Incidents: 10.5/year (30 percent reduction)
   - Cost Savings per Year: 4.5 incidents × $400,000 = $1.8 million/year
   - Four-Year Savings: $1.8 million × 4 = $7.2 million
3. Efficiency Gains:
   - Labor Cost Savings: $250,000/year
   - Four-Year Savings: $250,000 × 4 = $1 million
4. Compliance Penalty Avoidance:
   - $600,000 in savings over four years
5. Operational Improvements and Enhanced Observability:

- Improved system performance,
  faster incident response, and proactive threat detection
- Estimated intangible benefits: $800,000 over 4 years

Total Savings Over 4 Years:
- Downtime Reduction: $12 million
- Incident Reduction: $7.2 million
- Efficiency Gains: $1 million
- Compliance Savings: $600,000
- Intangible Benefits: $800,000
- Total: $21.6 million

ROI Calculation:
- Net Benefit = Total Savings – Investment
- $21.6 million – $1 million = $20.6 million
- ROI = (Net Benefit / Investment) × 100
- ROI = (20.6 / 1) × 100 = 2,060 percent

Payback Period:
- Initial Investment: $1 million
- Annual Savings: $5.4 million (downtime + incident + labor savings)
- Payback Period: $1 million / $5.4 million = 0.19 years (2.3 months)

Deploying digital resilience solutions at Panasonic delivers significant value, with a projected ROI of 540 percent and a fast payback period of 2.3 months. The investment fortifies Panasonic's security, reduces operational disruptions, and enhances overall system reliability.

ARTIFICIAL INTELLIGENCE THEORY

Pinpoint potential areas for improvement and provide tailored suggestions to executive leadership teams with accounts. Formulating comprehensive business within hours, allowing for rapid development of strategic initiatives.

Why change?

Challenge:	Do your teams leverage the latest AI capabilities to generate insights? 85 percent of discovery can be complete prior to your first executive meeting. Can you research an industry segment in the time as one account?

How do we differentiate?

Concept 37:	**Unparalleled Executive Insights** are now readily available thanks to AI, allowing you to craft business strategies in just a few hours instead of weeks. Sales teams can obtain crucial information, tailor their outreach efforts, and predict the needs of executives, leading to more effective business results.
Concept 38:	**The Strategic Stakeholder Exchange** consists of four components that make it compelling to the C-suite. The first is a story to provide context, use cases to identify persona, metrics to determine the size of the impact, and opportunity to make real with expert resource availability.
Concept 39:	**Content Writing Review** provides sales teams with the resources to create tailored messages, refine their outreach approaches, and foster more significant interactions with prospective clients. By examining audience demographics and behavioral information, sales professionals can generate content that connects with your audience.
Concept 40:	**Outreach Visibility** revolutionizes the way sales teams generate demand by automating engagement processes, monitoring performance metrics, and providing crucial insights into executive open rates to ensure your value proposition hits the mark.

What do we receive?

Result:	Access to executive insights outside-in to accelerate your knowledge. Proven AI prompts that **increase seller productivity +48%**. Add value in every interaction with executives with fast follow-up.

TIPS AND TRICKS FOR ARTIFICIAL INTELLIGENCE

- In today's fiercely competitive B2B arena, engaging with executives demands more than a run-of-the-mill pitch. Personalization, clear value articulation, and strategic follow-up are indispensable elements of effective outreach. Sales professionals are finding AI to be a game-changing tool, enabling deeper, more meaningful connections and boosting response rates. By leveraging AI, outreach efforts can be meticulously crafted and **tailored to resonate** with decision-makers at high-powered firms.

- Executives are constantly bombarded with sales emails, making personalization an essential strategy for standing out. AI can sift through public data sources such as LinkedIn profiles, company press releases, and earnings calls to generate insights that serve as the bedrock of personalized communication. For instance, a brief prompt for a summary of your client's latest quarterly reports can unveil growth priorities and strategic initiatives. Aligning your message with these areas makes your outreach far more relevant and engaging.

- At the core of executive outreach lies value-centric messaging. It's insufficient to merely highlight product features; the emphasis must be on how the solution advances your prospect's objectives, like enhancing operational efficiency, cutting costs, or fostering innovation. AI can emulate the perspective of firm leadership, helping sales professionals **preemptively identify** and address potential objections. Asking AI to role-play as a CFO or CIO offers invaluable insights into the objections or interests that may surface during the sales discussion.

- Subject lines are the gateway to your message and can determine whether an email is opened or disregarded. With AI, sales teams can produce multiple subject line variations, each capturing different tones and strategies. A/B testing these subject lines helps pinpoint the most effective approach. For instance, asking ChatGPT for "ten subject line options related to AI-driven supply chain solutions" ensures you can select the one that best aligns with the target audience.

- Condensing intricate offerings into **succinct executive summaries** is another domain where AI shines. Executives favor brief yet powerful overviews that spotlight key benefits. By asking AI to "summarize how AI solutions enhance data insights or operational efficiency," sales professionals can create compelling messages that underscore ROI, risk reduction, and competitive advantage.

- Managing objections is an inevitable aspect of the sales process, and being prepared is crucial. AI allows you to anticipate potential pushback by simulating the executive's concerns. For example, if a CIO is hesitant to invest in generative AI for manufacturing, AI can generate counterarguments addressing cost, integration, and ROI, thereby fortifying your overall pitch.

- Follow-up sequences are vital for maintaining engagement, but crafting personalized, multi-touch outreach can be labor-intensive. AI simplifies this by creating a series of emails or LinkedIn messages **tailored for different roles**. A customized three-email follow-up sequence targeting a CTO can sustain the conversation without being intrusive.

- Establishing thought leadership is a long-term strategy that builds credibility and trust. Sales professionals can employ AI to draft LinkedIn posts or white papers on industry-relevant subjects that align with the client's interests. By producing content on AI in manufacturing or sustainable technology, sales teams can position themselves as knowledgeable partners rather than mere vendors.

- AI can simulate potential executive meetings by generating common questions and ideal responses. This role-playing exercise ensures that sales professionals are ready to tackle the client's specific challenges and opportunities during live discussions.

- Keeping abreast of market trends and competitor activities is essential for **tailoring outreach**. AI can swiftly summarize the latest trends in AI-driven manufacturing or smart factory solutions, ensuring sales professionals are armed with current, relevant insights. Incorporating these insights into outreach materials showcases expertise and adds value to the conversation.
- Matching the tone and language of your client's communications enhances message receptivity. AI can adjust the wording of outreach emails to reflect the style found in their leadership statements or public announcements, fostering a sense of familiarity and alignment.
- After you prompt AI for a basic response, don't forget to prompt it for an enhanced result. Here are a few samples to get you started:
  - *Turn this into a more detailed formal and structured piece.* This will expand your response into a structured document with significantly more detail.
  - *Turn this into a written narrative.* This will convert your outline with bullet points into a written narrative.
  - *Remove the words _____ or replace them with the word _____.* This enables you to remove repetitive words.

By harnessing AI, sales professionals can revolutionize their outreach strategies, cultivating deeper connections with executives as potential strategic partners. From personalized messaging and objection handling to follow-ups and thought leadership, the potential is vast. Embracing these strategies will not only elevate engagement but also drive sustainable business growth.

ARTIFICIAL INTELLIGENCE WORKBOOK
DEVELOP WORLD-CLASS SPEED TO INSIGHT

Artificial Intelligence Frameworks

178 PERSONALIZE CONTENT	Tailoring content to meet the specific audience segment • Leveraging data to deliver relevant and engaging experience
179 ANNUAL REPORT INSIGHTS	Observations and conclusions derived from analyzing • Financial performance, strategic direction, and market position
180 INDUSTRY ASSESSMENTS	Industry structure, dynamics, trends, competitive landscape • Customer behavior, competitive pressures, and emerging opportunities
181 TIME TO VALUE	Realize promised value of solution after purchase • Customer satisfaction, product adoption, and effectiveness

Artificial Intelligence Sales Plays

182 UNCOVER	Process to identify and quantify the tangible benefits • Strategic account management and value selling
183 INTELLIGENCE	Gather and analyze to enhance strategic engagement • Personalized message for competitive advantage
184 RECOMMENDATIONS	tailored to individual client preferences, behaviors, or needs • Enhance executive engagement and conversion rates

185 PREDICTIVE	Data-driven insights to forecast timing for actions and to • Prioritize tasks and opportunities based on potential impact
186 NATURAL LANGUAGE PROCESSING	Interpret human language that is meaningful and useful • Text and speech to derive insights and automate tasks
187 CURATION	Sharing high-quality insightful content to establish brand • Become recognized expert in your field on domain expertise
188 ENHANCE	Data analytics to analyze competitive intelligence in real time • Strategic decisions to capitalize on new opportunities faster
189 COMPETITION	Competitive strengths, weaknesses, market position, and differentiators • Unique position to outperform competitors and drive growth.
190 PERSONALIZATION	Tailored document provides executives with critical insights • Equip executives with intelligence to make informed decisions
191 SOCIAL SELLING	Engage prospects to build relationships and share valuable insights • Connect with potential customers in a non-intrusive manner
192 ADAPTIVE LEARNING	Personalize learning style of each specific user • Learning paths based on user performance to ensure focus
193 VERIFY	Process of systematically testing which value proposition works the best • Message aligns with executive priorities' value of your solution

Diagram 10.1 How to Accelerate the Time to Insight for Researching Executives

EVERYDAY APPLICATIONS

In a world driven by rapid technological advancements and constant change, the ability to stay informed and continuously learn has become more important than ever. For professionals, leaders, and lifelong learners, pursuing growth requires efficient study. Fortunately, AI is ready to provide knowledge, insights, and ideas at a moment's notice.

Imagine standing in line for coffee, with a few minutes to spare before the caffeine hits your brain. Instead of scrolling aimlessly through social media, you open an AI app on your phone and ask about the latest trends in your industry. Within seconds, you receive a concise, **well-informed summary that could shape your next big project or decision**. This isn't just convenient—it's a shift in how knowledge is acquired and applied.

AI has evolved beyond simple question-and-answer tools. It has become a dynamic companion capable of understanding complex queries, synthesizing vast amounts of data, and delivering tailored insights that align with your professional interests. Whether you're seeking strategies to enhance leadership, monitoring market trends, or exploring new innovations, AI transforms idle moments into valuable opportunities for growth.

But the true power of AI extends beyond information retrieval. Say you're brainstorming ideas for a major presentation or project, but you're stuck. With a quick prompt, AI offers fresh perspectives, suggests innovative approaches, and even helps structure your thoughts. It's as if you have a personal advisor who not only answers questions but also sparks creativity and enhances problem-solving.

For executives and industry leaders, the ability to stay ahead of the curve is critical. AI ensures you remain informed about evolving markets, emerging competitors, and shifting global dynamics. It filters out noise, leaving you with the insights that matter most. This level of awareness can drive smarter decision-making, positioning you and your organization for long-term success.

AI also plays a key role in professional development. Whether you're refining leadership skills, practicing negotiation tactics, or exploring new frameworks for strategic planning, AI tailors learning experiences to suit your goals. It offers personalized resources and interactive content that fit seamlessly into your day, making skill enhancement part of your routine rather than a task you have to schedule.

Ultimately, the integration of AI into our daily lives represents more than just technological advancement—it symbolizes the merging of curiosity and capability. By embracing AI as a learning and insight tool, you open doors to continuous growth and empower yourself to lead with greater confidence and foresight.

So, the next time you find yourself with a few spare minutes, consider what AI can unlock for you. The path to knowledge is no longer distant or time-consuming: it's right there in your pocket, ready whenever you are.

ARTIFICIAL INTELLIGENCE KEY TAKEAWAYS

1. How can your GTM teams prepare for executive meetings within AI?

   Execute with world-class speed to discuss business strategies with executives.

2. Is it possible to be compelling without researching an executive's preferences?

   Information is available if you ask generative AI the correct series of prompts.

3. Unless you're an English major, why should everyone leverage a content-writing AI?

   Executive outreach lets you know right away if your message is on the mark.

4. Why is executive outreach daunting without real-time feedback from the messages you've sent?

   Outreach AI solutions let you know right away if your message is on the mark.

5. Can you create high-converting content which requires personalization with an edge?

Tailor your customer value creation approach with a feedback loop to know how to adjust.

6. How can specific Annual Report search terms allow you to dissect meaningful insights quickly?

Financial intelligence is required to gain C-suite attention to engage in a discussion.

7. What can you share with an executive who has been in their industry for twenty-five years?

Access to game-changing use cases that have created a proven competitive advantage.

8. How can AI generate an outside-in return on investment in seconds?

Generating projected economic benefit before your initial executive meeting.

SUMMARY

In a time when technology is rapidly reshaping industries, Artificial Intelligence (AI) emerges as a powerful force in strategic consulting. For executives managing complex business environments, AI presents a cost-effective alternative to traditional consulting services. Leveraging AI's capabilities, leaders gain access to deep insights, foster innovation, and streamline operations, all without the hefty fees typically associated with top-tier strategy consulting firms.

AI's strength lies in its ability to swiftly process and analyze vast amounts of data, making it essential for market and competitive analysis. By providing real-time insights, executives can stay informed about market trends, competitor actions, and industry changes. Lengthy reports and complicated datasets are no longer obstacles to decision-making, as AI transforms them into clear, actionable summaries. Strategic frameworks like SWOT, PESTEL, and Porter's Five Forces are developed with AI's assistance, offering a detailed understanding of the competitive landscape and positioning companies for success.

Beyond market analysis, AI excels in strategic brainstorming and scenario planning. By simulating different strategic scenarios, AI projects potential outcomes, allowing executives to assess risks and opportunities with accuracy. As a driver of innovation, AI sparks creative ideas for new products, services, and market entries, fueling growth and differentiation. With AI's support, organizations can develop multiple strategic paths, providing leaders with the insights needed to navigate uncertainty and seize emerging opportunities.

Operational Excellence, crucial for sustained success, is enhanced through AI-driven process optimization. AI identifies inefficiencies, suggests methodologies like Lean and Six Sigma, and highlights cost-saving measures. By pinpointing areas suitable for automation, AI reduces manual effort, speeds up workflows, and boosts overall productivity. This not only enhances efficiency but also strengthens resilience against operational challenges.

AI's value extends to leadership and change management, offering essential guidance during transformation periods. Whether following Kotter's 8-Step Process or other established frameworks, AI supports leaders in executing change initiatives. By analyzing employee engagement and feedback, AI proposes strategies to improve morale and performance, cultivating a culture of adaptability and continuous improvement. During crises, AI aids in developing effective communication strategies, helping leaders maintain stability and inspire confidence throughout the organization.

Financial modeling and strategic investment decisions are areas where AI's analytical power proves indispensable. AI performs sophisticated ROI calculations, assisting executives in prioritizing high-value initiatives. In mergers and acquisitions, AI evaluates potential targets, assessing their strategic fit and financial health. Moreover, AI identifies funding opportunities and monitors investor trends, guiding executives toward the best paths for growth and expansion.

Understanding and responding to customer needs is crucial for long-term success. AI helps map customer journeys, identifying pain points and areas for improvement. By aligning product roadmaps with market demands, AI ensures that development efforts stay relevant and forward-looking.

Additionally, AI designs comprehensive GTM strategies, setting up products for successful launches and sustained market presence.

Effective communication is critical for leadership, and AI enhances this aspect by generating executive summaries, drafting speeches, and creating visually compelling data presentations. By converting complex datasets into clear visual formats, AI ensures that executives can communicate insights and strategic directions with clarity and impact.

AI stands at the forefront of modern strategic consulting, equipping executives with tools to make informed, data-driven decisions. By integrating AI into their strategic processes, organizations unlock new levels of efficiency, drive innovation, and secure long-term growth. As AI technology continues to advance, its potential to offer sophisticated, cost-effective consulting solutions will only grow, solidifying its role as an invaluable asset for executive leadership. In Chapter 11, we will describe how your teams take all of this personalized outside-in research to create strategic engagements with executives that will be set into comprehensive launch plans.

CHAPTER 11

LAUNCH PLANS

Cascade Information

(Increase Sales Achieve Quota by 24 Percent)

CHAPTER 11

> **DRIVING REVENUE GROWTH:** Culture of Demand Creation

> **THE 13-WEEK CAPACITY PLAN:** Prioritize What Matters

> **PROVIDING STRATEGIC NARRATIVES:** Business Conversations

> **MULTI-THREADED PROSPECTING:** Every Account Is Different

> **THE TRUTH ABOUT EXECUTING A LAUNCH PLAN:** Initiate

> **BUILDING EXECUTIVE RELATIONSHIPS:** Top Down Wins

> **THE PERFECT EXECUTIVE MEETING:** Present New Ideas

> **CLIENT DELIVERABLES LEAD TO ACCOUNT PLANS:** Funnel

> **OPTIMIZING YOUR VIRTUAL TEAM:** Leverage Depth Chart

> **LAUNCH PLAN THEORY:** Increase Sales Achieve Quota 24 Percent

> **TIPS AND TRICKS:** Outflank the Competition

> **LAUNCH PLANS WORKBOOK:** Early Indicators Determine Success

---

> **EVERYDAY APPLICATIONS:** Create Demand

> **KEY TAKEAWAYS:** Anticipate Client Needs

> **SUMMARY:** Cascade Information

DRIVING REVENUE GROWTH

Jordan emerged as a beacon of transformative leadership, standing apart as the only sales leader in her company focusing 100 percent on growth accounts. Every account her team managed was a prospect, untouched by prior sales or existing relationships. This formidable challenge made Jordan's results all the more remarkable: Within only ten weeks of her arrival, her team went from struggling to secure on-site meetings to scheduling ten critical meetings with ideal prospects.

What drove this stunning turnaround? Jordan understood that success in sales didn't merely come from talent but from a disciplined and adaptive mindset. In week one, she introduced a meticulously crafted **growth playbook** to her team. More than just a simple list of strategies, Jordan's playbook presented a prescriptive approach built on three essential pillars: coachability, accountability, and resilience. It guided the team through the complexities of the sales landscape, helping each team member conquer obstacles that once seemed impossible.

In enterprise sales, there is often a sharp focus on forecasting opportunities that are already in play. Weekly meetings dive deep into the compelling event, next steps, cost of inaction, and the timeline to close. However, Jordan noticed a critical gap: Her company's pipeline management, the **foundation of future growth**, lacked structure. Because each sales professional managed pipeline creation in their own way, it was difficult to track and replicate success across the team. More importantly, the progress updates in their CRM system were inconsistent, making it hard to get a clear picture of the pipeline's health.

Recognizing this, Jordan instituted a bold new weekly routine: a one-hour, interactive pipeline team call. During this session, each sales professional was required to discuss their key meetings, account plans, and overall progress. Using the "popcorning" concept, one sales professional would present their updates and then select the next person to speak. This dynamic mechanism fostered both competition and best practice sharing, ensuring that everyone came prepared.

These calls brought immediate clarity, as Jordan could quickly identify who was ready and actively creating demand, as well as who needed targeted coaching and a potential course correction. Beyond the numbers, though, Jordan instilled a culture of learning and shared success. Just as athletes review game footage to improve their technique, Jordan's team analyzed their past performance, reflecting on successful tactics and learning from each other's experiences. This **peer-driven approach** reinforced best practices and encouraged the team to replicate winning strategies.

Jordan's story serves as a testament to the power of leadership, structure, and the unwavering belief that even the most challenging competitive environments can be conquered with the right mindset and approach. By fostering a culture rooted in coachability, accountability, and resilience, Jordan didn't just drive short-term results; her structured and thoughtful approach transformed the way the growth team operated, setting a new benchmark for sustained growth and excellence.

Along the same lines, this chapter presents several frameworks for planning and structuring your GTM teams' account management practices. Use them to identify ways to model and duplicate success in your company, to build a culture of excellence.

THE 13-WEEK CAPACITY PLAN

Not all territories offer the same opportunity, and success often depends on how well your sales professionals manage their time and resources. The key to consistent performance lies in developing a personal capacity plan that aligns sales efforts with the demands of each phase of the sales quarter. Without this structured approach, sales efforts can easily become misaligned, reducing the chances of meeting or exceeding quotas.

A typical sales quarter spans thirteen weeks, but the nature of work shifts dramatically as the quarter progresses. The final four weeks of each quarter are often dominated by closing activities, leaving little room for pipeline generation. Imagine a sales professional with a $1.2 million quota facing the opportunity to close a $3 million deal—demand creation simply cannot take precedence in such a scenario. Strategic planning is essential to ensure that you meet both short-term and long-term objectives.

With that in mind, start by dividing your quarter into three distinct phases, each with a specific focus:

- In the first month, prioritize **demand creation**: generate leads, conduct initial outreach, and qualify potential opportunities. This foundational work is crucial, as it sets the stage for future inflight opportunities.
- The second month is all about **opportunity management**: By this stage, initial contacts have matured into active deals. To advance these opportunities, focus on meeting with stakeholders, refining proposals, and addressing potential objections. The goal is to move deals through the pipeline efficiently, ensuring they are well-positioned for closure.
- The final month emphasizes **deal closure**: negotiations, contract finalization, and troubleshooting any last-minute concerns. This phase directly influences revenue and quota attainment, making it a critical component of the sales cycle.

However, not all sales professionals will have substantial deals to close at the end of the quarter. In that case, simply hit reset and return to demand creation. This proactive shift ensures that your pipeline remains robust, preventing dry spells in subsequent quarters.

TIME MANAGEMENT CADENCE

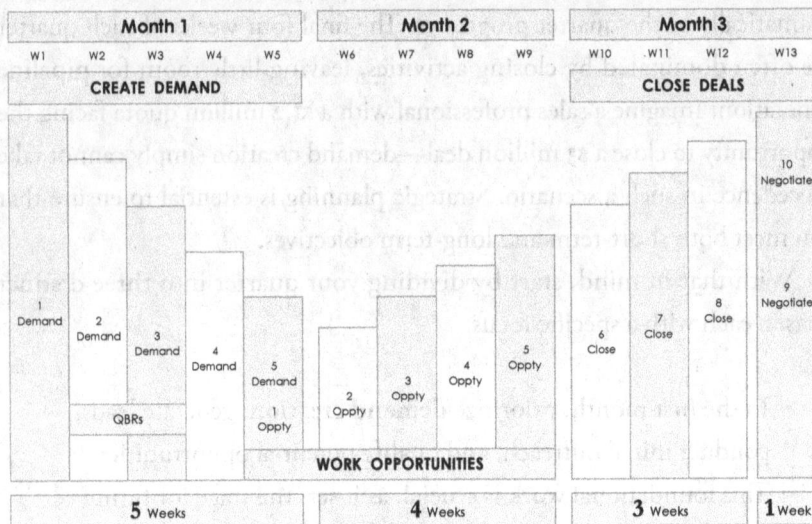

Month 1					Month 2				Month 3			
W1	W2	W3	W4	W5	W6	W7	W8	W9	W10	W11	W12	W13

CREATE DEMAND

CLOSE DEALS

1 Demand
2 Demand
3 Demand
4 Demand
5 Demand
QBRs

1 Oppty
2 Oppty
3 Oppty
4 Oppty
5 Oppty
6 Close
7 Close
8 Close
9 Negotiate
10 Negotiate

WORK OPPORTUNITIES

5 Weeks	4 Weeks	3 Weeks	1 Week

Diagram 11.0 Sales Focus by Month

Sales managers play a pivotal role in guiding and managing this process, both in terms of closing current-quarter deals and of monitoring team members without immediate deals. By encouraging these professionals to focus on lead generation and early-stage opportunity development, managers help maintain overall team momentum and balance short-term goals with long-term growth. Furthermore, you can leverage collaborative partnerships to identify and exchange leads, further broadening the scope of your opportunities. By actively engaging with partner networks, your sales professionals can unlock access to prospects that may have been previously out of reach, building credibility and trust within key accounts.

Sales success is rarely the product of random chance. It is achieved through disciplined effort, strategic foresight, and consistent execution. A growth playbook serves as an all-encompassing guide for cultivating a robust pipeline—one that is four times the value of their sales quota. Every outreach, meeting, and partnership is pivotal in shaping future outcomes. The key lies in understanding that daily disciplines, even those without immediate rewards, are crucial for driving long-term success. By adhering to this plan, sales professionals can set the stage today for the triumphs they will experience five months down the line.

Success begins with consistent and deliberate prospecting. Sales professionals should allocate two hours each day to pipeline generation activities, with a target of adding four hundred thousand dollars to the sales pipeline each quarter. This seemingly modest commitment can accumulate substantial results. Try to secure five customer meetings per week, with a focus on connecting with at least two executive-level stakeholders. As we've seen, these executive engagements are vital in driving larger deals and nurturing strategic relationships.

A focused outreach strategy is essential for maintaining momentum. Each week, your sales professionals should prioritize five target accounts and develop customized, value-driven messaging for each. Likewise, they should reach out to five executives within each account. Overall, each salesperson should secure three new prospecting meetings each week and add ten new contacts to your CRM system. These seemingly incremental activities culminate in larger milestones—say, contributing to two customer workshops per month and at least two visits to the executive briefing center (EBC) each quarter.

To maximize coverage, the Business Development Representative (BDR) on each account's executive outreach emails, extend the message to an additional forty-five contacts within the same organization. This creates a ripple effect, fostering continuous engagement and establishing a presence across multiple levels of the account. Consistency is crucial, as a steady progression ensures that opportunities are continuously nurtured and advanced.

By adhering to this plan, sales professionals can anticipate building a quarterly pipeline valued at four times their target. Regular engagement with executives not only increases deal size but also strengthens relationships, fostering long-term loyalty and trust. Moreover, by expanding contact networks through structured outreach, sales professionals open doors to new possibilities and solidify their standing within target accounts. Pipeline development is not a one-time initiative; it is a continuous process that demands dedication and foresight. By embracing this structured, methodical approach, sales professionals can ensure that they are consistently positioned for success.

SALES PROFESSIONAL EXPECTATIONS

1	Pipeline Coverage	4X	25% Close Rate
2	Pipeline Generation	2 Hours per Day	25% of Your Daily Time
3	Pipeline Additions	$400k per Month	Require $4.8M Pipeline to Close $1.2M
4	Forecast	Commit to Plan Quarterly	Require $1.2M in the Pipeline per Quarter to close $300k
5	Customer Meetings	5 per Week	To Achieve $1.45M in Pipeline
6	Executive Meetings	2 per Week	To Create Significant Transactions
7	Partner Meetings	1 per Week	Partner Momentum
8	Customer Outreach	50 per Week	Customer Value Creation
9	New Contacts Added	10 per Week	Create the Flywheel for Your BDR
10	New Meetings	3 per Week	To Achieve $3.36M in Pipeline
11	Customer On-site Workshops	2 per Week	To Achieve $4.8M in Pipeline
12	Executive Briefing Center Visits	2 per Quarter	Value Realization Quantify Benefits

Diagram 11.1 Demand Creation: Best Practices

At most sales organizations, these metrics are not typically managed on a weekly basis. But hyperscaled revenue requires optimized weekly schedules to maximize productivity. A sample calendar is below, but of course individual differences and specific territory demands will require unique time management strategies, so each professional can effectively address their unique challenges and opportunities. As long as everyone in your organization maintains a relentless focus on building a pipeline each quarter, you will achieve consistent revenue success.

OPTIMIZE YOUR CALENDAR FOR REVENUE

	Monday	Tuesday	Wednesday	Thursday	Friday
8:00 AM	Emails, Slack	Emails, Slack	Emails, Slack	Emails, Slack	Emails, Slack
8:30 AM	Current Deal Work	Pipeline Development	Pipeline Development	Current Deal Work	Current Deal Work
9:00 AM	Current Deal Work	Pipeline Development	Pipeline Development	Current Deal Work	Current Deal Work
9:30 AM	Prep 1:1	Pipeline Development	Pipeline Development	Pipeline Development	Industry Insights
10:00 AM	SE 1:1	Forecast Call	Flex Time	Pipeline Development	Industry Insights
10:30 AM	SE 1:1	Forecast Call	Flex Time	Pipeline Development	Prep Call
11:00 AM	Open	Forecast Call	Flex Time	Pipeline Development	Prep Call
11:30 AM	Players Call	Lunch	Lunch	Lunch	Pipeline Dev Call
12:00 PM	Lunch	Prep Call	Lunch	Prep Call	Pipeline Dev Call
12:30 PM	Prep Team Calls	Customer Calls	Prep 1:1	Customer Calls	Lunch
1:00 PM	Team Calls	Customer Calls	1:1 w/ Manager	Customer Calls	Pipeline Development
1:30 PM	Team Calls	Team Debrief	Prep Team Calls	Team Debrief	Pipeline Development
2:00 PM	Action Items	Open	Team Calls	Pipeline Development	Pipeline Development
2:30 PM	Open	Prep 1:1	Team Calls	Pipeline Development	Pipeline Development
3:00 PM	Pipeline Work	BDR 1:1	Action Items	Pipeline Development	Flex Time
3:30 PM	Pipeline Work	Flex Time	Pipeline Admin: Contacts, sequences, etc.	Pipeline Development	Flex Time
4:00 PM	Update SFDC	Flex Time	Pipeline Admin: Contacts, sequences, etc.	Update SFDC	Update SFDC
4:30 PM	Follow Up	Follow Up	Follow Up	Follow Up	Follow Up

Diagram 11.2 Create Your Weekly Schedule

PROVIDING STRATEGIC NARRATIVES

Industry trends evolve rapidly due to digital transformation, shifting consumer expectations, and heightened competition, so sales leaders must develop sophisticated, data-driven strategies to stay ahead. Crafting strategic narratives not only helps you deliver comprehensive insights but clarifies your client's enablers of success, the driving forces behind industry change, and the critical questions and KPIs that ensure continuous improvement.

For example, in the Consumer Packaged Goods (CPG) sector, the effectiveness of trade promotions is crucial for a company's market share growth and profitability. The CPG landscape is undergoing a fundamental transformation as technological advancements and changing consumer preferences reshape traditional promotion strategies. Already, CPG sales have surged by 35 percent year-over-year, necessitating digitally focused and omnichannel promotional strategies. With trade promotions representing 20 to 25 percent of gross sales, refining spending to maximize returns is essential. Furthermore, a notable 73 percent of consumers now expect personalized promotions, prompting brands to invest in data analytics and targeted marketing approaches. Over 60 percent of CPG companies are channeling resources into AI solutions that enhance forecasting, optimize spending, and improve overall efficiency.

Before you pitch your solution, however, you must demonstrate why traditional approaches to trade promotions are insufficient. Your strategic narrative might point out, for instance, that despite high investment levels, up to 30 percent of trade spend yields suboptimal returns. Meanwhile, disconnected systems and siloed data inhibit holistic decision-making, leading to disjointed promotional strategies. To avoid these pitfalls, companies in the CPG sphere must deploy smarter, more agile, and more innovative trade promotions that capture attention and drive loyalty.

Along with this warning, of course, your narrative should identify avenues for strategic growth and innovation. You might point out that the inability to diagnose underperforming promotions stems from fragmented data. Integrating analytics platforms would enable a more precise evaluation of promotional performance, driving better outcomes. Or you could highlight how disconnected marketing, sales, and finance functions often lead to inconsistencies. Centralized, cross-functional platforms would instead unify promotional efforts, ensuring consistency and alignment. Finally, you could show how fluctuating consumer demand requires more accurate, AI-driven forecasting tools that predict trends and inform promotional planning. The diagram that follows brings it all together.

SOLUTION PITCH PLAN WAVE CAMPAIGNS

WEEK	PITCH THIS	CRO	CMO	CDO	SVP CS	CIO	COO
1	Increase self-service success			X	X	X	
2	Boost online conversions	X	X	X	X		
3	X-channel service across physical and virtual stores	X	X	X	X	X	X
4	Data insights for segmentation and tailored treatment		X		X	X	X
5	Commerce and customer service	X	X	X	X		
6	Social customer service		X	X	X		
7	Raise margins with personalized offers	X	X		X		

Diagram 11.3 Define Your Five-Stage Wave Campaign

ENABLING SALES WITH SOLUTION PITCH PLANS

Increase Self-Service Industry: Retail	67% of retailers ranked customer satisfaction as their top initiative, 82% said customer service strategies are their primary focus
	National Retail Federation (NRF)
Research the Topic:	Self-service trends: Helping customers serve themselves
	Help is just a click away—increase web self-service success
Trends and Stats	58% of Americans research online before buying
	49% of online shoppers are comfortable having their info collected in exchange for personalized service and offers
	60% of consumers trust retail websites to keep their information secure
Business Challenges	Inability to provide a mobile-friendly support site
	Can't provide knowledge-based content, or advanced search capabilities, on product pages
	Unable to offer guided troubleshooting or automatically suggest answers a shopper hasn't seen yet
	Lack personalized service account where shoppers can submit, track, and close support requests
	No way to capture answer feedback to continually improve the knowledge base
Questions to Ask	Is your support site mobile-enabled for any device?
	Are knowledge answers and advanced search available on product pages for easy access?
	How do you provide guided troubleshooting— step-by-step decision trees, how-to-videos?
	Do you offer a virtual assistant or automatically suggest answers a shopper hasn't viewed?
	Do shoppers have personalized accounts to manage their own service requests? Can they provide feedback on knowledge-based answers?

KPIs	Self-service Rate = # of self-service interactions / # of interactions
	% Escalation from Self-service to Agent Help = # of self-service requests completed with agent self-service requests
	Content Effectiveness = average # of self-service answers viewed per visitor
	Customer Effort Score (CES) = use numeric scale via post-interaction feedback survey
Reference A	Connects 1,000s of suppliers in Reference A Sustainability Hub efficiently and cost-effectively
	Enables sustainability projects that have high impact and low transaction costs
	Reference A also reduces costs with web customer service deflection
	500+ agent seats in the contact center
Reference B	83,000 knowledge-based articles serving 200K online visitors/month
	38% drop in calls and 50% drop in emails with web self-service
	Web presence across 8 countries with 300K inquiries/ month answered within 24 hours
	99.5% CSAT and improved customer retention
	Saved millions with greater contact center efficiency
	One common knowledge base across all channels (phone, email, Web, chat)
	18% reduction in customer hold times
Sales Tools	Industry Accelerators—Retail
	Customer Reference eBook
	Customer Video on Help Is a Click Away
	Customer Video on Web Customer Service
	Benefits of Web Self-Service
	Business Value Assessment Tool

Diagram 11.4 Lines of Business Conversation

Using this insight, your sales professionals can engage brand managers in meaningful dialogue that uncovers pain points and opportunities for growth. You might start with questions like these:

- How do you currently assess the effectiveness of your trade promotions?
- What forecasting challenges hinder your promotional planning?
- How do you detect and address underperforming promotions?
- Which platforms are used to centralize and analyze trade spend data?
- How agile is your promotional strategy in adapting to evolving consumer preferences?

By adopting such a comprehensive and strategic approach to the issues your clients are facing, your sales leaders can solidify their position as indispensable partners to client companies. A focus on collaboration, AI-driven insights, and key performance measurement not only unlocks growth but fosters innovation, ensuring sustained success in an increasingly competitive market landscape.

MULTI-THREADED PROSPECTING

Sales professionals can't depend on just one prospecting method; instead, they must adopt a multi-threaded approach to engage accounts on several levels. This section delves into seven essential strategies that, when executed together, drive deeper engagement, build trust, and unlock new opportunities within target accounts.

ESTABLISHING CREDIBILITY WITH EXECUTIVE STAKEHOLDERS is often the initial step in forming meaningful client relationships. By conducting comprehensive industry benchmarking, sales professionals can pinpoint areas where target accounts may fall behind competitors or where growth opportunities exist. When prospects see the potential for tangible improvements, they are more inclined to engage in deeper discussions. Presenting tailored reports, executive summaries, and customized presentations reinforces the sales professional's role as a strategic advisor. This data-driven approach acts as a catalyst for initiating executive-level conversations, not just one-off pitches.

TRACKING YOUR PROSPECT'S DIGITAL FOOTPRINT offers invaluable insights into their interests and needs. Buyer intent platforms track online activity, providing visibility into behaviors such as website visits, content downloads, and search queries. Sales professionals can prioritize high-intent leads, crafting personalized outreach that directly addresses demonstrated interests. This proactive engagement boosts the likelihood of converting leads into pipeline opportunities, ensuring that prospects feel understood and valued from the first interaction.

No two operating units within an account are identical. By developing STRATEGIC ACCOUNT PLANS tailored to the unique needs of each segment, sales teams position themselves as expert advisors. As detailed previously, this involves conducting in-depth research, aligning proposed initiatives with overarching corporate objectives, and presenting customized plans during quarterly business reviews. Strategic account planning ensures that the proposed solutions resonate with each part of the organization, fostering alignment and increasing buy-in from all levels.

FACE-TO-FACE INTERACTIONS are powerful tools for relationship building. On-site strategic workshops create a forum for open dialogue, where sales professionals and client leadership can collaboratively explore current challenges and future initiatives. These sessions often lead to the co-creation of solution roadmaps and project timelines. The hands-on nature of workshops demonstrates commitment and fosters deeper trust, resulting in actionable insights and stronger partnerships.

STRATEGIC PARTNERSHIPS can significantly expand your sales team's reach. By leveraging relationships with technology and service partners, sales professionals gain access to new opportunities and untapped accounts. Joint account planning, co-selling initiatives, and shared insights allow you to develop comprehensive solutions that provide greater value to mutual clients. Regular engagement with these partners ensures that sales teams stay informed about emerging opportunities, fostering growth through collaboration.

INTERNAL ALIGNMENT is just as critical as external engagement. By collaborating with enterprise account teams, sales professionals ensure consistent messaging and a unified strategy. Regular internal meetings facilitate insight sharing and the identification of expansion opportunities. This collaborative effort maximizes the potential for upselling and cross-selling, driving greater value across the entire account portfolio.

The prospecting journey does not end with the initial sale. To sustain long-term engagement and drive ongoing growth, sales professionals must consistently reinforce the value of their solutions. Sharing case studies, white papers, and success stories serves as a reminder of past successes, while regular check-ins keep clients informed about product updates and industry trends. Your GTM teams should not just sell your products well but position themselves as continuous sources of value.

THE TRUTH ABOUT EXECUTING A LAUNCH PLAN

Aligning organizational teams around effective launch plans is crucial to sustained success. These plans are not simply about execution; they represent a strategic commitment to personalized engagement, ensuring every customer interaction feels uniquely relevant. By embedding this principle throughout your approach, you can consistently deliver impactful content tailored specifically to each customer's distinct business strategy.

Building a culture of personalized demand creation is foundational. Successful organizations understand that true engagement goes beyond typical transactional interactions. Thus, you should prioritize outreach that genuinely resonates with executives by leveraging deep industry expertise and offering value up front through strategic consultations. This advisory approach positions you as a trusted partner deeply invested in your customers' success.

This customer-first philosophy extends directly into quarterly sales planning. With deliberate, structured efforts, your sales teams can optimize their productivity through clear monthly priorities. In the first month, have them concentrate on building robust pipelines by proactively identifying and qualifying new opportunities. During month two, they'll transition seamlessly to nurturing these relationships, addressing concerns, validating proposed solutions, and setting the stage for successful negotiations. Finally, in the third month, their focus shifts decisively toward closing deals, overcoming obstacles, and securing executive-level commitments, ultimately driving measurable growth.

To engage stakeholders effectively, your team must skillfully tailor conversations for each line of business. Rather than prematurely promoting technological solutions, these conversations should initially emphasize strategic alignment with stakeholders' specific business goals. This targeted approach captures executive interest, driving deeper engagement and ensuring lasting commitment.

Moreover, understanding the complexities within each customer account requires a comprehensive, multi-threaded prospecting strategy. Combining top-down engagement with senior executives and bottom-up validation from operational stakeholders ensures thorough account penetration. Each method yields unique insights, enabling a holistic understanding of customer challenges and opportunities.

Top-down approaches, particularly involving C-suite executives, are powerful accelerators for sales cycles. Referrals from senior leadership expedite decision-making due to their strategic vision, oversight, and decisiveness. Crucially, organizations must first demonstrate genuine expertise and value before establishing these high-level relationships, creating a foundation of trust and credibility.

Strategic executive meetings are also key to influencing customer decisions. Effective meetings involve presenting innovative, compelling ideas clearly linked to executive-level strategic objectives. Additionally, proactively identifying and addressing potential concerns during these interactions minimizes adoption barriers, streamlining the path to approval and partnership.

Effective account planning further reinforces this strategy, relying heavily on direct feedback from customer executives. Instead of relying on external assumptions, successful account plans integrate insights gleaned directly from customers. This "inside-out" methodology ensures that your strategies resonate authentically, fostering deeper customer relationships built on transparency and trust.

Finally, the effectiveness of any organizational strategy is amplified through an optimized virtual team playbook. By systematically leveraging internal subject-matter experts and clearly defining roles within the broader team, you can ensure every interaction with customers is coordinated, informed, and impactful. This structured collaboration consistently delivers exceptional customer experiences, reinforcing satisfaction and loyalty.

BUILDING EXECUTIVE RELATIONSHIPS

The influence of internal champions plays a pivotal role in shaping deal sizes, revenue outcomes, and overall business growth. Sales professionals often find themselves engaging with champions at various organizational levels, from directors to senior executives. Effective engagement here can have profound implications for the revenue potential of each deal, highlighting the importance of understanding how different champions affect the sales process.

Director-level champions are frequently involved in smaller, transactional deals that align with their departmental budgets and immediate needs. These 1x opportunities represent steady, incremental growth, offering predictable and consistent revenue streams. The sales cycle for director-level deals tends to be shorter, requiring fewer layers of approval. Directors can advocate specific purchases, but their influence is often confined to their department's scope, limiting the overall deal size. While these smaller deals contribute to a stable pipeline, their impact on long-term revenue growth is often limited.

On the other hand, **executive-level champions**, such as C-suite leaders or senior VPs, have the authority to drive transformational change within their organizations. Their engagement is typically associated with large, strategic transactions—commonly referred to as 4x opportunities. These deals can be four times or more the size of standard transactions and must align with broader organizational objectives. Moreover, executive-level transactions frequently lead to multi-year contracts and expanded service offerings, increasing the overall customer lifetime value. By contrast, director-level deals may deliver short-term gains but are less likely to evolve into enduring strategic partnerships that drive future business.

Striking the right balance between 1x and 4x opportunities is key to a successful sales strategy. While director-level deals ensure a steady revenue stream, executive-level engagements unlock transformative growth. Sales teams are encouraged to cultivate relationships at the executive level by showcasing thought leadership and aligning solutions with long-term organizational goals. Additionally, mapping champions across multiple organizational tiers ensures broader stakeholder engagement, driving deal momentum and reducing potential barriers. By leveraging both types of opportunities, sales professionals can build a resilient pipeline that supports immediate revenue needs while positioning their organizations for long-term success.

THE PERFECT EXECUTIVE MEETING

Executive meetings play a pivotal role in shaping strategic direction, fostering alignment, and driving organizational growth. The comprehensive executive meeting framework outlined here is designed to provide a structured and detailed approach for your meetings, to ensure each key element is strategically and meticulously addressed.

Industry Assessment serves as the foundation for informed decision-making. By leveraging automated point-of-view tools and data-driven insights, executives can establish a clear understanding of prevailing industry trends. Specifically, a thorough examination of five industry case studies, coupled with insights from two highly respected organizations, allows benchmarking and highlights best practices. Peer comparisons and performance metrics are essential for recognizing gaps and setting ambitious but achievable targets. Regular engagement with industry news, thought leadership, and best practices ensures the organization remains at the forefront of innovation and efficiency.

Account Assessment delves into the internal landscape, providing a clear picture of executive compensation, strategic priorities, and areas for growth. By conducting a SWOT analysis, the organization can align use cases with overarching priorities, ensuring every initiative contributes to long-term success. Special attention is given to the evolving business climate, such as the impact of COVID-19, and to proactive competitor analysis, in order to maintain a competitive edge. Additionally, identifying key buyers and consolidating relevant documents lays the groundwork for successful engagements.

To ensure internal alignment, the Point of View Internal Review process facilitates collaboration across teams. This involves aligning solutions with sales plays, reviewing strategies with regional managers and industry principals, and thoroughly evaluating opportunities. Developing customer-facing account plans solidifies the organization's commitment to delivering tailored solutions.

Preparing for executive meetings requires rigorous planning. Relationship maps visualize stakeholder connections, while a three-horizon proposal helps structure initiatives across different time frames, promoting phased implementation. Comprehensive briefing books, enriched with client perspectives and detailed account plans, empower executives with the information they need to make informed decisions.

Securing meetings demands specific deliverables, such as agenda emails and investment strategies, which set the tone and objectives. As outlined in Deliverables to Secure Meeting and Deliverables Prior to Meeting, clarity and precision in communication ensure alignment and readiness. Summarizing key points and business cases further reinforces the strategic narrative.

The First Executive Meeting represents a critical juncture, highlighting relationship connections and project updates. Industry customer stories and best practices add credibility to proposals, while investment strategies and business case projections anchor discussions in tangible value. Demonstrating use case efficiency gains, implementation time frames, and total cost of ownership provides executives with a comprehensive view of the proposed initiatives.

Finally, don't neglect post-meeting follow-up. Benchmarking against admired companies, updating industry comparisons, and refining investment strategies ensure that the organization stays responsive to evolving priorities. Revising business cases and adjusting implementation timelines solidify the path forward, reinforcing the organization's commitment to continuous improvement and value delivery.

This framework, built on structured assessments, collaborative reviews, and detailed deliverables, ensures that your executive meetings are not only productive but transformative, driving sustained success and strategic advancement.

CLIENT DELIVERABLES LEAD TO ACCOUNT PLANS

Creating detailed client deliverables early in the executive sales engagement process is crucial for validating your strategic viewpoint and aligning with customer expectations, especially when pursuing significant, unbudgeted transactions. The hyperscale methodology emphasizes the development of comprehensive, customer-facing executive deliverables. These deliverables serve as foundational elements crafted specifically for presentation and iterative refinement based on direct customer feedback. The resulting deliverables become core components and structural pillars of a thorough and strategic account plan.

Strategic progression with each prospective customer demands careful selection from sixteen distinct sales frameworks (detailed in Diagram 11.5). Your choice of framework should closely match your tailored engagement strategy and the unique context of each customer interaction. By systematically applying these frameworks, you streamline and simplify the account planning process. This structured approach enables you to consistently gather critical insights from stakeholders at various organizational levels, facilitating precise adjustments in terminology, messaging, and strategic alignment to resonate deeply with the customer's evolving business goals and objectives.

SIXTEEN EXECUTIVE DELIVERABLES

ACCOUNT PLAN

CUSTOMER-CENTRIC RESEARCH	ALIGN TO BUSINESS OBJECTIVES	COLLABORATIVE PLANNING	VALUE REALIZATION
M	**A**	**C**	**O**
POINT OF VIEW	NEEDS ANALYSIS	ECONOMIC BENEFIT	EXECUTIVE PROPOSAL
Chapter 1	Chapter 2	Chapter 3	Chapter 4
1 CEO Email	5 Relationship Map	9 Value Realization	13 Executive Decision Document
2 Partner Summary	6 Three-Year Press Release	10 Account Plans	14 Procurement Scorecard
3 Business Strategy	7 Solution Imaging	11 Executive Demo Guide	15 Executive Proposal
4 Investment Strategy	8 Mutual Action Plans	12 Reference Matrix	16 Implementation Plan

Customer Value Creation

Diagram 11.5 Deliverable by the Four Pillars of MACO Framework

Each deliverable produced throughout this iterative engagement process serves dual strategic purposes: externally validating your proposed strategies and internally enriching the overall account planning documentation. Consequently, the customer directly influences the account plan's strategic orientation, ensuring the plan remains outwardly customer-focused rather than inwardly driven or speculative.

Account plans must be viewed as dynamic, continuously evolving documents requiring routine and deliberate updates, preferably conducted on a monthly basis. Regular updates are critical to accurately reflect current market conditions, evolving customer requirements, and shifting strategic priorities. Leveraging these sixteen sales frameworks as part of this iterative process enables timely and informed updates. Regular monthly reviews are instrumental in systematically incorporating direct customer feedback, recalibrating strategic objectives, refining stakeholder mapping, and proactively identifying opportunities and risks.

Treating account plans as dynamic, adaptable tools significantly enhances the accuracy of sales pipelines, deepens the quality of customer engagement, and ensures the lasting relevance and effectiveness of your sales strategies. This iterative, structured approach drives consistent growth, strengthens customer retention, and fosters long-term mutual value creation for both clients and your organization.

Moreover, quarterly business reviews provide a structured platform for conducting comprehensive evaluations of each strategic account. These reviews are crucial checkpoints for proactively identifying future collaborative opportunities and strategically planning upcoming project requirements, aligning closely with your clients' roadmap strategies, and ensuring a strong, mutually beneficial partnership trajectory.

OPTIMIZING YOUR VIRTUAL TEAM

Expanding modern client relationships goes beyond traditional one-on-one interactions: You must also coordinate with specialized virtual teams, each integral in building trust, providing insights, and ensuring smooth execution. This section explores the distinct roles of these teams, demonstrating how their combined expertise drives client growth and establishes enduring partnerships.

Forging Strategic Partnerships. Solutions Consultants are at the forefront of client engagement, a linchpin in driving strategic alignment with senior leadership. These consultants are not merely technical advisors but pivotal connectors to executive decision-makers. By engaging directly with CEOs, they cultivate strategic partnerships that align proposed solutions with overarching business objectives, transforming vendors into indispensable allies.

In short, Solutions Consultants articulate value propositions that resonate at the highest levels. They craft compelling narratives, leveraging success stories through reference matrices and visually mapping solutions that mirror client aspirations. This visualization process, known as **solution imaging**, breathes life into abstract ideas, bridging the gap between concept and tangible value.

Prioritization is central to accelerating adoption. By identifying high-impact use cases tailored to immediate needs, Solutions Consultants create an urgency that drives action. In parallel, executive dashboards provide real-time performance insights, reinforcing the ongoing value of implemented solutions. Ultimately, these consultants captivate audiences with solution demonstrations, offering a glimpse into the transformative power of the technology at hand.

Building Financial Alignment. No strategic partnership is complete without financial alignment, a domain expertly navigated by Business Value Advisors. These professionals translate technical capabilities into compelling financial proposals that speak the language of CFOs. Through meticulous cost-benefit analyses and ROI projections, they craft proposals that align with fiscal constraints while spotlighting long-term gains.

The narrative extends to investment strategies, positioning your solutions as catalysts for profitability and operational efficiency. Business Value Advisors conduct comprehensive business value assessments, quantifying potential benefits to reinforce the indispensability of the proposed solutions. This data-driven approach culminates in the formulation of value hypotheses, sparking dialogue and exploration into untapped opportunities.

Sustaining Success. Customer Success teams manage the journey past solution deployment, extending into the realm of sustained value realization. These teams shepherd clients through every stage of the solution life cycle, ensuring promised outcomes materialize into measurable results. Central to this effort is the client success framework, a structured pathway that guides organizations toward key milestones. Regularly scheduled Quarterly Business Reviews (QBRs) serve as checkpoints for reflection, adaptation, and reaffirmation of value delivery. Mutual action plans further solidify this partnership, fostering shared accountability and driving continuous progress.

Ensuring Seamless Execution. Transitioning from strategy to execution requires meticulous planning and analysis—a responsibility shouldered by Professional Services teams. Through deployment analyses, these teams assess feasibility, crafting tailored strategies that smooth the path to implementation. Comprehensive implementation plans lay the groundwork for success, detailing the necessary steps, resources, and timelines to mitigate risks. The concept of benefit by horizon underscores the phased delivery of value, ensuring clients experience both immediate wins and long-term growth.

Pioneering Technical Vision. Field CTOs dazzle executives in initial engagements to drive momentum and future-proof solutions. Acting as the bridge between technology and business vision, the Field CTO crafts reference architectures that ensure scalability and alignment with evolving client environments. Strategic roadmaps, developed in collaboration with clients, serve as blueprints for ongoing technology evolution. These roadmaps not only anticipate future needs but also unlock pathways for value expansion, driving iterative improvements and fostering upsell opportunities.

By leveraging the collective capabilities of virtual teams, sales professionals can foster and grow client relationships in groundbreaking ways. Each role is integral in crafting a unified narrative of trust, innovation, and lasting value. This collaborative effort drives organizations toward long-term success and enduring client partnerships.

LAUNCH PLAN THEORY

Develop strategic engagements with executives that align their business with your solutions. Consistently deliver quarterly business strategies to the executive leadership teams in your accounts.

Why change?

Challenge:	Does your seller send executives new strategies once a quarter? Will executives engage your teams if they don't know who you are? Are your teams proactively waiting for leads to be developed for them?

How do we differentiate?

Concept 41:	**Drive Revenue Growth** prescriptive approach built on three essential pillars— coachability, accountability, and resilience. Weekly one-hour pipeline team calls. Each sales professional shares updates on their key meetings, account plans, and overall progress.
Concept 42:	**Multi-Threaded Prospecting** among various stakeholders, while effectively managing information flow up and down the leadership hierarchy across departments and business units, to sustain and accelerate momentum within each account.
Concept 43:	**Building Executive Relationships** is achieved by sales professionals who grasp their industry's challenges and offer valuable insights. By staying updated on market trends, competitors, and industry shifts, they position themselves as strategic partners.
Concept 44:	**Optimize Virtual Team** by leveraging each expert resource to collaboratively develop executive deliverables. These should seamlessly integrate your deal strategy with the customer's journey map, incorporating feedback loops to continuously improve collaboration and outcomes.

What do we receive?

Result:	Create confirm fit evaluations with no competition to increase win rates. Proposing business strategies **increase sales achieve quota +24%.** Your teams should provide free strategy consulting to their accounts.

TIPS AND TRICKS FOR LAUNCH PLANS

- Engaging with executives is a key driver of success in 4x transactions. These high-level decision-makers possess the authority and strategic insight needed to advance deals, **aligning proposed solutions** with their organizations' broader goals. When account teams build and nurture relationships at the executive level, they secure buy-in, streamline processes, and distinguish their offerings from the competition. This approach positions them for sustained success.

- Sending messages to executives effectively requires careful planning and strategic timing. **Initiating communication at precisely 9 p.m.** local time allows your messages to stand out distinctly. Executives either see your concise and compelling message immediately during their quieter evening hours or at the top of their inbox the following morning, reinforcing its urgency and visibility.

- Each account is unique, demanding a tailored approach. Implementing at least five out of your eight routes-to-market from your growth playbook ensures customized strategies that address specific executive concerns and maximize engagement success. Continually refining your messaging through persona-based A/B testing further enhances this tailored approach, optimizing resonance with executive stakeholders based on their unique challenges and your solution's capabilities.

- A successful engagement strategy prioritizes interactions at the C-suite level. Carefully researching and **aligning your approach to strategic themes** valued by executives solidifies your relevance. Combining a top-down approach with a complementary bottom-up method, using a multi-threaded prospecting methodology, ensures comprehensive organizational engagement, driving internal buy-in across multiple levels and significantly accelerating revenue growth.

- Building credibility begins with presenting executives with compelling business strategies and value-driven insights before attempting to foster personal relationships. **Establishing yourself initially as a trusted advisor** helps lay the foundation for long-term, meaningful executive relationships.

- Leverage virtual teams to strengthen your relationships across technical and operational stakeholder groups. Internal advocacy from these stakeholders supports executive-level engagement and fosters organizational buy-in for your solutions. Complementing this effort, maintain structured, proactive pipeline development through meticulous planning within your thirteen-week capacity plan to ensure robust and **predictable quarterly pipeline growth.**

- Preparedness is crucial when engaging executives. Craft strategic narratives aligned directly with their objectives, clearly linking your solutions to measurable business outcomes and executive incentives. Preparation for executive meetings should include sending comprehensive content and structured agendas a day in advance, allowing executives to direct conversation priorities effectively. Prompt follow-up, within hours after meetings, maintains momentum and demonstrates respect for executives' time and objectives.

- Finally, systematically **documenting executive feedback** from engagements and incorporating these insights into your strategies ensures continuous improvement. This iterative process refines your approach, aligning your solutions closely with executive expectations and ultimately enhancing strategic alignment and relationship quality over time.

LAUNCH PLANS WORKBOOK
GAIN CONSENSUS

Launch Plan Frameworks

194 CAPACITY PLAN	Detailed planning framework that optimizes its resources • Balance workloads, meet demand, achieve strategic goals
195 STRATEGIC NARRATIVES	Compelling story about strategic vision, mission, priorities, and value proposition • Strategic direction that inspires alignment to achieve goals

196 PERFECT EXECUTIVE MEETING	Clear objectives that drive strategic outcomes to maximize engagement • Impactful collaboration with actionable outcomes
197 FRAMEWORKS TO ACCOUNT PLANS	Executive frameworks verify direction of account planning • Customer's business goals, pain points, and success metrics

Launch Plan Sales Plays

198 TARGETING	Identify targets' accounts based on strategic priorities • Ensure value messaging, solutions, and engagement strategies
199 DATA INSIGHTS	Data analytics create highly personalized messaging • Tailor interactions and recommendations for specific preferences
200 THOUGHT LEADERSHIP	Establish market leadership by educating and influencing • Create insightful, authoritative, and impactful content
201 MULTI-TOUCH	Running multiple channels and touch engagement strategy • Optimize seven different engagement strategies
202 UNSOLICITED	Investment made without request to create business strategy • Proactively initiate to generate value-focused proposal
203 INFLUENCERS	Individuals provide guidance to navigate the buying process • Organization priorities, decision-makers, and internal dynamics
204 DIFFERENTIATION	Clearly communicate your superior to competitors • Quantifying the financial value of your solution for customers

205 BUCKET LIST	Must-attend experiences due to your exclusive networking • Provide access to industry peers with strategic knowledge
206 TIMING	Determine best time to engage sending marketing messages • Measure when action will achieve desired outcome
207 CALL TO ACTION	Present direct actionable offer to take measurable action • Business outcomes that are compelling and results-driven
208 AGREEMENT	Ensure all departments align on strategic goals and vision • Work toward a common purpose to gain greater efficiency
209 BUDGET HOLDER	Determine person with authority to allocate initial budget • First point of financial authorization in the buying process
210 INITIAL LAND	Design clear efficient approach to securing an initial entry • Provide targeted, high-value solution that meets specific needs
211 VALUE EXPANSION	Systematically measure and communicate financial impacts • Solution values delivered to your customers

Diagram 11.6 How to Launch Strategic Engagement Content to Executives

EVERYDAY APPLICATIONS

For sales professionals aiming to optimize their productivity and achieve significant results, the initial two hours of the workday are exceptionally important. In the quiet of the early morning, the mind often operates at peak performance, free from the distractions that accumulate as the day unfolds. By dedicating this vital period to the most impactful tasks on their agenda, sales professionals can create a proactive rhythm that sets a positive trajectory for the rest of the day.

This is the ideal time for cold calling, lead generation, and crafting tailored outreach strategies—tasks that require undivided attention and sharp decision-making. By focusing on these efforts during their mental prime, sales professionals elevate the quality of their work and maximize efficiency.

Completing a difficult task early not only instills a sense of accomplishment but also generates the confidence and momentum needed to tackle subsequent responsibilities. This positive cycle fuels greater efficiency and minimizes the likelihood of procrastination. The proactive choice to handle complex work up front also ensures that high-value activities are prioritized and completed, leaving less room for avoidance.

As the day progresses, reactive tasks such as emails, meetings, and administrative duties inevitably demand attention. These activities, while necessary, can overshadow core sales efforts if not managed carefully. By focusing on demand-generating tasks during the first two hours, sales professionals assert control over their day, preserving vital time for actions that directly contribute to revenue growth. This strategic alignment of priorities allows for a balance between proactive selling and responsive administrative work.

A crucial advantage of early-morning outreach lies in accessibility. Decision-makers, often swamped by midday meetings and responsibilities, are more reachable during the early hours. By contacting prospects during this window, sales professionals increase their chances of engaging key stakeholders in meaningful conversations. This advantage can make the difference between a successful connection and a missed opportunity.

Ultimately, the first two hours of the workday represent an invaluable opportunity for sales professionals to create demand, set a positive trajectory, and stay ahead of the competition. Embracing this structured and strategic approach is more than just a productivity tip—it is a transformative practice that can unlock new levels of success in the sales domain.

LAUNCH PLAN KEY TAKEAWAYS

1. How do you measure if sales engage executives in their accounts monthly?

   Weekly team pipeline calls allow learning from teammates on what works well.

2. How much time should you allocate to pipeline development each week?

   Quarterly capacity plans are personalized for each sales professional.

3. Have you provided a line of business talk tracks to your sales teams by solution area?

   Strategic narratives provide sales the details they need on one page to engage effectively.

4. Each account is unique; how do you create momentum engaging each stakeholder?

   Discipline approach to multi-thread prospecting to engage across an entire account.

5. How do you build relationships with executives prospecting into net new accounts?

   Deliver complete business strategies based on proven industry case studies.

6. Can your teams anticipate executives' needs prior to having your initial meeting?

Surprise executives with new ideas that create a unique competitive advantage.

7. Have you validated your findings with client deliverables prior to account planning?

Receive customer buy-in from iterating on recommended strategies.

8. Does your sales team know how to leverage the virtual team to optimize client success?

Everyone knows their roles and works seamlessly together to drive customer value.

SUMMARY

The journey to hyperscaling revenue begins with discipline. It's not just about ambition or innovation; it's about consistency in pipeline development. Without a robust pipeline, even the most talented teams and groundbreaking products can falter. This is why prioritizing pipeline growth stands firm as the cornerstone driving scalable revenue.

Sales leaders play a crucial role here. By instilling the habit of early-day pipeline development across their teams, they create a rhythm that drives momentum. This window, often marked by peak focus and energy, becomes the safeguard against distractions and competing responsibilities. It's the time when deals are nurtured, opportunities are identified, and growth is strategically engineered. The teams that adopt this practice find themselves ahead, consistently filling their pipeline and advancing opportunities.

However, pipeline development doesn't happen in isolation. Scaling revenue requires the coordinated efforts of multiple departments, from marketing and product teams to customer success. Program management emerges as the linchpin, orchestrating these efforts and ensuring seamless collaboration. Through structured alignment, program managers ensure that lead generation, content initiatives, and product launches complement sales activities. This holistic approach eliminates silos and brings all departments into lockstep with the shared goal of pipeline growth.

Amid this orchestration, personalized content becomes the catalyst that accelerates the sales process. In today's market, generic pitches fall flat. Prospects expect tailored solutions that address their unique pain points and aspirations. Crafting this level of personalization requires deep insights and collaborative input from various teams. Sales teams provide frontline feedback, while marketing and data analytics translate these insights into targeted content. This synergy between sales, marketing, and product teams results in personalized content that resonates at every stage of the buyer's journey. It's not just about capturing attention but guiding prospects through the pipeline with precision and relevance. In Chapter 12, we will explore how sellers align awareness across each business unit within their accounts, their broader virtual teams, and key executives, enabling the seamless flow of information at precisely the right moment. This ensures optimal preparation for maximum productivity in every meeting.

UNIFY AWARENESS

Orchestrate Seamless Teamwork

(Increase Incremental Revenue by 14 Percent)

CHAPTER 12

➤ **STRATEGIC ENGAGEMENT FRAMEWORK:** Impacts CEO

➤ **MANAGEMENT CADENCE:** Operational Excellence

➤ **SEQUENTIAL ENGAGEMENT PLAYS:** Multi-Threaded Influence

➤ **TRAVERSING THE PROVING GROUND:** Top 1 Percenters

➤ **THE TRUTH ABOUT UNIFYING AWARENESS:** Orchestration

➤ **REDEFINING DECISION CRITERIA:** Enterprise Pursuits

➤ **THE C3 COMMUNICATION MODEL:** Written Confirmation

➤ **THE CALENDAR OF EVENTS:** Identify Hidden Client Constraints

---

➤ **ELEVATING BUSINESS ACUMEN:** Leverage the Depth Chart

➤ **UNIFY AWARENESS THEORY:** Incremental Revenue +14 Percent

➤ **TIPS AND TRICKS:** Fill in Where Needed

➤ **UNIFY AWARENESS WORKBOOK:** Take on Challenging Tours

➤ **EVERYDAY APPLICATIONS:** Uncomfortable Conversations

➤ **KEY TAKEAWAYS:** Develop with Empathy and Comparison

➤ **PARTING THOUGHTS:** Orchestrate Seamless Teamwork

➤ **VALUE FRAMEWORK:** Realization Creates Flywheel to Prospect

STRATEGIC ENGAGEMENT FRAMEWORK

Building deep, meaningful relationships with your key accounts is crucial for long-term success. The Strategic Engagement Framework acts as a guiding light for creating lasting partnerships and driving impactful results. This detailed approach, rooted in structured methodologies, sets the stage for enhanced client engagement and ongoing growth.

Executive engagement is marked by a distinctive approach—leading with answers. Rather than initiating discussions with exploratory questions, you should present clear, actionable solutions up front. This approach accelerates decision-making, demonstrates confidence, and highlights your organization's deep understanding of the client's needs.

At the heart of this framework lies the concept of outside-in account assessments. By stepping into the shoes of external observers, your team can unveil hidden challenges and untapped opportunities within your clients' business. This unbiased perspective allows you to address client pain points more effectively and craft solutions that resonate deeply with their long-term aspirations.

Benchmarking against industry peers and existing customers further amplifies the engagement process. By drawing from real-world data, you will gain valuable insights into the performance landscape of their target accounts. This comparative analysis not only highlights competitive gaps but also underscores areas of opportunity, helping you position your offerings as indispensable tools for industry leadership.

Needless to say, the best engagement strategies are meticulously tailored to reflect the ambitions and objectives of key decision-makers. This alignment evolves continuously, ensuring that engagement remains impactful and directly contributes to the client's overarching vision. As your Diamond Teams leverage their collective expertise to develop materials that speak directly to each client's challenges, you will demonstrate a nuanced and up-to-date understanding of executive goals and firm priorities.

Engagement transcends senior leadership, nurturing relationships across operational teams, mid-level management, directors, and executives. By building advocacy at multiple touchpoints, you can easily foster widespread support, mitigating the risk of engagement bottlenecks and increasing the likelihood of successful implementation.

Proactivity is a defining feature of this framework, shown especially through the creation of unsolicited proposals. You can seize the initiative by presenting innovative solutions even before your clients formally articulate their needs. This forward-thinking approach not only differentiates your work from your competitors but also positions your team as thought leaders capable of anticipating and addressing client challenges.

Each sales play in this engagement serves as a stepping stone, gradually intensifying engagement and reinforcing trust. This structured progression ensures that communication remains consistent and that clients view the organization as a continuous source of value.

STRATEGIC ENGAGEMENT FRAMEWORK

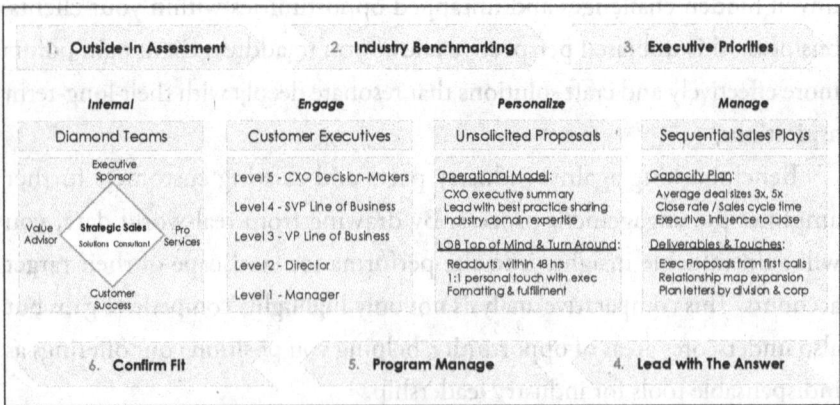

1. Outside-In Assessment	2. Industry Benchmarking	3. Executive Priorities	
Internal	Engage	Personalize	Manage
Diamond Teams	Customer Executives	Unsolicited Proposals	Sequential Sales Plays
Executive Sponsor	Level 5 - CXO Decision-Makers	Operational Model:	Capacity Plan:
	Level 4 - SVP Line of Business	CXO executive summary Lead with best practice sharing Industry domain expertise	Average deal sizes 3x, 5x Close rate / Sales cycle time Executive influence to close
Value Advisor — Strategic Sales Solutions Consultant — Pro Services	Level 3 - VP Line of Business	LOB Top of Mind & Turn Around:	Deliverables & Touches:
	Level 2 - Director	Readouts within 48 hrs 1:1 personal touch with exec Formatting & fulfillment	Exec Proposals from first calls Relationship map expansion Plan letters by division & corp
Customer Success	Level 1 - Manager		
6. Confirm Fit	5. Program Manage	4. Lead with The Answer	

Diagram 12.0 Strategic Operating Model

The ultimate objective of the framework is to confirm fit engagements, effectively eliminating all of your competition. By crafting tailored solutions that align seamlessly with client objectives, you don't just win deals but establish and nurture exclusive partnerships. Cultivating trust-based relationships leaves your competitors with no avenue for entry.

To lead GTM teams managing strategic engagement frameworks, a collaborative mindset is essential. Let me show you how one executive sales leader, JR, illustrates this mindset. In every engagement, JR aims to identify and address the core business challenges his clients face, developing solutions that are not only innovative but also profoundly impactful. His leadership is driven by a clear, forward-thinking vision—one that empowers his team by fostering autonomy and encouraging individuals to leverage their unique strengths. This trust among his team cultivates a culture of accountability and creativity, enabling each member to play a crucial role in driving customer value.

At the core of JR's methodology is his dedication to fostering enduring, trustworthy relationships with clients. For him, true success isn't just about immediate outcomes but the lasting influence his team has on client achievements. His skill in connecting with clients on both technical and operational fronts enables him to design customized solutions that resonate beyond IT departments, engaging business leaders and decision-makers alike.

Internally, JR acts as a catalyst for cultural transformation. He leads with optimism, championing growth and adaptability in an ever-evolving landscape. While forecasting and operational precision remain crucial, JR consistently balances these short-term priorities with broader, strategic initiatives. He trains his sales professionals to sharpen their business acumen, ensuring they are equipped not only to meet targets but to anticipate future opportunities. His focus on building a robust sales pipeline and fostering thought leadership ensures his firm's sustained growth and relevance.

One of JR's defining traits is his commitment to meticulous preparation and internal development. He advocates for tackling the most challenging conversations within the organization first, using the opportunity to help his team refine their strategies and enhance their approaches. Every internal briefing call is an opportunity to hone executive engagement skills, enabling sales professionals to anticipate needs and propose solutions with confidence and creativity. This disciplined internal practice ensures that, when engaging with economic buyers, his team is not only prepared but primed for success.

Moreover, JR is deliberate in nurturing future leaders. By empowering his leadership team with the oversight of key initiatives, he offers them chances to expand and hone their leadership capabilities. This commitment to leadership development not only propels organizational objectives but also builds a reservoir of skilled, confident leaders poised to drive the business forward.

MANAGEMENT CADENCE

To achieve consistent and sustainable revenue growth, you need a structured and disciplined approach that equally emphasizes demand creation, opportunity management, and the closure of deals. This framework establishes a comprehensive roadmap that facilitates alignment, accountability, and execution across your sales organization. By enforcing a regular weekly cadence, your sales leaders can synchronize efforts, optimize sales workflows, and drive significant revenue acceleration.

The foundation of this framework rests on revenue commitment, demand creation, and opportunity management. Each of these pillars contains essential processes and checkpoints to strategically align all the team's activities to propel growth and maintain deal momentum.

Revenue Commitment drives performance accountability. Through weekly personal commitment calls, sales professionals are held responsible for achieving their quarterly targets. These calls not only reinforce accountability but also ensure alignment with corporate objectives and provide a platform for addressing potential obstacles. Simultaneously, executive bridging plays a critical role in advancing strategic deals. By directly engaging with high-priority accounts, executives eliminate roadblocks and contribute valuable insights that propel deals forward.

Demand Creation generates a continuous influx of new leads, making it essential for long-term growth. A dynamic pipeline fuels the organization's future, which is why weekly targets for pipeline additions are so important. These efforts are supported by four-quarter pipeline management, ensuring visibility and planning extend beyond the immediate sales cycle. To sustain momentum, conduct executive and director meetings weekly, align your senior leadership with pipeline activities, and provide a venue to discuss escalations and strategic accounts.

A key component of demand creation involves expanding your professional networks by consistently adding relevant contacts. This broadens outreach, strengthens client relationships, and maximizes engagement opportunities. Weekly contract engagement is equally important, ensuring that new contracts are initiated while existing ones continue progressing toward closure.

Furthermore, regular solution-pitch plan reviews help sales teams refine messaging and tailor solutions to meet client needs, reinforcing the overall effectiveness of their presentations. Partnership summary reviews play an equally vital role in fostering collaborative growth, as they provide insights into co-selling opportunities and joint GTM strategies.

Opportunity Management transforms leads into tangible deals. A cornerstone of this process is the **Mutual Action Plan** (MAP), developed in collaboration with the customer and confirmed in writing. These plans establish clear timelines, responsibilities, and milestones, ensuring shared accountability for deal progression.

Accurate and timely price quotes reflect a company's responsiveness and reinforce trust with clients. This activity is complemented by win theme development—regular reviews of value propositions that differentiate your offerings from competitors. Thorough demonstration run-throughs further solidify preparedness, ensuring sales teams can effectively showcase solutions and align presentations with client pain points.

Comprehensive implementation planning is another critical element. By clearly outlining deployment phases, resource requirements, and risk mitigation strategies, implementation plans instill client confidence in the organization's ability to deliver. Finally, ongoing relationship mapping highlights key stakeholders and decision-makers within target accounts. This intelligence drives deeper engagement and aligns strategies to better influence purchasing decisions. Tracking each deal's maturity likewise enables sales teams to monitor close dates and prioritize high-probability deals, ensuring an efficient allocation of resources.

CLOSING DEALS

The final stage of the framework is dedicated to sealing agreements and converting opportunities into revenue. Executive proposal reviews ensure that every submission reflects strategic alignment and maintains the highest quality standards. Decision document reviews provide an additional layer of oversight, minimizing errors and ensuring that all necessary information is presented clearly to clients.

In particular, negotiation cover letters should be crafted and refined under executive guidance, reinforcing deal value and enhancing positioning during negotiations. Similarly, information document reviews ensure that all supplementary materials—such as case studies, white papers, and product guides—align with the overarching sales strategy and meet client expectations.

By adhering to this comprehensive framework, you will not only enhance your sales performance but also create a repeatable, scalable process that drives consistent, sustainable revenue growth in an increasingly competitive landscape.

SEQUENTIAL ENGAGEMENT PLAYS

Relying on a single engagement strategy can create blind spots and pose substantial risks to securing alignment and funding for your initiatives. Do your sales professionals actively execute three distinct engagement strategies within an account simultaneously to generate momentum, targeting different levels within the organization? Here's how it might play out.

The C-suite is focused on strategic imperatives for Engagement Play One. For this audience, your value proposition must revolve around high-level growth initiatives and operational excellence. These executives are driven by the need to expand market share, boost revenue, and enhance efficiency across the enterprise. To effectively engage them, it is critical to align solutions with their strategic priorities, ensuring that every conversation revolves around measurable business impact.

The first step is to position your solutions as drivers of growth. This means showcasing how your offerings enable market penetration, spark innovation, and unlock new revenue streams. Growth remains the top priority, but efficiency follows closely behind. Once the path to expansion is clear, emphasize how operational streamlining can further improve profitability and scalability. By aligning your proposals with tangible financial metrics—such as EBITDA improvement, cost-to-revenue ratios, and gross margin enhancement—you frame your solutions in terms that resonate deeply with executive leadership.

To solidify engagement, articulate the top business benefits your solutions deliver. You've already shown how your tools accelerate revenue growth, position the organization for market leadership, and leverage operational efficiencies to reduce costs and streamline processes. From there, address risk mitigation and regulatory compliance, reinforcing how your solutions safeguard the organization against potential liabilities. Last, emphasize the ways in which customer and employee experiences are enhanced, creating a more dynamic and productive ecosystem.

Anecdotal evidence plays a crucial role in reinforcing these points. Sharing success stories from peer organizations and industries builds credibility and trust. Use these narratives to demonstrate clear, measurable returns on investment, showcasing how similar businesses have realized significant value from your solutions.

Meanwhile, you can drive Line of Business engagement through tailored solutions in Engagement Play Two. Line of Business (LoB) executives operate within specific functional domains, each with its own set of objectives and challenges. Engaging effectively requires tailoring your message to resonate with the unique priorities of each buying center—be it marketing, finance, sales, operations, or IT. By aligning your solutions with the department's goals, you ensure that your proposals address their most pressing concerns.

Engagement at the LoB level is structured around acquisition, retention, and efficiency. Solutions that drive customer acquisition and enhance market penetration are paramount. A close second is strategies that bolster customer retention, as they can improve satisfaction and increase lifetime value. Finally, efficiency remains a universal concern: Leaders are constantly seeking innovations that can reduce manual processes, automate workflows, and optimize resource utilization.

To kick off the engagement, consider organizing workshops and discovery sessions to understand their pain points. Pilot programs are an excellent way to demonstrate rapid value and build confidence in your solution. Collaboratively develop success metrics that align with LoB objectives, ensuring that performance benchmarks reflect their goals and deliver measurable results.

Demonstrating competitive key performance indicators further strengthens your engagement. Benchmark KPIs that industry leaders monitor to reveal gaps in your client's current measurement capabilities. By highlighting these disparities and proposing ways to address them, you position your solution as essential to staying competitive.

Evaluation teams focus on advanced capabilities and technical viability in Engagement Play Three. Evaluation teams are tasked with scrutinizing solutions from both functional and technical perspectives. Engaging with these subject-matter experts requires detailed documentation, clear demonstrations of technical alignment, and the ability to map solutions to existing business flows.

To meet their needs, provide comprehensive insights into how your solution addresses functional and technical requirements. Showcase compatibility with existing infrastructure, ensuring compliance with regulatory mandates and internal security standards. Mapping your solution to real-world business processes is equally essential. Present use cases that mirror current workflows and highlight how your proposed solution enhances efficiency without causing disruption.

A key focus for evaluation teams—and especially CIOs—is platform consolidation. Highlight how your solution reduces tech sprawl by unifying disparate systems. Emphasize the cost savings and simplified management associated with platform unification, reinforcing the value of an integrated ecosystem.

Meeting critical decision criteria is pivotal. Demonstrate how your solution replicates and enhances current applications. Provide credible references from organizations that have achieved tangible success, reinforcing their trust and reducing perceived risks. Sharing your product roadmap further enhances confidence, outlining future innovations and demonstrating your commitment to continuous improvement.

Building long-term confidence requires ongoing engagement. Develop a feature release timeline, involve evaluation teams in beta programs, and regularly update them on industry trends. By positioning your solution as a forward-looking, evolving platform, you solidify its relevance and alignment with their long-term strategic goals.

TRAVERSING THE PROVING GROUND

Navigating the proving ground in complex sales engagements demands a thoughtful and strategic approach. As we've seen in previous chapters, success hinges on your ability to engage both the executive suite, operating above the line, and the evaluation team, positioned below the line. This dual-engagement model is essential for fostering alignment across decision-makers and influencers within your customer's organization. The best sales strategies bridge the gap between top-down and bottom-up communication, ensuring that critical insights uncovered during the evaluation process are shared consistently and effectively across all levels.

Engagement at the executive level focuses on strategic goals, business outcomes, and return on investment. Executives want to understand how a proposed solution aligns with their long-term objectives and drives competitive advantage. Conversely, the evaluation team, consisting of technical managers and practitioners, delves into the functionality, feasibility, and operational impact of each solution. They are tasked with ensuring the solution can be integrated seamlessly and can mitigate potential risks.

For effective executive engagement, providing concise summaries, articulating strategic alignment, and emphasizing value propositions are key. Executives appreciate high-level updates that demonstrate how the solution impacts key performance indicators and business growth. Meanwhile, the evaluation team benefits from technical workshops, regular feedback loops, and detailed implementation planning that address their day-to-day concerns.

In short, top-down engagement keeps initiatives visible and supported at the executive level, while bottom-up engagement ensures trust is built with the evaluation team through detailed demonstrations and collaborative planning. Bridging the gap between executives and the evaluation team requires sales professionals to act as information conduits. Executives and evaluators often operate in silos, making it critical to ensure insights flow across both tiers. Unified messaging that resonates with both audiences, regular check-ins involving cross-level participation, and encouraging evaluators to present findings to executives are all effective strategies for fostering alignment.

RUNNING MULTIPLE ENGAGEMENT TRACKS

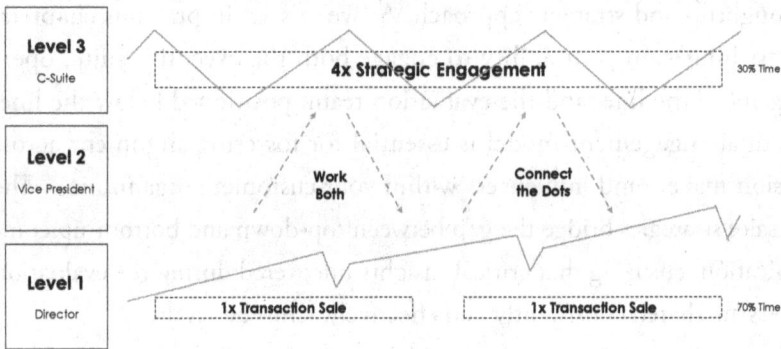

Diagram 12.1 Cascade Communication to All Levels

Common pitfalls in this process include neglecting one group over the other, failing to tailor messaging appropriately, and assuming internal communication happens naturally within the customer organization. Inadvertently focusing more on one group can stall deals, create misalignment, or lead to incomplete evaluations. Proactive communication and careful alignment of information prevent disengagement and ensure all stakeholders remain informed and invested.

Ultimately, navigating the proving ground requires a dual-engagement strategy that addresses the unique priorities of executives and technical evaluators. By fostering alignment through thoughtful communication, sales professionals can drive forward momentum, shorten the sales cycle, and significantly enhance their chances of closing complex deals.

THE TRUTH ABOUT UNIFYING AWARENESS

Building deep, meaningful relationships with key accounts is essential. By leveraging a robust Strategic Engagement Framework, a structured and deliberate approach, you can more effectively foster enduring partnerships and drive meaningful business outcomes. Through systematic methodologies and targeted client engagement practices, this framework enables continuous organizational growth.

The journey of executive engagement begins with presenting clearly defined, actionable solutions rather than posing exploratory questions. By proactively addressing client needs, organizations can effectively demonstrate their expertise, rapidly build credibility, and streamline the decision-making process. This up-front clarity signals a deep, nuanced understanding of client challenges, which is instrumental in building trust and forging lasting partnerships.

To sustain momentum and comprehensive account engagement, it is important to deploy sequential engagement plays. These strategic moves involve orchestrating multiple, coordinated interactions across various client business units, reinforcing relationships and promoting alignment within client organizations. The structured nature of these interactions ensures sustained visibility and proactive communication across all client touchpoints.

A crucial stage in the engagement process involves traversing the proving ground. This involves effectively sharing insights and successes from preliminary evaluations or pilot projects with client executive leadership. Sales teams play a pivotal role here by strategically cascading information upward, clearly articulating the partnership's value and obtaining essential executive recognition, thereby reinforcing confidence in the ongoing collaboration.

Another critical element involves aligning decision criteria between evaluation teams and executive leadership. Given that roughly 85 percent of decision-making criteria typically differ between operational evaluators and senior executives, sales professionals must leverage their credibility with key stakeholders to influence and reshape these criteria. Ensuring alignment with executive-level strategic priorities significantly enhances the likelihood of securing broader organizational buy-in.

To engage effectively at the executive level, sales professionals must continuously elevate their business acumen. High-level interactions demand precise alignment with executive strategic objectives, succinct yet impactful presentations, and a keen awareness of executives' limited time and extensive responsibilities. Respecting these factors maximizes executive engagement and ensures productive dialogues.

Furthermore, the framework emphasizes strategic engagement as a long-term commitment rather than a transactional exchange. Viewing client relationships through a lens of continuous improvement and mutual value creation supports long-term client retention, loyalty, and sustained revenue growth across multiple sales cycles.

Management plays a key role in reinforcing this engagement approach by maintaining a structured weekly cadence. Regular reviews and alignment to quarterly objectives ensure consistent attention on critical tasks, especially those that might otherwise be overlooked, enhancing the strategic execution and operational effectiveness of the sales teams.

Central to maintaining clarity and accountability in client communications is the C3 Communication Model (Conversation, Communication, and Confirmation). This method involves initiating dialogue verbally, documenting key discussion points in writing, and securing written client confirmation. This structured approach significantly minimizes ambiguity, increases accountability, and fosters mutual clarity.

Finally, proactive calendar management is critical. By mapping out client stakeholders' availability and recognizing when evaluation processes may experience delays due to absences, teams can strategically plan activities, ensuring the continuity of engagement efforts and accurate forecasting.

Ultimately, the Strategic Engagement Framework ensures focused, consistent, and strategic interactions, significantly enhancing an organization's capability to establish strong, lasting client partnerships, thus driving long-term success and sustainable business growth.

REDEFINING DECISION CRITERIA

The cornerstone of enterprise sales lies in your ability to influence corporate decision-making, establishing your solution as essential for your client's growth and market leadership. Redefining their decision criteria transcends feature presentation; it's about steering clients to see the long-term strategic value your solution offers. This requires a deep understanding of client motivations, aligning your solution with their objectives, and showcasing how other successful companies have leveraged your product to achieve differentiation and success.

To begin, you need a deep understanding of the client's business drivers. This means identifying their overarching objectives—whether they stress accelerating revenue growth, expanding into new markets, enhancing operational efficiency, or fostering innovation. Equally important is pinpointing the pain points and obstacles that may hinder progress. By engaging stakeholders from different departments, you can gain a holistic view of the internal dynamics that shape the firm's decision-making process.

A powerful way to reshape decision criteria is showcasing the success of existing clients. By profiling companies that share similar industry contexts or challenges, you can highlight how they harnessed your solution to achieve transformative results. Quantifiable metrics, case studies, and best practices paint a compelling picture of how your product drives operational improvements and competitive advantages.

From there, emphasize what sets your solution apart. In a crowded market, decision-makers need to see beyond standard offerings. By presenting unique features, superior capabilities, and innovative use cases, you can position your solution as a distinct strategic asset. Tailoring these differentiators to the client's specific industry or market conditions further enhances their relevance and impact.

Additionally, aligning your solution with industry trends and regulatory demands underscores its longevity and adaptability. Companies gravitate toward solutions that not only solve current problems but also future-proof their operations. Highlight how your solution evolves with market advancements or helps clients meet compliance requirements, in order to solidify your long-term value proposition.

Perhaps the most critical shift is moving the focus from product features to tangible business outcomes. Decision-makers are increasingly driven by ROI, growth projections, and long-term benefits. By framing your solution in terms of return on investment, scalability, and client success stories, you ensure the conversation centers around strategic impact rather than a checklist of functionalities.

Ultimately, redefining your client's decision criteria transforms the selection process into a collaborative journey, reinforcing your role as a trusted advisor. This not only increases the likelihood of a successful engagement but also fosters enduring partnerships that promote mutual sustained growth and market leadership.

THE C3 COMMUNICATION MODEL

Ensuring clarity in business engagements and alignment between parties is crucial for success. The C3 Communication Model is a structured and dependable framework, guiding interactions to foster mutual understanding, articulate the current situation, and chart a shared path forward. This section examines the significance and application of the C3 Model, demonstrating how it can transform professional engagements by enhancing collaboration and trust.

As you might guess, the C3 Model emphasizes three Cs: Conversation, Communication, and Confirmation. Each component serves as a building block to create a comprehensive and fluid process. Dialogue is initiated, documented, and validated, leaving little room for misinterpretation or ambiguity.

The process begins with **Conversation**—the initial exchange of ideas and insights. Whether verbal or written, this phase is designed to surface critical information relevant to the engagement. In this setting, both parties engage in direct discussions that bring to light pain points, objectives, and potential solutions. This stage is crucial, as it lays the foundation for mutual understanding by fostering an open dialogue and identifying areas requiring further exploration.

From this point, the model transitions into **Communication**—transforming the essence of the conversation into a more formal written summary. The communication phase acts as a mirror: It both reflects the critical topics you've already discussed and reinforces what you have shared and agreed on. Typically delivered through email or formal project documentation, this summary details key components such as timelines, milestones, success criteria, and budget considerations. This written account equips both parties with a reference point that ensures alignment and provides clear direction for subsequent actions.

However, communication alone is not sufficient without **Confirmation**. This final element serves as a seal of mutual agreement. Upon receiving the formal communication report, the client or second party is invited to respond, either by agreeing to the documented points or suggesting modifications. This process of confirmation plays a pivotal role in addressing any discrepancies or misunderstandings, securing alignment before progressing further. With formal acknowledgment in hand, the foundation for future collaboration is firmly established.

During the sales process, the C3 Model ensures smooth progression and alignment at every critical juncture. It is particularly effective during the qualification of opportunities, where initial conversations are structured to assess the presence of pain points or needs. The insights gathered are documented and validated, forming the basis for continued engagement.

As the process advances to solution definition, the C3 Model facilitates collaboration as you and your client map potential solutions to their business challenges. Through written communication and subsequent confirmation, both parties solidify their understanding and commitment to explore further. Similarly, during technical and business validation stages, the model continues to provide a structured pathway, ensuring that solutions are not only feasible but align with broader business objectives.

But the real payoff is in the contracting stage. As both parties prepare for negotiation and acquisition, the model's emphasis on transparent and documented communication ensures that their respective interests are prioritized and mutually understood. By confirming contract terms and expectations, the model mitigates risks and streamlines the path to agreement.

The benefits of adopting the C3 Communication Model are far-reaching. **Enhanced clarity, improved collaboration, and efficient decision-making** stand at the forefront, ensuring that projects progress seamlessly without unnecessary delays. Additionally, the model serves as a safeguard, mitigating risks by verifying critical information at each stage, reducing the likelihood of future conflicts. Its focus on continuous documentation creates a valuable archive of exchanges that can be revisited throughout the sales cycle, ensuring continuity and accountability.

THE CALENDAR OF EVENTS

A successful project doesn't just depend on great ideas or cutting-edge technology—it requires careful planning and the synchronized efforts of all stakeholders involved. In many organizations, the evaluation and selection phases of a project can encounter significant delays due to schedule conflicts, unanticipated absences, and poor visibility of stakeholder availability. Business travel, personal leave, and vacations can lead to missed milestones, throwing off the entire project timeline.

This is where the Calendar of Events becomes an invaluable asset, transforming abstract next steps into a tangible, visual roadmap. It maps out all crucial tasks, deadlines, and project milestones, offering a clear overview that enables teams to anticipate scheduling conflicts well in advance. By laying this groundwork, organizations can identify potential roadblocks, ensuring a smooth and proactive adjustment to project plans.

One of the calendar's most significant advantages is enhanced visibility: It allows stakeholders to pinpoint precisely when key team members will be in or out of the office. This level of transparency reduces the risk of last-minute disruptions and fosters a sense of shared responsibility, ensuring that everyone stays aligned with the project's goals.

Another key benefit is conflict resolution. By proactively visualizing stakeholder availability, teams can adjust their schedules before conflicts arise. This prevents bottlenecks and delays, preserving the integrity of project timelines. By working backward from the desired go-live date, the Calendar of Events ensures that milestones are not only met but synchronized seamlessly, guaranteeing a timely and efficient rollout.

Moreover, the visual nature of the calendar promotes greater engagement and accountability. When stakeholders see their commitments mapped out, they become more invested in the process. This collaborative environment enhances communication across teams and departments, fostering a culture of transparency and shared ownership.

Implementing a Calendar of Events is straightforward but requires deliberate steps. First, teams must define key milestones and deadlines that will shape the evaluation process. Engaging with stakeholders to gather information on their availability is critical—this ensures the calendar reflects realistic schedules. Using project management tools or calendar platforms, teams can then construct the calendar by overlaying stakeholder availability with major project activities.

Once the initial draft is ready, circulating it for feedback ensures that all voices are heard and potential oversights are addressed. With collective buy-in, the final calendar is ready to guide the project forward. Regular updates to the calendar as the project evolves keep the plan dynamic and aligned with any changes in scope or availability.

In conclusion, the Calendar of Events stands as a critical tool for enhancing project efficiency and reducing risks associated with delays. Its ability to provide a clear, visual representation of key activities ensures that projects stay on track, deadlines are met, and teams operate with greater cohesion. By leveraging this simple yet effective tool, organizations can ensure seamless transitions from evaluation to implementation, driving successful project outcomes and timely go-lives.

ELEVATING BUSINESS ACUMEN

The journey of a sales professional involves ongoing development and refinement, as they cultivate the skills necessary to provide greater value to their clients. This steady progression unfolds through distinct stages, each reflecting a deeper level of engagement, strategic influence, and comprehension of customer needs. Advancing through these stages enhances sales professionals' capacity to shape decisions, align with executive priorities, and deliver measurable business outcomes.

The initial stage is marked by Product Focus. Here, the emphasis is on product differentiation. Sales representatives rely on showcasing the unique features of their offerings, comparing them to competitors, and responding reactively to customer inquiries. Early-career professionals in this phase often rely heavily on their product knowledge. Incentive pricing and discounts are commonly used to accelerate decisions, while internal champions are developed to promote products within the client organization.

As sales professionals grow, they enter the realm of Persona-Based Selling. This stage reflects a shift from pure product selling to understanding the roles and challenges faced by different stakeholders within the client organization. Sales professionals start positioning themselves as domain experts, offering tailored guidance and relevant success stories that resonate with line-of-business executives. Rather than waiting for engagement, they proactively reach out, becoming trusted advisors to individual personas and offering solutions that address specific pain points.

The third stage, Value-Based Selling, represents a deeper level of engagement. Sales professionals can now present a strong financial case for change, linking their solutions to measurable cost savings, revenue growth, and strategic business outcomes. This stage is characterized by aligning the proposed solutions with the broader objectives of the customer's business unit. By articulating the financial benefits and demonstrating ROI, sales professionals begin influencing higher-level decision-makers and gaining access to executive leadership.

By the time sales professionals reach the Industry-Networked-Consultant stage, they have become deeply embedded within their target industries. At this point, their focus shifts to leveraging specialized knowledge and networks to drive influence. Sales professionals here demonstrate industry-specific use cases, process integrations, and thought leadership that reflect an intimate understanding of the client's environment. Competitive insights, emerging trends, and innovative strategies become key tools to differentiate their offerings, solidifying their role as invaluable industry consultants.

Finally, at the most advanced stage, sales professionals can Control the Complex Sale. At this level, sales professionals are perceived as trusted advisors and strategic partners to senior executives and the C-suite. Their role extends beyond selling a solution to influencing the very criteria by which decisions are made. These sales leaders anticipate executive needs, align their solutions with overarching strategic priorities, and craft compelling proposals that justify even unbudgeted investments. They redefine the customer's vision and play a pivotal role in guiding large-scale business transformations.

This evolutionary path is not linear, but most sales professionals progress in the following manner:

- **EARLY STAGE**: Product-centric selling (Product Focus).
- **MID-STAGE**: Persona-based engagement and value-driven approaches (Persona-Based and Value-Based Selling).
- **ADVANCED STAGE**: Industry specialization and complex sales mastery (Industry Networked Consultant and Controlling the Complex Sale).

Through continuous learning, adapting to customer needs, and developing industry insights, sales professionals can advance their careers and drive significant value for both their clients and their organizations. Ultimately, the goal is to evolve from product sellers into strategic business partners who play a transformative role in their clients' success.

UNIFY AWARENESS THEORY

Orchestrate the dissemination of information that delivers value to your customer while keeping your executives informed. Initiate proactive engagement with clients, even when they haven't requested a formal assessment of your solutions.

Why change?

Challenge:	How do you receive buy-in and participation to build consistent pipeline? Any concern about providing executives with high value updates? Can you measure the value of your solutions to share with executives?

How do we differentiate?

Concept 45:	**Sequential Engagement Plays** are essential to cultivate momentum across various tiers within accounts. These distinct pillars will collectively foster the necessity for an enterprise agreement.
Concept 46:	**Navigating the Verification Phase** requires a dual approach, working both from the bottom up and top down, to align decision criteria across an organization. This alignment is essential for gaining consensus and winning selections. Sellers often excel at one but not both.
Concept 47:	**Recalibrate Evaluation Criteria** is crucial for achieving excellence in enterprise sales. By offering industry expertise, executives will recognize you as a thought leader to make recommendations. Utilize past customer successes to inform and shape future strategies effectively.
Concept 48:	**Elevate Business Acumen** over time is crucial for consistently providing value to executives in every interaction. By adopting an infinite game mindset, you build on prior engagements, anticipate needs, and streamline the evaluation process, reducing customer workload and minimizing indecision.

What do we receive?

Result:	Proven results shared in frameworks to provide what good looks like. Add value in every executive interaction to **increase revenue +14%**. Develop business strategies that create quantified value for customers.

TIPS AND TRICKS FOR UNIFYING AWARENESS

- The ability to create unified awareness across an organization and with multiple clients is a critical determinant of long-term success. This unified approach ensures that strategies, messages, and initiatives resonate across departments, fostering a **shared understanding that drives progress**. Achieving this level of cohesion requires a focus on four key elements: strategic leadership, problem-solving excellence, stakeholder mobilization, and the orchestration of seamless teamwork.

- At the heart of this process lies strategic leadership. True leaders shape their vision, align their teams, and influence outcomes through clarity and inspiration. They do not simply dictate objectives but cultivate an atmosphere of trust and collaboration. By consistently communicating the organization's broader goals, these leaders ensure that every individual and **department feels connected to the company's mission**. This shared sense of purpose motivates teams to contribute their best, reinforcing the unity that drives collective achievement.

- Problem-solving is equally vital to sustaining this cohesion. In the face of market volatility and shifting client needs, organizations must be agile and innovative. Those that prioritize problem-solving foster a culture of adaptability and resilience. Employees are encouraged to think critically, collaborate across functions, and find solutions that not only address immediate challenges but also create long-term opportunities. This problem-solving mindset becomes a cornerstone of reliability, both within the company and in the eyes of clients.

- Mobilizing key stakeholders plays an indispensable role in amplifying an organization's value. **Mobilizers become champions** of the company's message, ensuring that consistent, impactful communication flows across all business units and to external partners. They extend the reach of leadership, embodying the company's values and reinforcing its priorities in every interaction. By empowering these stakeholders and nurturing their growth, organizations ensure that their value proposition resonates internally and externally.

- Seamless teamwork acts as the glue that binds these elements together. **Collaboration across departments** eliminates silos, strengthens operations, and ensures that everyone is working toward the same objectives. This coordinated approach not only enhances internal efficiency but also creates a unified front for clients, fostering trust and delivering smooth, consistent experiences.

- Maintaining momentum and having comprehensive account engagement is vital to implement sequential engagement plays. These strategic maneuvers involve orchestrating multiple, coordinated interactions across various client business units, reinforcing relationships, and promoting alignment within client organizations. The structured nature of these interactions ensures sustained visibility and proactive communication across all client touchpoints.

- **Navigating the Proving Ground** entails effectively sharing insights and successes from preliminary evaluations or pilot projects with client executive leadership. Sales teams play a pivotal role here by strategically cascading information upward, clearly articulating the partnership's value and obtaining essential executive recognition, thereby reinforcing confidence in the ongoing collaboration.

- Management reinforces this engagement approach by maintaining a structured weekly cadence. Regular reviews and alignment to quarterly objectives ensure consistent attention on critical tasks, especially those that might otherwise be overlooked, enhancing the strategic execution and operational effectiveness of the sales teams.

- Ultimately, creating unified awareness is a continuous journey. It requires consistent effort, refinement, and dedication to strategic leadership, problem-solving, stakeholder mobilization, and teamwork. Companies that commit to these principles lay the **foundation for resilient growth** and lasting client relationships. The result is an organization that thrives in the face of change, driven by a shared vision and collective determination.

UNIFY AWARENESS WORKBOOK
QUARTERLY OPERATIONAL CADENCE

Unify Awareness Frameworks

212 STRATEGIC ENGAGEMENT FRAMEWORK	Plan your interactions in key accounts and with key stakeholders • Commit to business outcomes with decision-makers
213 MANAGEMENT CADENCE	Managing leading indicator performance measures • Organizational goals, monitor performance, and drive strategic execution
214 C3 COMMUNICATION MODEL	Three-part communication framework to ensure clarity • Executive communication, messaging, leadership updates, and stakeholder agreement to deliver impactful messages
215 CALENDAR OF EVENTS	Time-based schedule of planned activities, meetings, milestones jointly executed by two organizations • Ensure all parties align on timelines and key actions required

Unify Awareness Sales Plays

216 UNIFY	Ensure all teams share GTM strategy, objectives, initiatives • Collaborate toward common goal to drive market success

217 FLYWHEEL	Expand executive relationships continuously driving value • Increased trust, stronger relationships, and greater influence
218 CREDIBILITY	Engaging executives as trusted, credible, and strategic partners • Provide valuable insights demonstrate expertise, commitment to their success
219 VIRTUAL TEAM	Ensure team members work together to achieve common objectives • Promote collaboration, eliminate silos, team alignment
220 ACCOUNT-BASED MARKETING	Strategic engagement with high-value accounts treating them as individual markets • Personalized content, messaging, and solutions tailored
221 PROGRESS	Leverage initial meeting to tailor your value proposition • Demonstrate credibility to solving executives' challenges
222 SUCCESS	Strategic initiatives maintaining engagement with stakeholders • Business objectives to enhance long-term customer value
223 CASCADE	Coordinate the sharing of information at all levels in an organization • Ensure all teams have clear understanding of performance goals
224 QUICK WINS	Implement high-impact use cases that drive business case • Amplify early wins as a growth engine to build credibility
225 COMPETITIVE ADVANTAGE	Generate new ideas that adapt to changing market conditions • Proactively create value to solve customer challenges

Diagram 12.2 Orchestrate Communication with Multiple Levels

EVERYDAY APPLICATIONS

The cornerstone of effective account management is robust communication. Ensuring seamless internal alignment among teams and providing clients with clear visibility into the value delivered is fundamental to building stronger relationships, enhancing client satisfaction, and unlocking future growth opportunities. Without a structured and transparent communication strategy, even the most dedicated efforts can go unnoticed, potentially hindering deeper engagement and limiting your expansion opportunities.

To drive meaningful client outcomes, it is essential that your internal teams work in unison, each understanding their role in the broader account strategy. Establishing clear roles and responsibilities across departments—be it sales, customer success, technical support, or product management—creates accountability and streamlines efforts.

Frequent internal syncs, whether weekly or bi-weekly, provide a forum for these teams to exchange updates, discuss potential challenges, and refine strategies collaboratively. These structured meetings, driven by performance metrics and client feedback, ensure that no aspect of the account is overlooked. Meeting outcomes must be documented thoroughly, with actionable next steps clearly defined to sustain momentum.

Equally important is the establishment of a centralized platform, such as a CRM or internal collaboration tool, that serves as a single source of truth for all account-related materials. Housing account plans, meeting records, and client interactions in one place enhances transparency, facilitates knowledge sharing, and enables consistent messaging across all touchpoints. Quarterly strategic planning sessions further reinforce alignment by allowing teams to reassess progress, realign priorities, and adapt to evolving client needs.

Clients need to see the value being delivered, and quarterly business reviews serve as the ideal vehicle for this. A well-crafted QBR offers clients an in-depth analysis of performance, results achieved, and future initiatives, painting a clear picture of how the partnership is contributing to their success. Visual aids, case studies, and concrete data points transform these reviews from routine check-ins into compelling narratives of success.

In addition to QBRs, consistent performance reporting—whether monthly or bi-monthly—keeps clients informed between reviews. Tailored to align with client objectives and industry benchmarks, these reports highlight key milestones, areas for improvement, and actionable next steps.

Sharing client success stories and case studies further enhances visibility, providing tangible examples of the organization's impact. By proactively engaging clients for feedback—through surveys, informal check-ins, or structured interviews—organizations not only demonstrate responsiveness but also show a willingness to adapt and grow in line with client expectations.

Transparency breeds trust. By maintaining open lines of communication and proactively updating clients on project developments, risks, and milestones, organizations cultivate a sense of partnership and reliability. Addressing potential issues head-on, with solutions in hand, reinforces the perception of a committed and proactive partner.

Celebrating shared successes, whether through formal reports, press releases, or social media acknowledgments, further strengthens your bond with clients. Recognizing project completions or significant performance improvements underscores your organization's dedication and highlights the collaborative effort involved in achieving results.

Moreover, involving clients in strategic conversations, such as roadmap planning and innovation workshops, cements their role as partners rather than mere customers. This collaborative approach not only enhances trust but also ensures that solutions are more closely aligned with their evolving needs.

The pathway to expanding client relationships is paved with demonstrated value and proactive problem-solving. Expansion proposals must clearly articulate the ROI and additional benefits of your new products or services, tying them directly to the client's strategic goals. Positioning these proposals as solutions to pressing challenges or enablers of growth increases their relevance and appeal.

Anticipating client needs and presenting innovative ideas consistently positions the organization as a forward-thinking, indispensable partner. Sharing thought leadership content, such as white papers or market analysis, not only highlights expertise but also reassures clients that they are working with a company that is attuned to industry trends and future opportunities.

By prioritizing internal alignment and enhancing client visibility, organizations set the stage for long-term, mutually beneficial relationships. Proactive engagement, transparent communication, and a relentless focus on delivering value ensure that clients not only appreciate the work being done but become enthusiastic advocates for expansion and deeper collaboration. In doing so, you'll secure the foundation for sustained success and continuous growth.

UNIFY AWARENESS KEY TAKEAWAYS

1. Do you have a method to create strategic engagements in net new accounts?

   Arrive with business strategies that impact the CEO's strategic priorities.

2. Do you have a management cadence that archives sustainable revenue growth?

   Time allocation metrics across pipeline, opportunity management, and closing deals.

3. How does your sales team prioritize sequential engagement plays in accounts?

   Establish multi-threaded influence across multiple business units.

4. Do teams engage bottom up and top down to maximize their opportunity?

   Develop as many top-1-percenter sales professionals as possible in your organization.

5. Do your GTM teams establish credibility to redefine decision criteria?

   The key to enterprise sales is providing guidance as thought leaders to client executives.

6. How often do your teams manage the complex sales with your clients?

Receive written confirmation from economic buyers confirming next steps in the process.

7. Can your team identify hidden client constraints ahead of time?

Leverage a Calendar of Events to uncover down weeks during the evaluation.

8. Do you have a methodology to elevate your GTM team's business acumen?

Sales professionals apply subject expert knowledge during client engagements.

PARTING THOUGHTS

Sustainable businesses must go beyond simply responding to customer needs. A proactive approach to customer engagement, driven by valuable insights and executive alignment, can foster long-term partnerships and drive significant revenue growth. This book has outlined a comprehensive strategic plan to deliver consistent value to customers while ensuring executives remain informed and involved, ultimately increasing your revenue and enhancing customer satisfaction.

At the core of this initiative is the dissemination of proven results, executive engagement, and the development of a customer-centric business strategy. By systematically engaging with clients even before they request formal assessments, your organization can position itself as a trusted advisor and solutions provider.

The first pillar of this strategy is creating and sharing sales frameworks for proven results. Success stories and case studies serve as powerful tools for your sales team, showcasing real-world implementations and quantifiable benefits. To operationalize this, you must first develop a comprehensive library of use cases that highlight specific challenges addressed, solutions deployed, and the outcomes achieved. These cases will span various industries, offering versatility and relevance to different client segments.

To ensure accessibility and efficiency, house this content in a centralized digital repository. Organize your knowledge base meticulously, allowing sales teams and executives to quickly locate relevant materials. Further, use regular enablement workshops to empower sales teams, providing them with the skills and confidence needed to leverage these materials effectively during client engagements. Moving forward, establish a continuous feedback loop to refine and improve these frameworks. Sales teams should have structured channels to communicate their experiences and suggest enhancements, ensuring the materials evolve in alignment with client needs and market dynamics.

Executive engagement plays a pivotal role in driving high-level decision-making and fostering trust with clients. This framework emphasizes the importance of curating tailored executive briefings, designed to showcase the latest market insights, performance metrics, and ROI from deployed solutions. These briefings should be personalized to reflect the strategic priorities and objectives of each executive audience.

Beyond briefings, implement exclusive executive programs, such as round-tables and leadership summits, to provide ongoing value. These platforms will foster collaboration, thought leadership, and the exchange of innovative ideas, reinforcing your position as a market leader. Key performance indicators will guide these engagements, with a focus on achieving a 14 percent revenue uplift by aligning your solutions with your clients' critical business challenges. By analyzing the direct impact of executive interactions on sales conversions and deal velocity, you can fine-tune your specific approach for maximum effectiveness.

To further solidify long-term client relationships, conduct value mapping workshops, designed to align solutions with client objectives and operational pain points. These workshops will foster collaborative planning and ensure that the proposed solutions deliver measurable value. Complementing this initiative, ROI modeling will play a key role in demonstrating the financial benefits of specific solutions. By presenting data-driven ROI scenarios, you give clients clear insights into the immediate and long-term advantages of their investments.

After the sale, deploy customer performance scorecards to track satisfaction, solution adoption, and value realization. These scorecards will provide a comprehensive view of the client relationship, helping to identify areas for expansion and address potential churn risks proactively. This helps you embed a continuous improvement mechanism into your sales strategies. Insights gathered from scorecards and engagements will inform ongoing enhancements to service offerings and client interactions, ensuring sustained success and growth.

By prioritizing proactive engagement, fostering executive relationships, and consistently delivering quantifiable value, this strategic framework can position any organization to enhance customer loyalty and drive sustainable growth. This structured approach ensures that your company remains agile, competitive, and firmly established as an industry leader.

Remember, CEOs are increasingly tasked with not only maintaining growth but also driving transformative, hyperscale revenue. By strategically investing in elite, cross-functional Diamond Teams and developing reusable sales frameworks, you can unlock unprecedented opportunities and secure large-scale transactions that redefine market positioning—both for you and for your clients.

VALUE FRAMEWORK (JOIN CHAPTERS 9 TO 12)

Assessing the **value** you deliver is the cornerstone of any successful business endeavor. While it's crucial to develop innovative solutions, you'll never achieve hyperscale revenue growth until you can consistently quantify measurable benefits across your customer base. No client will risk their future on the chance that your technology might gain traction some day; they need clear evidence of how your solution will drive results before they even consider reading your case studies.

Give them that evidence during the rollout of Phase 1, then reinforce it quarterly during customer business reviews to ensure ongoing value expansion. Offering the entire C-suite performance scorecards of your solution, every quarter, will distinguish you from competitors and let you unlock specific best-of-breed capabilities that might attract new decision-makers. Demonstrating the ROI by implementation horizon allows executive leadership to justify more substantial investments in future phases, often sooner than anticipated. All in all, providing and documenting tangible value is essential to strengthening your relationship with every key decision-maker in your accounts.

The unprecedented access to information provided by **artificial intelligence** offers unparalleled insights into those same accounts, revealing opportunities for process improvements. Engaging executives necessitates thorough research to develop compelling business strategies. This approach enables the creation of a powerful strategy from an external perspective, increasing the likelihood of securing a referral from a C-suite executive, who can then advocate for collaboration with their direct reports to generate significant, unbudgeted transactions. Executives can always reallocate funds for new projects if you can demonstrate proven results that foster unique competitive advantages. Many sales professionals struggle with writing, so crafting a strategy that ChatGPT can refine into a comprehensive guide and then using content writing tools like Anyword to personalize the tone and incorporate engaging, positive terminology can be highly effective in capturing executive interest.

To achieve hyperscale revenue, it's crucial for your GTM teams to feel at ease creating personalized content, but even more critical is the **launch plan**. Delivering your message at the optimal time and cascading it across multiple business units generates the necessary momentum, while employing a multi-threaded approach with accounts helps identify what works best for each organization. Personalization enables you to start building executive relationships based on your proposed business strategies, a far more effective tactic than relying on a personal relationship approach. Executives can't risk their careers on a personal relationship, but they might go all in on the business strategy you're proposing. Your virtual team of subject-matter experts can assist in refining your message to establish the required credibility with executives. It's up to you to leverage your valuable resources to create a unique competitive advantage for your accounts. Focus on the customer, not on yourself or your solutions. This mindset is essential when recommending solutions that align with the needs of the customer's business and industry drivers.

Finally, executive bridging is crucial for **unifying awareness** between your organization and a strategic account you aim to build a lasting partnership with. Crafting specific messaging for the three different levels within the organization allows you to execute sequential engagement plays effectively. As a proficient enterprise seller, you should be enthusiastic about navigating the proving ground, capturing your differentiation with the evaluation team, and delivering a concise readout to client executives twice a quarter. This method often makes sellers uncomfortable, to the point of avoiding updates to the executive leadership team. However, securing a significant transaction is challenging if the executives are unaware of your presence. The only way to redefine decision criteria is through collaboration with the executive leadership team, as they possess unique requirements (and resources) for selecting strategic partners that the evaluation team cannot access. With consistent practice, each of your sales professionals will enhance their business acumen over time, gradually becoming comfortable in conversations with the C-suite. This transformation doesn't occur overnight, but you will begin to notice a shift in how they continually add value for influential executives—and bring in life-changing revenue to your company.

This is how all twelve chapters align through these three steps. Step 1, your GTM teams learn to adopt the approaches CEOs use to engage their most strategic clients. Step 2, your domain experts articulate your unique differentiation, crafting a competitive advantage that translates into actionable frameworks your global sales force can utilize to establish themselves as thought leaders in the industry. Step 3, your teams prioritize value, presenting a perspective grounded in a fully developed business strategy that drives meaningful impact.

THREE GO-TO MARKET MOTIONS

Strategic Engagement	STEP 1	How elite GTM focused CEOs sell today
		Enable GTM teams to engage the C-suite
		MACO Demand Creation Framework

Value Differentiation	STEP 2	Invest in personalization for the customer
		Access to Sales Frameworks Library
		DEFINE Business Strategies

Customer Buy-In	STEP 3	Execute your launch plan at scale
		Expand influence from a single champion to many
		VALUE Creation of Customers

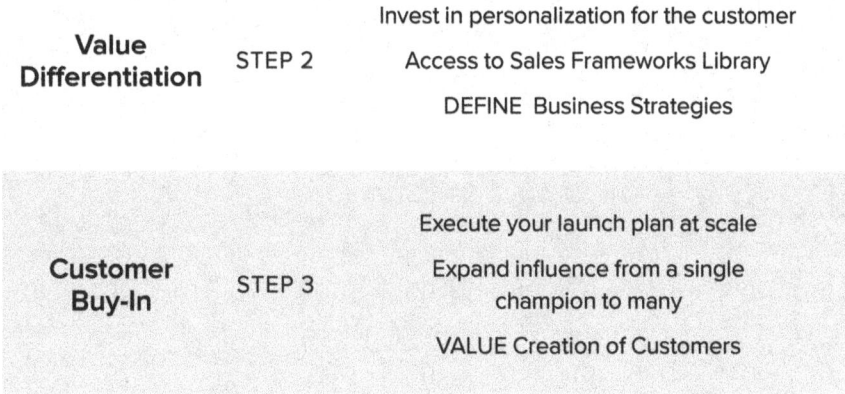

Diagram 12.3 Three Phases to Implement the Sales Operating System

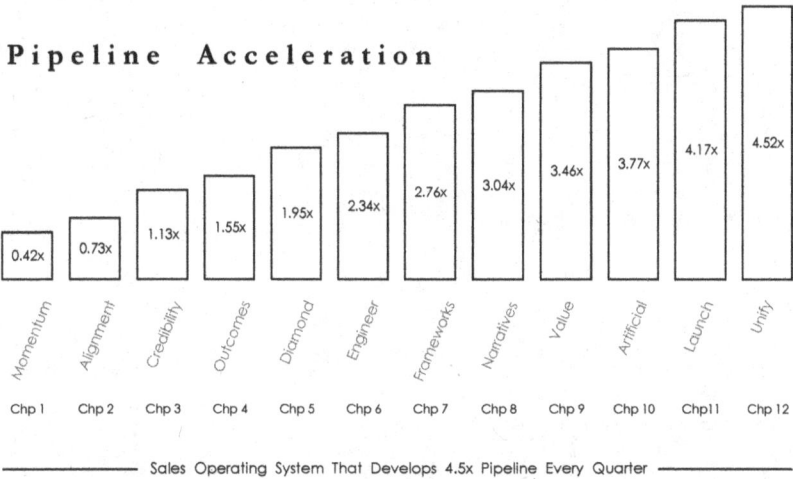

Pipeline Acceleration

Chp 1	Chp 2	Chp 3	Chp 4	Chp 5	Chp 6	Chp 7	Chp 8	Chp 9	Chp 10	Chp 11	Chp 12
Momentum	Alignment	Credibility	Outcomes	Diamond	Engineer	Frameworks	Narratives	Value	Artificial	Launch	Unify
0.42x	0.73x	1.13x	1.55x	1.95x	2.34x	2.76x	3.04x	3.46x	3.77x	4.17x	4.52x

———— Sales Operating System That Develops 4.5x Pipeline Every Quarter ————

Diagram 12.4 Building Blocks to Generate High-Value Pipeline

INDEX

We live our lives to connect through stories.
Do you have ones that leave a lasting impact?

This is your chance to elevate how you
communicate with executives.

Using the frameworks in this book will
guide you toward building transformative strategies.

Structuring deals requires far more precision
than simply closing them.

This book provides clear, actionable steps
to master complex enterprise sales processes.

The goal is to empower you with proven insights
to design your own revenue blueprint.

www.hyperscalerevenue.ai

www.ingramcontent.com/pod-product-compliance
Lightning Source LLC
Chambersburg PA
CBHW011158220326
41597CB00026BA/4662

* 9 7 9 8 8 9 5 1 5 1 2 7 3 *